TURBULENCE

HOW DEREGULATION DESTROYED CANADA'S AIRLINES

WAYNE SKENE

DOUGLAS & MCINTYRE
VANCOUVER/TORONTO

Douglas & McIntyre Ltd.
1615 Venables Street
Vancouver, British Columbia V5L 2H1

The publisher gratefully acknowledges the support of the
Canada Council, and of the British Columbia Ministry of
Tourism, Small Business and Culture for its publishing
programs.

Canadian Cataloguing in Publication Data

Skene, Wayne, 1941-
Turbulence

ISBN 1-55054-164-1

1. Aeronautics, Commercial—Canada. 2. Airlines—Canada. I.
Title.
HE9815.A4S53 1994   387.7'0971   C94-910450-7

Editing by Brian Scrivener
Jacket design by Tom Brown
Typeset by Vancouver Desktop Publishing Centre
Printed and bound in Canada by Best Gagné Book
    Manufacturers, Inc.
Printed on acid-free paper ∞

Contents

This book is dedicated to my father, Richard Skene. He was born a year before the first Canadian flew at Baddeck, Nova Scotia. He often stared into the sky above him and watched, in his quiet but curious way, the growth of twentieth-century aviation technology—from fabric-clad biplanes to helium-filled dirigibles, from turboprops to 747s. Through it all, he was always less impressed with this glittering march into the heavens than he was with the power and cooperation he felt through the reins of a team of finely matched Morgans.

Preface and
Acknowledgements

"We may define business in a broad, general way as the art of losing money."
　—Stephen Leacock
"Every government is a device by which a few control the actions of many."
　—I.F. Stone
"Nothing can preserve the integrity of contact between individuals, except a discretionary authority in the state to revise what has become intolerable. The powers of uninterrupted usury are too great. If the accretions of vested interests were to grow without mitigation for many generations, half the population would be no better than slaves to the other half."
　—John Maynard Keynes, *Treatise on Monetary Reform*

THIS BOOK TAKES AN UNORTHODOX APPROACH to the issue at hand. Some of the ideas in this book will no doubt seem quite outrageous. The tone may seem irreverent. The approach will seem nationalistic. And for that, I make no apologies whatsoever. I went looking for another lost symbol of our nationhood and culture—in this case, a once vibrant, healthy and growing aviation industry proudly serving all Canadians—and became increasingly outraged at what I found. I discovered another of our familiar institutions dismantled in the name of political expediency and of theories—some business, some academic—that were foreign and largely unproven, often supported by questionable assumptions, and seldom taking into account our national integrity. I found we were increasingly a nation with much too much of our policy agenda—social, as well as economic—being drafted by the Canadian business sector, particularly Corporate Canada. To little surprise, I found the average voting Canadian had less influence in the political process than one would dare hazard, at even the most cynical moment. And by the time I had finished the book, I had begun to fear we were now entering a dangerous political era, one in which the very principles of parliamentary democracy were being questioned by excessive supporters of a misconstrued version of capitalism.

With those thoughts, we may seem a long way away from airplanes. But read on. And first, let me state my biases:

1. Airlines are too big, and their chances of financial success too limited, to be run like mom-and-pop grocery stores.
2. Cooperation, not competition, makes businesses, corporations and national economies stronger.
3. Participants in the free marketplace can tend to self-destruct. Market-driven competition destroys as often as it builds.
4. Knowing how to make money in business does not mean you know how to run a democratically elected government, or know how to design appropriate government policy.
5. Government policy-making is most often designed in an atmosphere of expediency, confusion and doubt.
6. You cannot base the foundation of a strong nation on self-interest; a nation cannot just be a place in which to make money.
7. You cannot make the consumer the sovereign element in a nation without devaluing the nation itself. A consumer demands. A citizen gives back.
8. When you heedlessly diminish the role or effectiveness of government, you diminish yourself as well.
9. Capitalism is only one element within a democratic nation's belief system. It is not the other way around.
10. Without enlightened government to set the rules and regulations by which we may all benefit, we are little more than anarchists. In some cases, well-to-do anarchists, but anarchists, nevertheless.

As usual, I am indebted to many people for their help and guidance. In writing this book I availed myself of a number of published works that proved invaluable from both a historical and a research point of view: Max Ward's *The Max Ward Story*; Ronald A. Keith's *Bush Pilot with a Briefcase: The Happy-Go-Lucky Story of Grant McConachie*; Philip Smith's *It Seems Like Only Yesterday: Air Canada—The First 50 Years*; and Anthony Sampson's *Empires of the Sky: The Politics, Contests and Cartels of World Airlines*, to name only a few. But one of the most helpful and most enlightening works was *The Politics of Canada's Airlines from Diefenbaker to Mulroney*, written by Garth

Stevenson, a professor of political science at the University of Alberta when he wrote the book.

I sincerely thank the many people who volunteered their time, who spoke with me and shared their experiences and points of view, particularly Sidney Fattedad, William Jordan, Bill Farrall and Ross Healy. My son Cameron once again assisted me in research. His enthusiasm and diligence opened many delightful new information doors for me. I owe my publisher, Scott McIntyre, a special thank you for his support and guidance on this project, particularly for sensing there was a more important story to tell Canadians—behind the too-romantic notions about airplanes, bush pilots and the business of flight. Brian Scrivener stood by me with his humour and his insight, proving again that there is a virtuosity to the editor's craft, one that so often can make the mundane seem masterful. And as always, thanks to my wife, Connie. Without her patience, encouragement and insightful, refining comments on work-in-progress, writing books would never be as challenging, nor as much fun.

1 / Flying the Unfriendly Skies

"Perhaps the worst financial devastation has been that of the nation's airlines. Here an ill-considered deregulation—faith once again in the market in a public service industry where utility regulation is normal—has been combined with corporate raiding and leveraged buyouts on an impressive scale. The results have been heavy debt, the bankruptcy of several of the larger airlines . . . a chaotic muddle of fares and available routes, an inability to replace aging equipment and, in the end, quite possibly an exploitive monopoly by the survivors."
—John Kenneth Galbraith, *The Culture of Contentment*

THE SKY FINALLY BEGAN TO FALL for Canada's airline industry on Monday, July 27, 1992. On that date, the board of directors of the Calgary-based PWA Corporation, the parent company of Canadian Airlines International Ltd., announced that discussions with AMR Corporation of Fort Worth, Texas, the parent company of American Airlines, regarding a possible alliance between the two air carriers had been terminated. The announcement severely jolted the industry, if not the entire country. It perplexed some politicians, gratified a number of federal bureaucrats, shocked most airline employees, spooked investors and creditors, stunned analysts and airline transportation academics, and marked the beginning of the end to Canada's hope of ever being a major force in international airline transportation.

After months of negotiating, like the billing and cooing of courting love birds, PWA Corp. had seemed finally ready to consummate an airline partnership between Canadian Airlines International Ltd. (CAIL) and American Airlines, the largest U.S. carrier in the world by revenue, and one that was five times CAIL's size. CAIL was a foundering airline, requiring immediate financial help. PWA had performed its mating dance with American Airlines for the better part of a year, building in feral anticipation to the point in mid-July when an alliance between the two was all but a done deal. Approaching the end of the fourth week of July, it appeared to most observers that Canada's No. 2 airline was about to marry a foreigner.

But suddenly, at 4:30 P.M. EDT on July 27, 1992, PWA's board of directors announced that the CAIL-American Airlines nuptials had been called off. PWA had, inexplicably, changed partners right in front of the altar. PWA would now enter into merger discussions with CAIL's despised competitor—Air Canada. The announcement reverberated throughout the country.

The nation had been caught unaware. Airline industry observers scrambled to make sense of PWA's sudden about-face. PWA shareholders, already at ragged nerve ends after watching the value of their holdings plummet over the past few years, began calling their stock brokers to discuss bailing out. With a previous spate of Canadian charter airline failures fresh in mind—failures that had left travellers stranded in various foreign locations—CAIL ticket holders began wondering whether their return fare tickets meant what they said. The Canadian public began wondering what was happening to their once reliable and stable airline industry. The Mulroney government in Ottawa, the people largely responsible for this sudden chaos that masqueraded as an industry, headed for the bunkers, perhaps to pray. Analysts and airline watchers started scratching their heads over the serendipitous way PWA Corp., along with its battered airline, continued to defy financial gravity. According to CAIL's financial picture, the Calgary-based airline should have crashed months, some said years, earlier.

Before it merged itself in a series of buy-outs and re-emerged as Canadian Airlines International Ltd., Pacific Western Airlines had been the darling of the Canadian airline business, with eighteen straight years of profitable operation. The accumulated debt and administrative load from absorbing four carriers (Eastern Provincial Airways, Nordair, CP Air and Wardair), plus a number of feeder or commuter airlines, the impact of a recession, and the results of a tough fare war had all backed PWA Corp. into a very tight financial corner. Its board had been shopping for a strategic alliance (roughly translated: get someone to buy a chunk of CAIL in return for some badly needed cash) with another North American carrier—*any* carrier it seemed—since the autumn of 1990. They had concluded that the long-term viability of their airline was in jeopardy unless a rich partner could be found.

Although PWA's financial problems looked relatively recent, some airline analysts had taken the temperature of the ailing company and concluded, as far back as May 1990, that Canada's second major carrier was functionally insolvent. Both CAIL and Air Canada were in bad shape and prospects for improvement seemed remote. Competition between the two airlines was killing them. Both airlines were selling seats at a loss. Both airlines were highly leveraged, with roughly eighty per cent of their fixed capital loaded with debt, compared to less than seventy per cent for struggling U.S. air carriers. Together, they were losing close to $2 million dollars a day. And the bills just kept piling up.

As early as February 1991, PWA even began talking with its nemesis, Air Canada, about possibly buying out CAIL in its entirety. But Air Canada had only been interested in acquiring CAIL's lucrative international routes—an idea PWA flatly rejected. This led to discussions about a merger between the carriers. Many analysts had already said a merger between the two Canadian airlines would just result in one very sick airline. Air Canada had also started to bleed from its bottom line in 1990 and was headed toward a large net loss for 1991.

In September 1991, CAIL president Kevin Jenkins told his employees the airline "was running out of cash and is running low on time to pull off a deal to survive." The airline was "dead in a year" unless it received wage concessions worth at least $116 million a year over the next two years from its 18,000 employees. The airline also wanted to lay off 1,300 employees. As well, Jenkins was shopping for more favourable terms from creditors, possible help from governments, and/or an infusion of capital in the form of a beneficial alliance with a foreign carrier.

CAIL was in serious financial trouble, even at this early point. The factors at issue did not just add up to a case study of a sputtering corporation. This was the prelude to what should have been a full-scale corporate collapse. Speculation about a new PWA share issue, the second major dilution of stock in mere months, helped drive PWA's share price to a new low of $4.20. With options dwindling to digital proportions—one for alive or zero for dead—PWA broke off its earlier discussions with Air Canada in March 1992 in order to enter into serious negotiations with AMR. In between the various wooing pitches, PWA had also tried shopping a deal with numerous other American carriers, as many as a dozen, according to industry reports.

Pacific Western Airlines, the little Calgary-based airline-that-once-could, had started after World War II as tiny Central B.C. Airways, with nothing more than a stagger-wing Beechcraft biplane operating in the far northern Fort St. James region. Growing steadily, it became the nation's No. 3 domestic carrier by the early 1980s. With the surprise acquisition of Canadian Pacific Air Lines on January 1, 1987, and then Wardair, and the amalgamation of these takeover initiatives (along with the remnants of Eastern Provincial Airways and Nordair) into CAIL, the Calgary-based airline would become the virtual equal to Air Canada by 1989. Now, by the summer of 1992, it was on the blocks, large parts of it for sale to the highest bidder—any bidder at all, really. Except, apparently, Air Canada.

After witnessing PWA Corp. reject Air Canada's offers throughout 1991 and the spring of 1992, most Canadians had been under the impression that now, for better or for worse, PWA was about to strike an equity deal with American Airlines. A PWA–AMR deal might put to rest almost six years of turmoil in the Canadian airline business. Suddenly and inexplicably, those discussions with AMR were terminated. And now merger talks with Air Canada were on again.

The turbulence arrived after decades of relative peace, order and what many Canadians perceived to be the relatively good management of the nation's airline industry. In fact, by the time the PWA–AMR deal was finally consummated—almost two years later—the clouds of chaos that enveloped Canada's airline industry would just get thicker. In retrospect, PWA's troubles were just getting off the ground in July 1992. Things would actually get worse.

"These days no one can make money in the goddamn airline business. The economics represent sheer hell."
    —Cyrus Smith, on resigning from American Airlines in 1968, quoted in Anthony Sampson, *Empires of the Sky*

It has been said many times that, more than any other business, airlines take on the personality of their owners or chief executive officers. The history of the airline business, particularly in North America, is really the story of the men who—with their enthusiasm, their energy and their sometimes romantic notions—built and operated the airlines. Some called them dreamers. Some called them cavaliers. Others called them barroom gamblers. To many they were evangelists. And the promise of human flight was like the promise of the gospel.

The airplane has always symbolized the possibilities of a better future. These men dedicated themselves to its promise with a mixture of idealism, hope and, too often, a self-destructive zeal that edged out beyond the boundaries of good business practice, out even beyond the ether of spirituality. Their fervour resembled a kind of secular religion.

Before the invention of the airplane, people had always associated flying with spiritual matters. If flight seemed wondrous, the advent of the airplane seemed miraculous. In the early days of human flight, particularly in the United States, the celebration quickly reached messianic proportions. If flight was divine, then pilots had to be gods. The conquest of the skies—by the likes of Charles Lindbergh, Eddie Rickenbacker, Richard Byrd and Amelia Earhart—was a particularly profound spiritual activity for Americans. World War I flying ace Eddie Rickenbacker, who went on to head Eastern Airlines, believed what they were doing was all part of "some mysterious Universal Plan," that they "were just chosen pawns of the Creator." The creed of this "winged gospel" also restated for Americans, in twentieth century terms, the idea of progress. But this time, it was guided by the hand of The Almighty.

"Aviation was a religion," wrote Joseph Corn in *The Winged Gospel: America's Romance with Aviation*, 1900-1950. "Like traditional faiths, its belief system gave meaning to existence and provided a grand design for future life . . . Indeed, aviation was a kind of crusade for believers." Lindbergh, with his lone voyage to Paris in 1927, was mythologized in letters, articles, books, poetry, speeches and sermons. It has been said that more poems were written about Lindbergh's exploit than about any other person or event in western history. Beyond fulfilling their aviation contract with God, Corn described how Americans also believed their mastery of the airplane symbolized the continuation of their struggle to dominate nature, or what was left of their wild frontier. It helped reassure them of their continuing vitality as a people and a land with a glorious destiny. America's air pioneers would enable the nation to bridge the gaps between spirituality and the new religion of technology.

On a more mundane level, the fresh air now available to travellers flying above America's smoggy, industrial atmosphere would bring improved health. Exploring America's remaining frontier would now be easier and faster when done from above. Real estate agents were expected to improve their sales by providing prospective customers with views of property from thousands of feet in the sky. And hunters would improve their marksmanship against birds on the wing, given their vantage point from within the open cockpit of an airplane.

Flying would "alter aesthetic values and taste," wrote Corn, clearing the skies for better understanding and appreciation by poets and artists. Finally, the airplane would, perhaps by virtue of its altitudinal connection with the Saviour, generate a new universal sense of peace. It would curb violence and, by bringing different peoples closer together in time and space, bring about an end to war. As many Americans believed, "only 'fools' would dare fight when armies employed flying machines."

"Where prophets erred most consistently, however, was not in the technical but rather the social and moral realms," Corn wrote. "They consistently overestimated the airplane's capacity to effect social change, yet this was what really interested most observers about the conquest of the skies, particularly those outside the aeronautical field."

Americans would remain almost entirely alone in this spiritual and technological reverence toward its new, mechanical messiah. Even before World War I, the British, the French and eventually the Germans were predicting the opposite of the American winged gospel. They were not blinded by spiritual euphoria and instead focused their use of the airplane on transportation and military action. Most observers outside America saw no flight-induced transformation of social values, behaviour or tastes. Early twentieth century critics faulted the U.S. for its romantic and utopian notions, pointing to the same type of romanticism that Americans had wrapped their hopes around during the coming of the railroad in the second quarter of the nineteenth century. Then, Americans had expected railroads would eventually weld their country into one seamless city, bring about a new democracy and reduce crime. Railroads, it was also believed, would put an end to slavery.

The fact that airplanes and passenger flight were, if not a "veritable religious cause" to Americans, then at least a technological miracle to be taking advantage of, did not evaporate as readily and as early as one might expect. The echoing sound of the winged gospel would continue through the early half of this century, burning itself into the belief systems of the men who would run the nation's modern airlines.

From Rickenbacker's view they were simply "pawns of the Creator" working out some "mysterious Universal Plan" for the beneficial uses of airplanes, to the free enterprise, deregulated atmosphere of the 1980s, these robust devotees would patch together their made-in-America doctrines with messianic enthusiasm for airplanes and flight, along with large dollops of investment capital—and call it the airline industry.

Some personalities—Rickenbacker of Eastern Airlines, Cyrus Smith of American Airlines, William Patterson of United Airlines—were engrossed in opening up the continent to the airline business. Others, like Pan Am's Juan Trippe, started out in the 1920s using a fleet of surplus warplanes to fly New York socialites to their country retreats. From that humble beginning, Trippe would make Pan Am, for a time, one of the most influential airlines in the world.

These cavaliers took huge risks—as often in life and limb as in investment terms—and survived for a time in the romantic ether of the early air passenger transportation industry. They saw themselves more as conquerors, less as businessmen. Trans World Airlines even formed an aviation club in 1939 called *Conquistadores del Cielo*—The Conquerors of the Sky.

They called running an airline a business, yet they fought with each other, pausing only long enough to gather in financial exhaustion, then in collusion. They defied the laws of gravity and the laws of anti-trust. And although they long enjoyed the substantive benefits—almost to this day—of the guiding and supportive hand of government, they persisted in ignoring that fundamental fact of their success. They believed the success of their mission came solely from their own courage and risk-taking. Yet their ability to fly, in business and in personal terms, depended not on the risky and romantic notions attached to air travel, but on a careful combination of disciplines that were the opposite of a carefree spirit they most liked to believe made their airlines successful. Quite naturally, it was their habit of linking flight with transcendent hope rather than with business acumen that would bring them back to earth so markedly by the 1990s.

Flight in general, and the business of passenger flight in particular, were not natural functions of man, no matter how hard one might pray. The successful operation of an airline was actually the antithesis of the personal freedom and belief in technological evangelism most cavaliers followed. Flight, Anne Lindbergh wrote, "rests firmly supported, on a structure of laws, rules, principles—laws to which plane and man alike must conform. Rules of construction, of performance, of equipment, for one; rules of training, health, experience, skill and judgement, for the other." The rules were there to sustain the business of flying as much as they were to keep aircraft from colliding with the ground.

One of the irrefutable rules upon which the American airline industry would be built was that government, in one fashion or another, was essential to the industry's growth and development. Break that rule and there would be an enormous price to pay. It would be a rule by which the *conquistadores* played until another group of dreamers appeared upon the airline scene in the 1970s and changed the rules. By 1992, they would both begin to flutter back to earth—more broke than rich, more ideologically chastened than sure of themselves.

> "Some delusions, though notorious to all the world, have subsisted for ages, flourishing as widely among civilised and polished nations as among the early barbarians with whom they originated."
> —Charles Mackay, *Extraordinary Popular Delusions and the Madness of Crowds*, 1852

The early development of the airline transportation business in Canada would follow similar romantic notions about cavaliers and their faith and their courage. But Canadians would lean less on the dramatic crutch of the gospel to find their way through the early skies. Perhaps it was the nation's retarded development or our historic struggle with this large piece of geography, but our approach would be decidedly less Episcopalian and more Methodist than that of our friends to the south. While Americans tended to gaze fondly, and with excitement, at the heavens, Canadians would stare, undaunted, at the bush.

The heroes of Canada's air space would be almost as large in our minds and imaginations as those of the U.S. The difference would be that, whereas their air heroes often carried out their business in the spiritual stratosphere, ours would fly closer to the ground—aeronautically as well as commercially. Strangely enough, when the industry began to unravel in the 1980s, the financial results on both sides of the border would be roughly the same, though the flight plan to the destination would be different.

Canada's aviation history is dotted with the names of brave and adventurous men who flew either as bush pilots with dreams and visions or as airline executives with serious business purpose. The honour roll is long and proud. It most often speaks of W.R. "Wop" May and Vic Horner, C.H. "Punch" Dickins and Walter Gilbert, Grant McConachie, businessman James Richardson, Air Canada's Gordon McGregor, up to the rollicking stories that surround Max Ward and his dream of a Canadian sky filled with planes carrying his name.

Most of them began in the bush—Canada's largely unmapped and untamed wilderness—where as young adventurers they often flew half-blind and half-crazy over rock and lakes and forests, with little more than a strong sense of future possibilities and a large amount of luck. They flew fragile Gypsy Moths and rattling Fokkers, with one eye on the horizon and the other on an Imperial Oil road map propped on their knee. They crashed and took off and crashed again. They bought their airplanes with promises and debt and a belief in a blue-sky future. They flew them with a business recklessness—right into the 1980s—that defied bankers and accountants. To pay the bills, their planes had to be in the air as often as possible, carrying goods and people, regardless of whether the price paid for their transport covered the costs of flying. That was the beauty of the airline business in Canada; once aloft, the hard practicalities of business disappeared in direct relation to the distance they flew from the ground.

The legendary Grant McConachie kept alive his shaky dream of one day owning and operating a major airline by flying fresh fish. The McConachie flying-fish story is a metaphor for the airline business in Canada—for the way it began and for the way it ended up in 1994.

In December 1931, McConachie had more plane then business. His blue Fokker sat idle in an Edmonton hangar. It was the time of the Great Depression. Businessmen were not flying, and the government mail contracts, which almost all budding airlines relied upon to survive in the early days, had all been handed out. McConachie stumbled across a scheme to use his Fokker to fly fresh-caught whitefish from Cold Lake, Alberta, to the railhead at Bonnyville, for eventual shipment to eager buyers in Chicago. McConachie's Fokker would replace the horsedrawn sleighs used to move the fish. He was anxious, even frantic for a contract to fly thirty thousand pounds of fish weekly over the thirty miles between the two remote Alberta towns.

McConachie received one-and-a-half cents a pound for his work. He happily estimated that this cash flow would nicely cover his costs of gas, oil and hiring expenses. But "he gave no thought to depreciation, funding for major overhaul, wages, other indirect costs or profit," biographer Ronald A. Keith wrote in *Bush Pilot with a Briefcase*. McConachie later admitted he lost about fourteen dollars for every hour he flew. "If there had been a bonus for ignorance, I would have made a fortune on that fish haul," the grand air pioneer was quoted as saying. "As it was, I was going broke happily, losing money on every hour's flying, but I thought I was making money."

Six decades later the industry's cargo would be different—double-breasted business executives instead of flopping Cold Lake whitefish—but the commercial flight plan would be roughly the same, as would the financial results.

"I fly because it releases my mind from the tyranny of petty things."
—Antoine de Saint-Exupéry, *Wind, Sand and Stars*

The many traces of personality that mark the history of the Canadian airline business began with those famed bush pilots who lived to fly, who gave way to engineers captivated by the mechanics of flight, who in turn made room for chartered accountants—concerned with controlling costs. In the 1980s and 1990s, the accountants would start to make room for MBA graduates and lawyers, concerned perhaps with having a job that allowed them to rub shoulders with the myths. From bush pilots to MBAs, the industry's financial track record would not change significantly. As romantically attractive as the business is, and as earnest and hard-working as the airline's leaders have been, few of them have been able to keep the profits flying with any consistency. In that respect, perhaps, the business is like the aircraft they fly. As high as they get, for as many moments or hours as it takes, the airplanes always have to come back down to earth.

"Harris pledged to restore [Air Canada] to operating profitability within a year," *Maclean's* magazine reported in July 1992, five months after Hollis Harris took over as Air Canada's president and chief executive officer. Harris's previous position had been chairman of Continental Airlines. When he joined Continental in 1990, he also predicted profitability for the Houston-based carrier. "But two months later, he was recommending bankruptcy protection under Chapter 11," the *Montreal Gazette* reported in March 1992.

Hollis Harris, in 1994 chairman as well as president of Canada's largest airline, was born in Carrollton, Georgia, seventy kilometres west of Atlanta. An American running the nation's former crown carrier was no anomaly. Trans-Canada Air Lines' first chief administrative officer had been American Philip Gustav Johnson. Johnson was appointed vice-president of operations for TCA on June 24, 1937, when Mackenzie King's transport minister C.D. Howe (himself born in the United States), reasoned that the only way the fledgling TCA would be able to compete with the Americans—and narrow their ten-year advantage—would be to hire an American. Johnson had been one of America's foremost business executives and was responsible for the remarkable early growth of the Boeing Airplane Company. His record in putting TCA on track was almost as impressive as the work he accomplished at Boeing.

The first son of a Methodist minister, Hollis Harris studied aeronautical engineering at Georgia Tech before joining Delta Air Lines Inc., where he worked over thirty-six years from ticket agent to president and chief operating officer of the Atlanta-based company. In 1990, after being passed over for the top job at Delta, Harris took over as chairman of Continental Airlines from the infamous Frank Lorenzo. Harris's profitability projection for Air Canada would not be quite as embarrassing as the one he uttered for Continental. Continental would quickly land as close to bankruptcy as the American law allows—the temporary financial protection provided by a legal stipulation called "Chapter 11." In Air Canada's case, the airline would simply continue to lose money after Harris's prognosis about its financial future.

Harris was building model airplanes at age seven and dreamt of becoming a pilot, though he never did acquire a license. "Hard-working," "people-oriented," "a stickler for detail," "devoutly and humbly Christian" are some of the terms used to describe the man who, according to the *Montreal Gazette*, once called on Continental's employees to pray for the company three times a day in the conviction that "God will show us the way to survive."

"For someone who's been in the airline business as long as he's been in it, he still feels like a kid on his first plane ride when he gets in a plane," Harris's daughter Patti Harris-Chalker told *The Financial Post*. "He still feels that newness, that passion, that euphoria."

Saddled with the haemorrhaging legacy of Frank Lorenzo, Harris's best professional and spiritual efforts did not have the desired results and Continental lost $314 million in the first half of 1991. His board wanted to cut six hundred jobs and one hundred and thirty-three flights and park twenty-two planes. Harris quit in disagreement.

At Air Canada, Harris inherited an airline with operating costs thirty per cent higher than those of major U.S. carriers. It also carried $3 billion in debt and had suffered $218 million in net losses on $3.5 billion in revenues for 1991. He would proceed to sell off money-losing parts of the airline, cut management by ten per cent and reduce the airline's workforce to about 19,500 employees—down from a previous high of 23,000. At the same time, Harris would stun some industry observers by increasing Air Canada's seating capacity in a market that had twenty-five per cent more seats than passengers and had been shrinking since 1989.

Unfortunately, Hollis Harris could not make good on his prediction to make Air Canada profitable within a year. By the end of his first year on the job, the Montreal-based carrier would suffer its largest net loss in history—$454 million for 1992 (- $6.13 a share), on the same $3.5 billion in operating revenue as 1991, followed by a further net loss in 1993 of $326 million.

Harris's predecessor, Claude Taylor, who had been president of Air Canada since 1976 and later its chairman, had hand-picked Harris as his successor. Taylor also started as a ticket agent. Moving steadily upward in the management hierarchy and earning his accountant's wings along the way, he worked, almost from the moment he became president, to have Air Canada privatized—taken out from under Ottawa's wing, distanced forever from federal politicians and bureaucrats, where it would be allowed to fly the increasingly competitive airline skies as a public company. In 1989—the last year Air Canada saw a net profit—the last of Air Canada's shares were sold to the public and the once-proud symbol of Canada's crown-owned enterprise became just another airline with thousands of shareholders and a huge cargo of debt.

"We were not as ready for the life beyond privatization as we thought we were," Taylor admitted to *Report on Business* magazine in February 1991. "We knew we had changes to make but we thought that growth would take care of everything. I regret I didn't have enough vision to say, 'What if growth doesn't happen?' "

Privatization did not help make Air Canada stronger and more competitive; just the opposite. The airline now stood a good chance of being reduced to a marginal player in the global marketplace. In 1989, the year the Mulroney Conservatives finally freed the crown carrier from the federal government's grip, Air Canada had been the free world's eighteenth largest passenger carrier. By 1990 the financial bottom began to fall out and it would be Taylor's job to slash the airline's costs, reduce staff and make its services more attractive to travellers. It was a whole new competitive world now, for which Air Canada was not, as Taylor admitted, all that well prepared. "We thought because we knew how to fly airplanes well, the rest would happen automatically," Taylor was quoted as saying.

Rhys Eyton, Taylor's counterpart at PWA, was, according to *Canadian Business* magazine, "the first head of a western Canadian airline to come from accounts payable rather than the cockpit." He was born in Vancouver in 1935, graduated with honours in business administration from the University of Western Ontario and obtained his chartered accountant's designation in 1966. He joined PWA's finance department in 1967 and, building a solid reputation as an inventive financial manager, was made president in 1976. "The key to this business is operating from a strong balance sheet," Eyton told *Canadian Business* in 1990. "If you don't have that, you won't make it." Eyton used his "balance sheet wizardry" to engineer the series of airline take-overs, rolling five sizeable airlines into one and building controlling stakes in five affiliated carriers. PWA's staff complement went from three thousand to more than seventeen thousand.

Between 1976, when Eyton became president, and 1989, PWA enjoyed thirteen consecutive years of profit. Operating revenue grew over that period from $102 million to $2.2 billion. Net income in the same period added up to an aggregate total of $234 million. Unfortunately, it would take only the next three years to wipe out that total. Between 1989 and 1991 PWA would suffer accumulated net losses of $233 million. And the following two years would be astronomically worse.

Fare wars diagnosed fatal virus threatening Canada
"Insolvent airlines lower fares to generate cash, forcing [other] insolvent

carriers to match them. If nothing is done to treat the virus the results will be more airline bankruptcies . . . within three years, there will possibly be no healthy domestic airlines without some significant government action now."

—Airline analyst Douglas Frechtling, *Vancouver Sun*, March 3, 1993

Once upon a time this country had two companies involved in the transportation business. The first was blessed by its government connections. It grew large, fat and complacent, but it always found a way to make money. The second company started out on its own, struggled in the shadows of the larger company, found innovative ways to compete and eventually began to take large amounts of market share away from its competitor. Little company No. 2 began cutting seriously into the larger company's profits, angering the latter's upper management and forcing it to fight back with a vicious marketing campaign that cost both firms dearly. It became clear the country could not support two transportation companies, which were intent on achieving profits only by damaging each other in wasteful competition.

Eventually, after four decades of bare-knuckle competition and commercial warfare that almost financially exhausted them, both companies, guided by the light of common sense held by government, merged to form one transportation company that ended up—appropriately, given the size of the market and the damage open competition did to both companies—controlling the entire marketplace.

After merging with the North West Company in 1821, the new Hudson's Bay Company (HBC) went on to become twice its original size, operating on almost an entire continental scale. At one point, the HBC was geographically the largest commercial enterprise in the world: after the merger and under regulation by the British government, HBC's market interests—in furs, in trade goods, in trinkets— would cover one-twelfth of the earth's surface.

Once upon a time this country had two transportation companies. Both were the invention of government. One grew fat and rich and arrogant by living off the public purse. The other struggled, decade after decade, loaded down with the debts accumulated from a ridiculous and costly rash of competition and expansion that only proved some industries are too large—in capital investment and in

14

14

TURBULENCE

social responsibility terms—to allow free and open competition. In this story, it was clear all along that what the country really needed was a government-regulated monopoly to ensure the proper growth of the company's services and fair prices for its customers—and to avoid the commercial and social damage that comes with wasteful competition.

By 1994, having fobbed its passenger responsibilities back on to the federal government with a withering entity called Via Rail, and after closing down many miles of its underutilized rail lines, Canadian Pacific (CP) and Canadian National Railways (CNR) began working together toward a merger of their eastern Canadian railroads. Having lost a combined $2 billion over the previous five years, the two competing railways were facing "a grave and immediate financial crisis." A merger would help "avert impending disaster" for both companies.

The railroads' problem? Overcapacity. Both management groups were admitting what many Canadians had known for decades. There was too much railroad for the size of the market.

When that merger is completed, and the damage from their continued competition in other parts of the country is computed as well, Canadians can expect that both companies will eventually seek a merger of their remaining operations. CN and CP will become one, just like HBC and the North West Company. It will only make business sense. The problem will then be that the national railway system will be an unregulated monopoly, free of government restrictions and able to charge whatever it pleases in a totally uncompetitive commercial environment. The prairie farmers, who fought against that usurious reality in the 1920s and 1930s in the form of the Canadian Pacific Railway, will then turn over, quite uncomfortably, in their graves.

Once upon a time this country had a proud and healthy airline industry. It was led by an airline owned and regulated by the federal government on behalf of the Canadian public. Guided by legislation to provide a transcontinental airline service that was safe, efficient and affordable, this airline—Trans-Canada Air Lines, later renamed Air Canada—went on to become one of the most respected air carriers in the world.

Along the way, and to some degree because of its effectiveness, TCA was complemented by a host of safe, well-run and cost-effective air carriers, each with a responsibility for providing air services in regions of the country where the national flag carrier no longer was required. Routes, performance standards and even air fares were regulated by a government agency to ensure Canadians enjoyed safe and fair-priced air travel. Government regulation of the country's airline industry existed, as for the fur trade after 1821, to avoid wasteful and damaging business competition among companies, to help the aviation industry grow, and to provide a broad range of national airline services to the consumer at the best possible price. Destructive head-to-head competition was kept to a minimum or avoided entirely.

The services provided by this regulated airline industry were some of the finest in the world. Regular air fare prices were competitive with those in the United States. In some cases, Canadian fares were even cheaper. This nation's airlines held one of the world's finest safety records. Many Canadian cities—Saskatoon, Edmonton, St. John's, to name just a few—enjoyed daily, direct flight service to major centres such as Toronto, Ottawa and Montreal.

Today, this country has what is essentially a two-airline industry, or duopoly. The industry is no longer regulated by the federal government. Canada's airlines now fly in more or less free and open competition with each other. Neither major Canadian airline makes money. With the exception of international flights, both airlines largely fly where they want, when they want.

Both carriers often fly to the same destinations, often at the same time of day and, usually, with both planes one-third to one-half empty. The chances of either airline making substantial profits in the future are marginal, if not arithmetically impossible.

This kind of competitive behaviour, hatched and enlarged by deregulation, is inherently self-destructive, leading certainly to the "bankruptcy virus" George Washington University's Douglas Frechtling pointed to in a 1993 study. If airlines are free to set fares by the perceived choice of the marketplace, the virus doesn't simply spread: it reaches absurd levels of competition frenzy, to the point where airlines do not just compete at irrational levels, but begin to dine upon themselves.

Both Canadian carriers, in the true spirit of destructive competition, also continue to deliver Canadian travellers to connecting *foreign* airlines—which then fly routes in direct competition with the other Canadian carrier. In other words, instead of Canadian carriers competing solely with the world, they compete with each other, effectively putting money into a foreign carrier's bank account rather than a Canadian bank account. It could only happen in Canada.

Canada has always been a nation that could only support one major transcontinental airline. The load figures of the two battered carriers prove that fact. But the debt burden carried by the Canadian airlines in 1992 was so immense they could not even do what HBC and the Nor'Westers did in 1821—merge together into one reasonable entity that made sense for the domestic, or for the international, marketplace. The other significant difference between then and now is that the merged HBC went on to commercially control the better part of an entire continent. Canada's airline industry no longer can be said to control even the airspace over its own country.

2 / Hello Cruel World

"The deregulators were determined from the start to extend the new competitiveness around the world, wherever American airlines were flying. But their campaign, which looked relatively straightforward inside the United States, became far more confused in other countries where airlines were owned by their governments and deeply interlocked with national policy, and where the appearance of free competition was never quite what it looked."
—Anthony Sampson, *Empires of the Sky*

THE PROBLEMS FACING ALL AIRLINES, but particularly Canada's two battered carriers, were complex and confusing. The tranquillity that typified the Canadian airline industry for so many decades had been shattered by a series of interrelated events beginning as early as the mid-1960s in the United States. One contributing factor was the introduction of wide-body passenger aircraft and the influence they had in providing low, charter-style air fares. The sharp rise in fuel prices triggered by the Organization of Petroleum Exporting Countries in late 1973, a series of recessions, and the levelling off of passenger traffic growth would also be contributing factors.

But the spark that would ignite more than a decade of consumer confusion, collapsing airlines and lost investor wealth was an initiative introduced by the American Congress in 1978. It was called "airline deregulation." The term would eventually come to stand for everything that seemed to go wrong with the world's—not just the U.S.'s—airline industry. In Canada, the introduction of full airline deregulation a decade after the Americans would not only prove inappropriate and costly, it would help tear the structural heart out of what once was a relatively stable and effective national airline industry.

Canadians were promised more airlines competing for their travel business, cheaper air fares, greater frequency of flights, better service and a stronger airline industry. Canadians got fewer competing airlines, fares that stayed the same or rose, less service on most major routes, and a domestic industry that was in such bad shape it could only be saved from collapse by selling itself to the highest foreign bidder. Under Canadian deregulation, Canadians would have a weaker, not a stronger, domestic air industry.

Canadians have a bad habit of borrowing ideas too quickly from other nations, particularly our friends to the south, rather than formulating our own based on our history, our social or business needs and our cultural aspirations. The lesson airline deregulation would teach us is that you can gravely damage the nation's economic and social fabric by jumping on inappropriate bandwagons. As we would later witness by the middle of 1994, even many Americans in the land-of-the-free-market were beginning to have grave second thoughts about the two economic initiatives they had spawned—deregulation of industries like airlines and privatization of public enterprises.

The lesson Americans were slowly beginning to learn from their free trade foray into global competition was that their most effective competitor nations—Japan, Germany, France, Korea, even Singapore and Thailand—made bold and aggressive use of government as a means of achieving competitive ends. Governments in these countries were a highly valued part of their economic success story. Government provided much-needed stability for the conduct of successful global trade. Government was there to set policy, to negotiate international agreements, to financially support the most promising business initiatives with research and development assistance, to maintain business-labour harmony, to check the damaging excesses of unrestricted competition, and to regulate domestic industries to ensure the most promising domestic corporations were strengthened for the global fight.

Americans had been preaching to one another for almost a quarter-century that "the less government, the better." They lived by a doctrine that said it made sense for domestic businesses to beat each other's financial brains out in the name of liberty of the individual, advantage for the consumer and free enterprise. Government's role was to get out of the way. Many claimed to be following the economic tenets laid down so challengingly by the eighteenth century Scottish economist Adam Smith who wrote that the success of commerce should best be left to the "invisible hand" of the marketplace. This simple translation of a complex theory fit the ideologically blinkered minds of people like President Ronald Reagan and his supporters. They would pound the drums for an economic doctrine that pressed for less government involvement in trade and commerce—often to America's detriment.

After totalling up the price of deregulating the savings and loans industry—as well as other costly misadventures in the name of getting government "off the backs of American business"—and after assessing their nation's comparatively poor economic performance against its major international competitors (in the midst of one of its worst economic periods since World War II, Japan still had an unemployment rate in early 1994 of only three per cent compared to the U.S.'s 6.4 per cent and Canada's eleven per cent), some Americans were now questioning the dogma that said there was a diminishing role for government where business and commerce were concerned. This dogma, they realized, might be handicapping their country's international aspirations.

It was becoming clear to some Americans that belief in the "Reaganomic" shorthand version of Adam Smith might make some people rich, but it would not build a stronger economy or a stronger nation. Because Canada traditionally followed the American drummer one or two decades after the beat, we had not yet, by 1994, reached that realization. Canadian business groups and federal politicians would still be so caught up in the flow of economic theories rolling across our border that few would hear the political alarm bells.

In fact, the brutal state of Canada's two major airlines would be blamed on everything *but* the industry's deregulation by the previous Mulroney government. Federal politicians, business leaders, many large corporations and a host of analysts would continue to insist that, despite how bad things were with Air Canada and CAIL, it still made sense to just let the two carriers continue to batter each other over a marketplace that could only support one of them. Canada's deregulated airline industry was, at this point, free enterprise not at its finest, but at its most chaotic.

Deregulation, particulary of Canada's airlines, made as much sense as holding the Stanley Cup playoffs without referees. Like them or not, referees were there, as were government regulators, to keep the players from mutilating or maiming each other.

"Don't sell your stock in Japan Inc. . . . [Y]es, economically it is suffering from an inflated yen and faces a serious threat of triple-dip recession . . . But far from being on the brink of collapse, Japan may be undergoing the restructuring that will deliver it into the 21st century as an unapologetic leader on the world stage . . . Since the end of the Second World War, Japan has valued stability above all things."
—*Vancouver Sun* editorial, April 30, 1994

The unstable air the Canadian airline industry had weathered until July 27, 1992 would be low level turbulence compared to the violent buffeting that hit the industry, Parliament Hill, investment houses and the Main Streets of the country after the PWA board announced they had suddenly, and inexplicably, changed their minds about a corporate marriage with AMR. PWA's compass had spun 180 degrees and the company was now willing to talk partnership with its bitter opponent, Air Canada.

PWA was in such a devastated condition that it apparently did not have enough cash to stay aloft long enough to close that life-saving deal with AMR. Incongruously, the only avenue of salvation that seemed open to the battered CAIL was a bail-out from the Mulroney government—the very politicians who had finally deregulated the business in the first place. That sobering discovery, followed by an almost clandestine voyage by a PWA board member in search of a Tory bail-out, set in motion, as the *Globe and Mail* reported, "a sequence of events that has since rattled the Canadian airline industry to its foundation."

The board member's visit to cabinet minister Don Mazankowski in Vegreville, Alberta, was the cue that PWA was at the brink of bankruptcy. The airline had no one but the federal Tories to turn to. There was no last minute equity bail-out to be had from private sector investors. The reality was finally sinking in. Canadian Airlines International was a financial basket case. Nervous shareholders were forced to watch their already battered shares in PWA drop by the month's end, to the $2 range, from what had once been a high flyer at $29.50 per common share.

About seventeen thousand Canadian employees, most of them in western Canada, now faced the possibility of unemployment. Analysts, academics and travel business representatives were staring at the possibility of a return to monopoly airline control and, in their minds at least, an inevitable increase in air fare prices, a reduction in service and flight frequency, and less rather than more of the competition two federal governments had promised when they began the process to deregulate the industry. Hypersensitive Conservative MPs, suddenly caught in the prelude to the anguish of the Charlottetown Accord round of constitutional wrangling, found themselves with another issue that could drive a wider and deeper wedge through the national unity debate: Calgary-based Canadian Airlines (the West) versus Montreal-based Air Canada (the East).

The Tory cabinet had been worried about PWA's viability and survival since the spring of 1990. CAIL was literally exhausted. It had run up $162 million in net losses in 1991 (-$3.66 a share), a follow-up to $71 million in losses over the previous two years. CAIL had last seen profit in 1988, a squeaky $30 million ($1.25 a share) on $2.2 billion in operating revenue. But the real issue was a political one.

Politics had started this mess and politics was standing in the way of a solution. The Tories were facing a no-win situation. They were an indebted and cash-strapped government which had made much of the issue of the national benefits of robust competition and free enterprise. To be seen to be doling out funds and/or loan guarantees for an indebted and cash-strapped private sector airline that had gotten corporate indigestion, as much as anything, from eating too many of its competitors, was an ideological nightmare for the Mulroney government. They had other problems as well. Air Canada wasn't doing much better financially than CAIL.

The world's airline business was in trouble and had been for a decade or more, but the two Canadian carriers were a special case. In that horrid year of 1992, when, worldwide, the industry would lose US $4.8 billion, Canadian Airlines and Air Canada would stick out as disproportionately heavy losers. While representing less than three per cent of global airline business, the losses of the two Canadian carriers would add up to more then eleven per cent of the world's total. They were bleeding at a much faster rate than the rest of the industry.

Both airlines were struggling to control costs. In 1992 CAIL would lay off thirteen hundred airline workers, attempt to cut aircraft capacity and still be heading for a hard landing. Air Canada in 1992 would unload its *en route* credit card operations on Citibank for $282 million, lay off roughly thirteen per cent of its workforce and try to lower its overall costs by ten per cent. But the airline's long-term debt had risen to over $3 billion by 1991, from $1.8 billion two years earlier, and Air Canada would still be budgeting for $1.9 billion in new aircraft purchases. The whole process had a whiff of unreality to it, as though Canada's largest carriers, not unlike the pace of the climb in the deficit or the national debt, could not implement cost-cutting measures fast enough. Frugality wasn't working any more. The bills and the debts were growing faster than management could cut or trim. The Canadian airline industry seemed less a business at this point than an example of financial anarchy.

At this juncture, almost seventy per cent of Canadian travellers were flying the skies of southern Canada on discount fares—with an average reduction of thirty-four per cent—which meant travellers were flying at less than cost. The two carriers had locked themselves in a travel war with cut-rate fares. The slip into another recession and flat domestic travel growth had not helped. Each July day, beginning as the ramp crews in St. John's readied the first aircraft for flight in the wee hours of the morning, and ending as the last crew member tossed the final piece of luggage onto the carousels in Vancouver's International Airport, Canada's answer to supremacy of the skies— CAIL and Air Canada—would have dropped more than $2 million just by existing.

Both air carriers would continue to exhibit a tremendous capacity for defying the normal gravitational pull of the factors of commerce. At the end of 1991, they also carried long-term debt and debt commitments totalling $4.5 billion. Their debt-to-equity ratio, the conventional test of solvency, would be an unbusinesslike 3.65:1. But while other carriers around the world were unloading expensive and burdensome commitments for new aircraft delivery, Canada's two major airlines still had over $3.1 billion in future aircraft contracts.

Air Canada was planning to buy as many as thirty-six new aircraft in 1991 and 1992, while CAIL had dibs on sixteen. To pay for this glut of new aircraft, both airlines would have to come up with operating margins of six to nine per cent per year. Air Canada had never achieved more than five per cent and CAIL had not come close since 1987. Bleak economic forecasts or no, Air Canada and CAIL continued to operate almost business-as-usual, continuing as one government study revealed, "with an aggressive program of fleet expansion."

The incomprehensible would become the bizarre in November 1991 when Air Canada would announce, with great brio, that it would take three of its Boeing 747 jumbo jets out of mothballs in the Mojave Desert for the spring of 1992. The $450 million worth of aircraft had been sitting idle since delivery from the factory. This sudden addition of extra seating capacity—in an industry reeling from two consecutive years of consumer contraction and at a time when most of their planes were flying one-third to one-half empty—was considered suicide by some industry observers. Air Canada would call it gaining "additional productivity" and getting ready for anticipated growth in 1992—a year which would turn out to be the worst in the airline's history.

For CAIL, the chickens from two major acquisitions—the agreement at the end of 1986 to buy 100 per cent of CP Air for $300 million and the takeover of Wardair in 1989—began coming home to roost with a vengeance in 1992. PWA debentures would be downgraded in the marketplace to the equivalent of junk bonds.

In a February 1993 article titled "A Litmus Test for Corporate Lemons" in *Canadian Business*, Ross Healy, president of Solvency Analysis Corporation of Toronto (SAC) pointed out that PWA had been in "deep, first order insolvency" since May 1990 thanks to the long-term debt it was carrying, largely the result of the two takeovers. The Wardair buy-out would prove to be the cause of the most balance sheet indigestion.

"At the time [May 1990] we identified clearly that PWA had the dollar volume of assets to bring their balance sheet back into a condition in which they could service their debt," Healy recalled in 1994. But to be solvent, PWA had to "immediately sell $700 million of assets—immediately."

SAC's formula for judging balance sheet viability (the operational activity ratio) was considered somewhat unorthodox to members of the airline industry and some investment dealers. SAC focused on a company's balance sheet and tested its ability to pay its bills rather than on the somewhat inert conventional debt/equity test of how much is owed versus how much equity exists.

By 1992, PWA had long passed the point where it could pay its bills by selling off its assets. PWA was all but dead. It would take a miracle on the order of Lazarus to keep CAIL from heading into bankruptcy.

"As the recession deepened in 1990 and 1991, and began to hurt all airlines, the ability to sell assets fell away extremely rapidly," Healy said of the storm PWA had chosen to fly into. "Worst of all, [PWA] had our analysis." SAC had performed the analysis on behalf of a client with a sizeable investment in the airline. The client showed the SAC findings to PWA for a response. "The feedback we got said basically these guys don't understand airline accounting, to which we responded to our client: that may be but it's clear [PWA] just doesn't understand accounting."

By early July 1992, PWA's board was trying to make a miracle happen. They were looking for government help to bridge the haemorrhaging CAIL to a "strategic alliance" or an investment offer in CAIL by AMR. Long before the wooing of AMR began, PWA had been holding discussions with Air Canada about a buy-out. Air Canada offered $238 million for CAIL's international routes, rather than buy the struggling airline. But one-half of CAIL's revenue came from its international operations. A sell-off of those routes would spell certain doom for the airline. Its counter-offer to Air Canada was for a merger. But Air Canada would prefer to hang back in the weeds and bid for the best parts of CAIL when and if it fell apart, leaving the non-revenue-bearing carrion for creditors. At the same time, talk was circulating within the industry about a twenty-five per cent purchase of PWA voting stock by a foreign carrier, either Delta, American or United airlines. The speculation kept the financial spotlight on a shaky CAIL.

On February 5, 1992, chairman, president and chief executive officer of PWA Corp. Rhys Eyton announced that the company had not ruled out a "made-in-Canada" solution—meaning a PWA merger with adversary Air Canada was still a talkable issue in his mind, a year after talks had stalled. A month later, on March 19, 1992, PWA did its first in a series of pirouettes and announced it had broken off all talks with Air Canada and was now in detailed negotiations with AMR. The airline said, yes, it had "given full and careful consideration to Air Canada's proposals," but the board had decided that continuing discussions with American Airlines was the best way to "maximize shareholder value."

Air Canada's new president, Hollis Harris, responded with the announcement that his airline intended to lodge a strong protest with the National Transportation Agency (NTA) in an effort to block any potential PWA–AMR deal. Air Canada feared the sudden appearance of the successful American giant on Canadian soil. CAIL was one thing, in terms of competition. American Airlines was decidedly another.

PWA argued that any deal that might be consummated with American would not be a take-over. Any foreign carrier buying into a Canadian airline was restricted by federal legislation to a twenty-five per cent voting share of the domestic airline. But a sobering statement by AMR's chairman Robert Crandall in Toronto on February 6—that American Airlines was not interested in "minority holdings" of other airlines—seemed a pretty clear signal to some that American, even at twenty-five per cent, would have a substantial say in how CAIL would be operated in any future partnership. Either that or there would be no deal at all.

At Air Canada, Harris was clearly agitated by events. He claimed a deal between AMR and PWA would turn Canada into "a country whose airlines could be relegated to junior partners of U.S. mega-airlines." Whether his fears were real or not, this did seem a rather strange position for Air Canada, whose management was also actively seeking a partnership with USAir of Arlington, Virginia, a U.S. carrier with 1990 revenues of US $6.6 billion. When the USAir opportunity fell through, Air Canada would eventually tie up a marketing alliance with the then–No. 2 U.S. carrier, United Airlines, plus buy a piece of bankruptcy-prone Continental Airlines. But it was clear by early 1992 that, after the ride through deregulation, both Canadian airlines needed American partners just to survive.

Harris was also trying to bolster a major Air Canada weak spot. Since the spring of 1990, Air Canada officials had been pounding on political doors attempting to gain route access into the Orient, particularly Tokyo and Hong Kong, both long-held CAIL destinations. Air Canada eagerly wanted to expand its international service into the booming Pacific Rim, an area traditionally served by Canadian Pacific Air Lines, before it was merged by PWA into CAIL. The International Civil Aviation Organization predicted passenger traffic in the Asia-Pacific region would grow by as much as 8.5 per cent by the year 2000, versus six per cent for the entire world's airline traffic. Other projections had the Asia-Pacific market expanding to almost forty per cent of the world's airline traffic over the next two decades.

Air Canada badly wanted a piece of the action. But its pleas had been falling on deaf federal ears.

In April 1992, Tory Minister of Transport Jean Corbeil would tell Air Canada to wait for a decision on its request until CAIL and American Airlines had worked out their potential commercial partnership. Frustration turned to fear for Air Canada. In effect, both Air Canada and American were aiming at the same route target. Neither airline had access to the rich Asia-Pacific market at the moment. A partnership deal with CAIL would instantly insert CAIL's Tokyo and Hong Kong destinations into American's routing system.

Air Canada could see itself up against American Airlines on two very important fronts. Even if it was to receive a favourable nod from Corbeil to fly a Toronto-Japan route, Air Canada would be pitted against the aircraft might of American rather than simply CAIL on the latter's existing routes. As well, American was eyeing the possibility of using CAIL's dominant position at Toronto's Pearson International Airport Terminal 3 to offer more transborder flights into the northeastern U.S., reducing its competitive pressures at New York's La Guardia and Washington, D.C.'s National airports. This would run head-to-head with Air Canada's northeastern U.S. services.

On April 14, CAIL president Kevin Jenkins announced PWA had signed a preliminary share purchase agreement with AMR. The agreement, subject to NTA review, was the first step in the effort to save CAIL.

Like the previous November, when it announced it was flooding the airline seat market by bringing three jumbo jets out of mothballs, Air Canada reacted by announcing it would increase its summer seating capacity. According to CAIL officials, this move by Air Canada was clearly "part of a plan to kill off Canadian" before the airline could close its life-saving deal with AMR. Hollis Harris replied that the initiative was "just good business."

But Air Canada's move was less good business than pure battle tactics. Although Air Canada's passenger traffic would edge up slightly, by five per cent over 1991, the deterioration in "yields" prevented any significant increase in operating revenues. (Yields are the number of cents earned in revenue from each passenger multiplied by the distance flown.) Previous cost reduction efforts implemented by Air Canada to try to control its bottom line were offset by the increased seat capacity. The gains Air Canada may have achieved with cost-cutting measures would be wiped out by the losses incurred by the extra seats they threw on the market.

AMR's proposed investment in CAIL was based primarily on CAIL jumping out of the Gemini Automated Group Distribution Systems Inc. computer reservation system it shared with Air Canada and joining AMR's SABRE system, a move that Gemini and Air Canada officials claimed would destroy Gemini. An angry Hollis Harris would eventually threaten to sue, claiming that PWA was legally bound to the Gemini partnership until 1997. Harris said every effort would be made to stop a PWA–AMR deal.

Harris also demanded Ottawa give his airline immediate access to Canada-Japan routes and fifty per cent of the slots at Japanese airports, as a sort of competitive concession. He then said Air Canada would "break even within eight to 12 months." At that time, in the spring of 1992, Air Canada was on its way to a third consecutive annual net loss, which was followed by a $326 million net loss in 1993.

Good numbers or bad, a preliminary agreement between PWA and AMR or not, Harris was still after a merger of the two money-losing Canadian airlines. It had been reported that on his first day on the job. he declared he intended to "engineer a takeover" of CAIL and, if possible, to follow that up with a merger with a major U.S. airline, preferably USAir, to keep pace with the growing trend toward globalization or "international partnerships," as a survival tactic for large carriers.

In the spring of 1992, CAIL seemed clearly partial to an AMR deal. For one thing, many more jobs would be saved. A PWA–AMR deal might result in the loss of 1,500 to 2,000 jobs, compared to an estimated 8,000 to 10,000 in a merger with Air Canada. The PWA board would still be piloting a Canadian operation. In theory at least, their seventy-five per cent voting control would mean Canadians would still be running Canadian Airlines, just like the good old days, whereas a merger with Air Canada was just a quick step to disintegration of the proud Calgary-based carrier—just as it had been for Wardair when it merged with PWA in 1989.

But both moves had potentially large political down sides. A merger with Air Canada still appeared to be the simplest solution. Air Canada chairman Claude Taylor trotted out a Decima poll showing, according to the *Montreal Gazette*, that eighty-five per cent of

Canadians would prefer a merger to a takeover by American interests (though a later Decima poll would lower that number substantially to forty-seven per cent, with only nine per cent favouring a U.S. partnership). PWA's Rhys Eyton trotted out a poll showing "Canadians are more concerned that a deal maintain domestic airline competition." But a merger also sparked other fears in many quarters. "A merger would leave just about the entire domestic industry controlled by one company," wrote the *Montreal Gazette*, "and would make a mockery of Canada's deregulation policy."

The Canadian travel industry as a whole could foresee a deterioration in efficiency, a drop in levels of service and an increase in air fares. They could also see the loss of lucrative override commissions from the competing Canadian carriers—incentive commissions that agencies receive for increasing their sales with one airline or the other. Investors, staring at a combined debt estimated to be about $4 billion, with long-term capital commitments of about $3 billion, and already spooked at losing more than $500 million in investment wealth on these two airlines in the past three years, were unlikely sources for the new infusion of equity the merged airline would desperately need. And creditors and aircraft manufacturers could see nothing but down side for them, with payment commitments shelved as the merged entity struggled to keep aloft, and with as many as eighty excess airplanes thrown on the international market, boosting capacity and stalling future aircraft purchases by other airlines.

On the other hand, a twenty-five per cent takeover of PWA by AMR had its drawbacks as well, the first being that somewhat ethereal issue of Canadian independence and sovereignty. With a majority of Canadians polled displaying their distaste for an encroachment from Fort Worth-based American Airlines, how might that sentiment translate into passenger preference when it came to buying tickets? Harsher critics were predicting the end of the domestic airline industry in Canada with the arrival of American on the scene. An already financially weakened Air Canada—living now in the private as opposed to the public sector, and no longer able to reach back into federal government pockets to bail itself out when times got tough— would be fighting the world's most successful airline on pretty porous home soil.

The Mulroney government had backed itself into an ideological corner with its dedication to airline deregulation and competition between two domestic carriers. Added to this was the cultural *realpolitik*, in which fretting Tory MPs from Quebec helped fuel a caucus split by circling their provincial patronage wagons around Air Canada, arguing protection for the Montreal-based airline against their western counterparts—who were arguing just as vociferously for the right to allow the Calgary-based CAIL to head south. Instability, wrote *The Financial Post*, "is the dominant feature of the Canadian industry."

Both airlines were stuck with too many aircraft for the number of passengers they could potentially carry. If surplus aircraft were not being parked in the Mojave Desert, they were being sold as quickly as a soft market would allow. In 1991, despite the fact industry analysts thought the airline could do even better, PWA had been fortunate to unload a handful of Airbus A310-300s and DC-10s, but there were still too many new planes on order.

Despite all this uncertainty, things looked as if they might be close to resolution. On May 5, 1992, AMR and PWA confirmed that a North-South deal was as good as done. In a maximum of six weeks, they claimed, they'd be able to wrap up talks and aim for a written agreement shortly thereafter. The deal at this point called for AMR to invest $200 million in CAIL, but according to AMR executive vice-president Donald J. Carty "that figure is not written in stone," and there were a couple of issues that needed to be ironed out.

On July 9, PWA's director of corporate communications Jack Lawless told the *Calgary Herald* a final deal with AMR could be reached "within a few weeks." The parties were still negotiating on marketing issues, such as the frequent flyer programs, but they planned to make a formal application to the NTA immediately after announcing a deal had been reached. As the acrimony began to die, Air Canada went on record as saying it no longer opposed a marriage between AMR and PWA. It seemed, in retrospect, a blissful end to a stormy couple of corporate years.

As late as July 23, PWA informed the *Montreal Gazette* that an agreement had been reached on the principal issues between the two airlines, such as AMR's one-third ownership of CAIL for now roughly $250 million and its request for a revised structure of the PWA board of directors. The wedding invitations had been sent out. Everyone knew the names of the happy couple. Consummation seemed moments away. The relief seemed palpable. Then, inexplicably, on

Monday, July 27, PWA announced that "discussions with AMR Corporation regarding a possible alliance have been terminated."

> *Transportation deregulation called failure*
> *"The prospect of a merger between Canada's two largest airlines proves the Conservatives' hands-off attitude has failed, critics said yesterday. While a merger might be the only salvation for Air Canada and Canadian Airlines International, it would end the competition that was supposed to be the hallmark of the Conservatives' transportation-deregulation program. It would also leave other Tory transportation policies—increased air links to U.S. cities, airport privatization and expansion—in tatters . . ."*
> —*Southam News*/CP, July 29, 1992

Instead of a North-South marriage with American Airlines, CAIL now stood before the pulpit with another suitor—Air Canada. The two Canadian airlines had "agreed to enter into merger discussions starting this week. The Government of Canada is aware of the pending discussions and will be monitoring them closely." The media release did not say *how aware* the Tories were or how closely these new discussion would be monitored. If the truth be known at this stage in this strange tale, the Conservatives were now an unexpected new guest in the wedding party.

"Merger with Air Canada has always been an option, and now we're pursuing it," the *Montreal Gazette* reported PWA's Lawless as saying. "It makes sense to pursue the option that has the greatest likelihood of preserving the airline industry in Canada," he added, as if the sudden shift of potential mates seemed little more than a young girl's license for whim. Lawless understandably ignored public comment on the acrimony that had built up between Air Canada and PWA over the past year: the seat capacity wars and the badmouthing that had gone on between the now-to-be-wed airlines—not to mention the repeated spurning by CAIL of Air Canada's advances in the past.

The country's newspapers exploded in a fury of speculation and general agreement that Air Canada had won a major victory—somehow. But what was going on? Who was pulling the strings? Once again Canada seemed headed for a single, national carrier—a monopoly. The Mulroney Tories had promised open competition, free enterprise and freedom-to-fail. Canadians now had lots of the latter and little benefit from the former. Some newspapers termed the potential merger the birth of "Mapleflot," in reference to the former Soviet Union's government-owned, trouble-plagued carrier.

The Conservatives had been primarily responsible for introducing airline deregulation with all sorts of promises. Now Canadians faced the prospect of even higher fares, less service and only one ticket agent to complain to. For those working in the industry, there was also the prospect of ten thousand fewer jobs. In the minds of most Canadians, the country had started out with one publicly-owned transcontinental air carrier dominating the marketplace; now we were being quickly flown into a situation that was potentially worse than anything the crown-owned version of Air Canada had ever perpetrated upon us—in reality or in myth.

At one time the taxpayers at least owned the monopoly carrier's assets and enjoyed the years of profit. Overall, regulation kept fares reasonable and service levels high. Now the prospect was that a private monopoly carrier—if it could remain aloft with all its debt—would be in a position to tell us where we wanted to fly to and for how much—and there wasn't much Canadians could do about it.

"We had an industry that was competing head-to-head," Deputy Prime Minister Don Mazankowski said in an effort to quiet the maelstrom after July 27, "but obviously both are losing money and there has to be a remedy found to this situation . . . the only other option is a merger." The words must have been tough to swallow for charter members of the Adam Smith Fan Club. Three days into the merger fiasco, shares of PWA plunged forty-seven per cent in massive volumes of trading on the Toronto Stock Exchange.

Mazankowski was effectively saying the Mulroney Tories had just been hoisted with their own petard. The modern application of Adam Smith's theories—about leaving the matter of the economy and money making to market forces, the "invisible hand" of fate and business competition—had failed. The other shaky shibboleth used by the Tories—"getting the government off our backs"—did not seem to be working either. If a merger did transpire, one of the first things the Tories would have to consider would be reintroducing regulation for the airline industry they had just deregulated.

As the howls began from the editorial side of the daily newspapers—about the need to "reregulate" this battered and bleeding industry, or to open Canadian skies to U.S. carriers to compete with Mapleflot—the July 30, 1992 *Globe and Mail* put its finger on an even more confusing contradiction: that the Tory cabinet might have been responsible for killing PWA's deal with AMR. "The government was instrumental in scotching Canadian's planned alliance with American and with persuading it to restart talks with Air Canada," the *Globe* announced, citing "sources knowledgeable about the events." So much for government in hands-off mode.

According to the story, PWA had been running drastically short of cash—more than even sceptics suspected—and had asked for government loan guarantees to bridge its way to the closing of the AMR agreement that, without the interim guarantees, would not be the done deal everyone thought possible. The Tories stiffed them. They then laid out conditions that forced PWA to terminate its love-talk with AMR and—as if the world is not a strange enough place—crawl back into bed with Air Canada, its old nemesis and competitor.

Backtracking on ideology aside, the Tories also had a problem with style. The Department of National Defence, it was reported, had long been in discussion with cash-strapped CAIL to buy three of its A310-300 Airbuses, surplus from the Wardair takeover, for a price of roughly $150 million. A telephone call from a highly placed Ottawa bureaucrat had informed PWA that if it did not break off talks with AMR, and reopen negotiations with Air Canada, Ottawa might not buy the three A310-300s as anticipated. If the sale did not go through, the struggling PWA stood to lose at least $40 million in cash it badly needed.

Most observers were convinced this was intervention by Ottawa to dictate a deal it preferred. To many western Canadians, it meant more concessions to Quebec, especially since it was theorized that Minister of Defence Marcel Masse had played his usual, heavy pro-Quebec role by using the hammer of the A310-300 purchases as a way of strengthening Montreal-based Air Canada's position. A combined CAIL-American Airlines would mean Air Canada would be going head-to-head with the world's most successful airline. Who knew what impact that might have on Air Canada business and jobs in Montreal?

The Tories were livid about the *Globe*'s story and the accusation that a federal official had intervened and strong-armed PWA back to the table with Air Canada. The newspaper stuck to its story. The Tories fumed. Air Canada officials rushed in with their first merger offer to PWA. It was less an offer of a hand in marriage than a shotgun between the ribs.

Air Canada's three main demands were that more than sixty per cent of the merged company would be owned by Air Canada shareholders, and that the big bosses—chairman and president—would come from its side of the family. Two other heavy consider-ations shook the PWA board: the fact the majority of the ten thousand employees out of work came from Canadian Airlines, and the headquarters for this new airline entity would be Montreal, as Corbeil later confirmed. This was not a merger proposal. It was a complete takeover proposition.

CAIL employees marched in the streets of Calgary, Vancouver and Toronto to protest Air Canada's terms. One employee group offered $60 million in deferred wages as an alternative, but it was considered too little too late. As each page of each company's balance sheet was turned, it became clear that this would be, if ever consummated, a marriage made in hell.

A casual review of the numbers had the combined airline losing more than $600 million in 1992. At the time, Air Canada was outlosing CAIL as much as $1.8 million-to-$800,000 a day. The future combined debt of the merged airline would be in excess of $7 billion. The debt-to-equity ratio was estimated at as much as 15:1, compared to American Airline's 3:1. And the new all-Canadian monopoly airline would still require more than $1 billion in new capital if it wanted to operate successfully. Many of the players—the boards and man-agement of the two airlines, the federal government, the employees, the investors and the creditors—began to think there might be *no* solution to this mess.

It was now being suggested in a number of quarters that a merger was not required. All Air Canada had to do—with cash-on-hand from the sale of *en route* and other downsizing ventures, estimated to be more than $700 million at the time—was float an offer to buy all of PWA's shares. Even by offering a premium price of $10 a share (PWA stock was trading at $2.33 a share in July) the whole company, minus debts, could be had for less than $500 million, based on forty-eight million PWA shares available at the time. For that figure, people theorized, Air Canada could solve everybody's problems and end up with a bunch of extra aircraft, buildings and property assets at fire-sale prices. But as enticing as the possibility looked, Air Canada management reportedly had doubts about the stability of the political process. Who knew what the Mulroney government might do next to screw up people's business plans?

3 / Too Much Geography, Too Much Politics

"The major problem in the airline industry is which major American airline will prop up Air Canada or the basket-case Canadian Airlines International, which desperately wants to save itself from Air Canada, run by an exile from Georgia who thinks the only solution to save his airline is to appeal to San Francisco. This is a country? God help us."
—Alan Fotheringham, *Maclean's*, December 27, 1993

THE AIRLINE INDUSTRY IS LESS A BUSINESS than a series of annual romantic fictions, wherein boards, accountants and investors try to erase the awkward reality of the financial present, relying on spiritually uplifting memories of the struggles of the past to keep them in the air. Flying, defying the ominous but inevitable tug back to the earth, they hope to rise into the blue-sky future they have been chasing since the industry began.

In January 1914, the St. Petersburg-Tampa Airboat Line probably started the first airline passenger service between St. Petersburg and Tampa, Florida. The company was belly-up by springtime. It was an omen for the industry as a whole. What began as endlessly exciting possibilities for flight in Kitty Hawk, North Carolina, in 1903—and in Baddeck, Nova Scotia, in 1909, with the first airplane flight in the British Empire—kept stalling over the decades, losing more and more altitude until the international airline industry finally returned to earth with a dull thud. In 1992, the accumulated losses of the world's airlines finally surpassed all the profits gained by the industry since its inception in 1914.

Between 1990 and 1993 alone, the International Air Transport Association (IATA), an organization made up of over two hundred of the world's airlines, estimated the industry's global operating losses totalled an unprecedented US $15.6 billion. Significantly more carriers were flying and losing money than were making money. It was roundly accepted that by the end of the century there would be fewer than eight, perhaps only six, large international air carriers—"mega-carriers"—in existence. Many of the familiar names on the global airline list would disappear. Many in the United States already had—Eastern, Pan Am, Braniff to name a few. In Canada, CP Air disappeared under PWA's wing in 1987, as did Wardair in 1989. Many of the once-proud national flag carriers would be relegated to feeder status in the future, delivering travellers through massive hub airports to the waiting mega-carriers—or they would be out of business.

The airline business is a perfect example of an industry that, in efforts to "shake itself out" and remain competitive and profitable, has driven itself—with a large degree of help from politicians, in Canada as well as around the world—into something resembling bankrupt purgatory. There they will remain for perhaps years, carrying on the pretence that running an airline is just like running any other kind of enterprise. It is only the times that are troubled, boards, politicians, airline academics and airline management will argue, not the way they set policies, stroke theories or manage companies.

One way the industry rationalizes its financial plight, not unlike the circumlocution used in large corporations' annual reports, is to pretend that very normal circumstances—the sudden inconsistencies associated with the economy, the spin of politics, the erratic stabs of human behaviour—do not apply to them. The April 14, 1994 issue of *Canadian Travel Press* announced that thanks to enforced cost-cutting and the various death's-door, eleventh-hour alliances—like the eventual agreement between PWA–AMR—the industry was enjoying a "new optimism." Air Canada, it reported, actually recorded a small profit of $1 million in 1993. Although Air Canada had suffered a $326 million net loss for the year, the trade periodical explained away the $327 million discrepancy by maintaining the airline "was driven into the red yet again by interest on its debts, write-offs on its shares in Ireland-based GPA Group Ltd. aircraft leasing, the cost of dissolving Gemini CRS, and staff-reduction buyouts."

Items such as costs related to laying off workers, interest on debt, and even income tax payments can be considered "unusual" items or nonoperating expenses in assessing a company's annual performance. These designations are certainly within generally accepted accounting standards. Still, designating interest, for instance, as a nonoperating expense in an industry that perennially carries massive debt with interest—as regular an expenditure item as fuel for their planes, wages and the cost of maintenance—might seem odd to the average citizen. After all, the cost of deciding to lay people off (like the cost of employing them), the money paid to borrow money to buy airplanes, and the taxes everyone pays (when they make money) are just regular costs of doing business, one would think. With creative accounting justifications like that, Treasury Board could no doubt eliminate much of the national debt.

The entire world airline industry was in a deep tailspin by 1992. That multi-billion-dollar worldwide aggregate loss was only another blinking red light on the pilot console. International airline yields had declined on average almost three per cent a year between 1960 and 1990, falling from roughly nineteen cents per passenger/kilometre to about eight cents in 1990 values. Greater competition, the replacement of propeller-driven aircraft with jets, and jets with jumbo jets, meant airlines today were earning fewer and fewer dollars from each passenger they carried. Companies would react to this problem by trying to further the cause of corporate suicide. They would begin fighting competitively to fill as many vacant seats as possible, primarily by flying more aircraft than demand warranted and by cutting ticket prices to below cost in an effort to attract more passengers.

Thanks in part to increased competition and the introduction of new and larger aircraft, "load factors" (the percentage of seats occupied on an airplane) predictably fell. By 1992 the average passenger plane was flying at less than sixty per cent capacity—more than two percentage points below the estimated break-even point. In the United States, the increased competition for airline travellers meant that by that year, ninety-five per cent of all passengers were travelling on discounted fares—at an average of about sixty per cent off the listed price.

Except for East Asia and the Pacific Rim, growth in global air travel had been declining since the late 1980s. The decline in business travel caused the most concern to the world's airlines. They had traditionally relied on business and first-class travel (the "high-yield" air traveller) to offset cheaper economy and bargain-class fares. The industry's measuring stick had been that the business traveller should represent about one-fifth of the passenger load, but two-thirds of the revenue, on an average flight. Battered by a series of recessions between 1981 and 1992, many companies slashed travel budgets and slapped restrictions on air travel. Company officials began flying less, and when they did, many began opting for discount fares.

Alternatives to air travel became attractive to businesses, including high-speed rail travel and even automobiles (saving time and some money by avoiding congested commutes to and from the airport). The alternatives went from the simple (more facsimile transmissions and telephone conference calls) to the complex (video conferencing). According to IATA, one-half of business travellers surveyed in 1993 expected telecommunication technology to replace at least some portion of their future air travel. The industry's forecast indicated that business travel, as a percentage of total domestic travel, would fall even further by the turn of the century. It was not a great prospect for any airline's future when your most valued customers were wandering away.

For all but the exceptionally focused air carrier, such as the no-frills, short-haul Dallas-based Southwest Airlines—a carrier that offered no meals, few amenities but cheaper fares, thanks to low labour costs and more efficient operations—all these trends were working against future financial success. By 1993 the profit margins for the industry were slim or all but nonexistent (even though IATA estimated that if every airline had raised its average ticket price just $14 in the previous three years the industry would have broken even—rather than lost U.S. $11.5 billion). It was getting harder and harder to believe there was a viable future for much of the international airline industry. *The Economist* pointed out in June 1993: "If competition is allowed to increase with the spread of airline privatization and deregulation, then the contest will become even closer as carriers scramble to earn every cent of additional revenue." There evidently was the possibility of even more airline death-and-destruction to come.

In a fourteen-page survey of the state of the world's airline business, which included a litany of failures and lost investment wealth associated with the errant philosophy called deregulation, *The Economist* found it difficult to conclude unequivocally that deregulation worked. Deregulation "needs policing" if it is to be successful, the prestigious magazine waffled.

The Economist's projections did not matter much for Canada. By 1993 the Canadian airline industry had about as much damage done to it as anyone could imagine. Air Canada had been privatized and the entire industry was in the midst of counting its dead after the Mulroney government's imposition of deregulation and the damage suffered by fuel increases and recession. In the five short years between 1989 and 1993, Canada's two major airlines incurred net losses totalling just shy of two billion dollars. One government study called the numbers of "crisis proportions."

Both Canadian airlines were sadly uncompetitive. Air Canada's unit costs were a lumbering 18.2 cents per available seat mile in 1991. CAIL's was slightly better at 14.6 cents. But neither compared with American Airline's 11.0 cents. By 1992 the two Canadian airlines' unit costs combined were 50 per cent higher than the average unit cost for the seven largest U.S. carriers. As both haemorrhaged with daily losses, Air Canada increased its seat capacity by fifteen per cent, forcing CAIL to increase its capacity as well, sparking a fare war that resulted in almost seventy per cent of passengers flying in southern Canada travelling below cost. This, in a business presumably bent on making profit.

In September 1993, Moody's Investors Services reviewed the financial state of Air Canada rather kindly and declared that the former crown carrier, so hastily privatized under the Mulroney government, "lacks the characteristics of a good investment." Air Canada had not seen a net profit since 1989.

In February 1994, Air Canada reported it was prepared to spend $1 billion on six long-range, European-built Airbus A340-300s, with delivery to begin in 1996, in the hope of "improving efficiency" and making it "more competitive" on light-density routes not profitable with older aircraft. At least one economic study indicated any airline's profits can be predicted to fall—in a regulated or a deregulated environment—within two years of an airline placing large orders for aircraft. The gargantuan cost of acquiring new aircraft in batches of two or three dozen runs easily into the billions of dollars. When the aircraft are delivered, those huge bills suddenly must be paid—driving down operating profits drastically.

Given that Air Canada had been operating in a net loss position over four consecutive years and that more new aircraft were on the way, the prospects for long term viability were not, as they say, within the realm of probability. The announcement the airline intended to buy more "iron" (a nice, masculine term often used within the industry for planes) may be a fiduciary kiss-of-death for Air Canada in 1996, and probably beyond.

PWA lost a record $543 million in 1992 and, according to industry estimates, would have had to *double* its fare prices if it intended to make money. Despite its financial track record, PWA announced in February 1994 that it was "poised for a return to profitability in 1995." After reporting its 1993 net loss of $292 million (a vast improvement from the $543 million lost the previous year), PWA chairman Rhys Eyton predicted another loss for 1994, but he was encouraged enough by "the trend toward profitability" that 1995 might show a profit. Tracking backwards, that would mean PWA would have lost money for six consecutive years, a best case scenario of the most troubling kind.

The battle for Canadian Airlines International's survival would take the better part of three years. During that time the airline would come within hours of collapsing more than once. Its year-end cash position often looked like a busker's pocket change. Its plight alerted the entire nation to the financial condition of the country's airline industry—and how unbusinesslike their numbers were.

By February 1994, PWA stock was sitting at $1.35, later to tumble to the forty-cent range. Stockholders were facing the massive stock value dilution about to take place with the forced trade of $722 million debt-for-equity as part of its AMR survival package. Even with the pending entry of American Airlines onto the ownership scene, some investment reporters were calling PWA overpriced at $1.35 and were recommending that readers sell.

> *"One of the things that makes writing about business so much fun is that you get to write the same stories over and over, because people keep making the same mistakes."*
> —Alan Sloan, *The Financial Times*, March 19, 1994

The explained reasons for the plight of Canada's airlines were many, varied and roughly similar to the ones used by other international airlines trying to explain their wobbly financial situations. Fewer people were flying. Operating costs had not gone down fast enough. Increased competition drove down revenues and profitability. Too many aircraft meant too many seats to fill with too few passengers. Steep fuel price increases were cited, though oil prices would reach record lows by 1993. Government taxes, such as the GST, it was claimed, helped make the nation's two principal carriers uncompetitive. Then there was the Gulf War and the impact it had on consumer demand, though the war itself had been over since 1991 and the bulk of the related drop in air travel had been in the international, not the domestic, sector. And, of course, there were a number of recessions which took place since 1981. All serious contributing factors.

But as troubled and beleaguered a business as it had been over the past decade, nothing stirred the turbulence in Canada so dramatically as the Mulroney government's initiative in 1988 to fully deregulate the airline industry. Deregulation of the airline business— U.S. style—had about as much application to the Canadian business experience as the American legislative structure has to our parliamentary democracy.

In 1978, the U.S. government introduced the *Airline Deregulation Act*, after almost a half century of federal government regulation of that nation's airways. The initiative had its roots deep in the country's capitalist beliefs about the efficiency and effectiveness of the marketplace, about American commerce, unfettered by government regulation, free to compete, free to succeed or free to fail. The entire deregulation premise was based on the goal of advantage to the consumer. Get costly regulation out of the way, and business and service would increase and drive down prices. But it did not happen.

Rising out of the beating heart of post-World War II American commerce, eliminating or reducing government regulations was a hymn that echoed partly with the thoughts about comparative advantage declared by nineteenth-century British economist David Ricardo, but more significantly with the hovering ghost of Adam Smith.

Deregulation freed the airlines from having to seek government permission about going in and out of business, where they could fly, and when and what they could charge passengers for air fares. An airline could close down a route if it so desired or change its mind about another. The idea was that air carriers were now free to do what they wished, including fail.

The circumstances surrounding American deregulation were decidedly different from the Canadian experience in a number of ways. First, there was no crown carrier operating as a public enterprise. Other than getting out from under government regulation—something that had helped make many a U.S. airline more profitable and its shareholders wealthier than they should have been—Americans had little to distract them on the issue of "public enterprise." It was all simply a matter of making the business more efficient and profitable, and of giving the travelling customer a price break.

Second, the opportunity for real "open competition" between carriers was substantially greater in the U.S., given the number of carriers flying at the time, the size of the American market, and the number of eager carrier participants waiting in the wings. Third, shortage of large amounts of investment capital was seldom a problem in the U.S. as it was in Canada. Fourth, there was a large population base that meant business competition on a grand, national scale was possible. Finally, that large population was spread out, lending itself to the hub-and-spoke distribution system American airlines began using.

Deregulating the Canadian airline business made about as much sense as opening Toronto's public transit system to free competition. The result, inevitably, would be too many transit companies fighting each other to carry too few passengers on too many buses or trolley cars. Each company would increase its debt to buy new vehicles, tracks, equipment—and competitors. The now-struggling transit companies would consolidate by merging and acquiring each other— the exact opposite of the "more competition" expectation. The one or two surviving road warriors, short on operating cash and themselves heavily burdened with debt, would appeal to municipal or provincial governments for protection from their creditors and from each other.

Government would then reregulate the transit business, carving the territory out so neither company failed—even though common sense would tell anyone that only one company was needed, given the passenger load factor and high capital costs related to public transit. Transit fares would go up accordingly for the rider, even though it was supposedly in his or her interest that healthy competition had first been generated. This little metaphor is pretty much what happened to the Canadian airline business between 1984 and 1994.

In Canada's case, deregulation was a major cause of the disaster from which the airline business will not likely recover, certainly not as healthy, domestically controlled, competitive carriers providing Canadians with the best service at the cheapest price possible. The Canadian airline business, despite occasional protests to the contrary, needs government regulation to survive. It has always needed government, since the birth of air travel.

The challenge of operating an airline—the immense and largely uncertain capital investment, the perishability of the product (an empty seat on an airplane in flight cannot be salvaged), the paper-thin profit margins—makes the industry like a public utility. Only the most dogmatic entrepreneur or neoclassical economist would argue that there are no limits to the ability of business to compete. Otherwise, we would by now be enjoying the advantages of space travel, brought to us by all that competitive fervour to get paying passengers to Mars.

Large public utilities, with their immense capital needs, can be a target of disdain and derision, but you will seldom see corporate giants enthusiastically arguing to be allowed to compete in the utility arena—not without monopoly protection provided by government. The exception, as in today's telephone and telecommunications market, comes when strict regulation of a sector of the economy has historically protected businesses against the self-destructive effects of competition and allowed for the successful growth of the utility. The characteristics of today's airline industry are not demonstrably different from utility models.

Most of an airline's capital commitment is tied up in the buying of aircraft. This is a fact of the industry's life that moves from the realm of necessity to a dependence bordering on addiction. Nothing makes airline management's eyes widen with envy and lust, their hearts beat with anticipation, more than the sight of a new airplane coming off the production line, dressed in their company colours. It becomes their chariot to the heavens.

Until the 1980s and the tapering off of traffic growth, the value of used aircraft had often been equal to or greater than their original purchase price, making the resale of aircraft a lucrative business. In fact, some veteran airline executives claimed most Canadian airlines made more money over the years by buying and selling airplanes than they ever did carrying passengers.

"I can understand when [PWA] said we don't understand airline accounting," said SAC's Ross Healy. "Prior to 1990 there was such a shortage of aircraft that you could sell your used planes at a profit." Even when an airline was in a queue waiting to receive delivery of its new airplane from the manufacturer "you could still sell your place in the queue for a heck of a lot of money—I think PWA did sell their place once and I think they got $100 million for it."

Around the Canadian airline industry, it was well known that the shrewd buying and selling of aircraft was one of the ways Max Ward carried his airline with a very skinny balance sheet. "He kept upgrading all the time—continually selling his old aircraft at a profit over his carrying costs—and that was one of the ways he made money," according to Healy.

But when the market for surplus aircraft began drying up, more than a few airlines were left with the daunting task of servicing loans and leases for hundreds of airplanes parked in mothballs at various desert locations.

"I guess PWA kind of thought things would carry on this way," said Healy. "That was the business Max Ward was in—buying and selling equipment—but that was not the business PWA was in. They were in the business of acquiring aircraft and acquiring market share, so they had no intention of blowing away all those [surplus] airliners."

The cost of today's modern passenger aircraft is staggering. A new Boeing 747-400 costs at least US $150 million, with spare parts and training. A new Airbus A340-330 costs US $120 million, not including parts and training. It is nothing for an airline to place orders for two dozen aircraft at a time, whether the potential for making money is there or not. In 1991, as both Air Canada and Canadian Airlines International were bleeding financially after three years of accumulated losses, the two carriers had outstanding orders for forty-two assorted new airplanes, from Boeing 767s and 747s to A320s.

The choices that must be made to buy and operate the right aircraft for the routes available to the airline—with up to two-year time frames for delivery—are like shooting craps for hundreds of millions of dollars at a throw. Sometimes decisions about when to rev up the engines on the new planes can border on corporate suicide.

The airline industry also faces peculiar financial hazards. Millions can be made or lost in a few weeks. Losing $2 million a day is not out of the question, providing the working capital pockets are deep, the balance sheet strong and the prospects for turn-around good. By simply reducing per-seat-per-kilometre costs by a single cent, an airline like CAIL can increase revenues as much as $130-140 million more a year. "The industry operates on very thin margins," said Sidney Fattedad, a former vice-president of CAIL and the man who eventually helped orchestrate the employee plan to save that airline. "The gamble is huge and you can go from a hundred million dollar loss a year to a hundred million dollar profit, just like that," he said with a snap of his fingers. "The airline industry is really crazy. It's like a bazaar. You take your bloody oranges to the bazaar, and its 120 degrees of heat, and if you aren't sold out by the end of the day, those oranges aren't good any more. So you sell them at whatever price. The same thing with airlines. Look at it this way: a seat goes off empty and it's another orange perished."

One additional passenger will contribute revenues but not generate any additional costs, no matter how low the price the airline charges to fill that empty seat. Most aircraft fly with empty seats, so there is a built-in incentive for management to discount fares and try to get some revenue—any revenue at all—from that empty seat. But the danger is that the airline might lower its fares to a point where it is no longer able to cover its costs. And just as management thinks it has revenue coming in to cover that once-empty seat, consumers can change their buying behaviour, putting even more pressure on airlines to juggle prices in an attempt to cover costs.

Business travellers, for instance, may take advantage of heavily discounted fares and begin scheduling their trips over a weekend, thereby pocketing price savings aimed, not at them, but at the discretionary flyer. Even with the shrewdest pricing tactic, management may fill the aircraft, but they could be losing money at the same time.

"The airline industry has a high degree of 'operating leverage,'" a 1992 National Transportation Agency study of the nation's airline performance pointed out. "A small drop in traffic can precipitate a severe decline in earnings. The product's perishability, and the difficulties of reducing costs in the short run are the immediate causes of the high leverage. This in turn is a major cause of volatile earnings and airline industry uncertainty."

It is the airplane itself, paradoxically the fundamental component of the industry, that makes it difficult, if not impossible, to run an airline as a profitable business. The basic rule in the industry is this: you don't want to have too much capacity—too many airplanes—for the airline's route structure. The extremely high cost of an aircraft contributes to the high leverage.

But the way many airline managers and boards have treated the acquisition of new aircraft has probably been the most significant factor contributing to their company's financial woes, and often, their demise. In relative terms, the price of one Boeing 747 is the equivalent to the cost of constructing a building complex the size of the Toronto Dominion Centre. The decision to go ahead and build the TD Centre was a major real estate venture. Yet airline executives and boards will easily make a decision to go ahead with the purchase of a batch of new aircraft with a cost from *six to twenty-four times* the cost of a TD Centre. In other words, the purchase of two dozen expensive, modern aircraft is the investment equivalent of the construction of *two or three square blocks* of high-rise buildings or office towers in Ottawa, Vancouver or Toronto.

One apocryphal story tells of an executive of Western Airlines who decided to go against the industry flow in the mid-1960s and, instead of buying DC-9s or 727s, bought two dozen Boeing 720 aircraft (a relatively unpopular short-fuselage, short-range version of the Boeing 707), against the advice of his own management. The decision was made during a golf match with a manufacturing representative. "The decision broke Western," said one knowledgeable observer.

As the survivors of the world's deregulated airline industry were still licking their deep financial wounds in April 1994—awash with excess aircraft capacity and debt—Boeing Co. of Everett, Washington, rolled out its newest passenger airplane: the giant twin-engine Boeing 777. The 777 has a slightly wider body than the Boeing 747 and about the same seating capacity. With two engines, it should be twenty-five per cent cheaper to operate, but will still cost as much as US $146 million to purchase, versus a Boeing 747's US $160 million price. The concept for the 777 blossomed in 1986. The design process began in 1990. The first aircraft will be delivered to customers in May 1995. The total value of the orders and options placed for 124 new 777s in April 1994 by the world's battered airline industry added up to over US $16 billion. Boeing expects the world's airline business will buy as many as 12,000 new aircraft by 2010—worth US $815 billion!

Success in the airline business seems simple. It depends on matching capacity (the number of aircraft and the number of seats you have available) with passenger demand. In the manufacturing sector, a producer can react to low demand by slowing the production line or by letting inventories stockpile until consumer demand raises prices to a level that covers costs and makes a profit. But reducing an airline's capacity to meet a drop in consumer demand is extremely difficult. It is not easy to simply stop flying all the Boeing 747s in the fleet until business picks up. In the short term, it is almost impossible. Schedules are heavily dependent on the integration of aircraft and deployment of crews. If flights are cancelled, crews must still be paid, and aircraft, buildings and normal operating costs must still be taken care of.

The only real option for airline management during a short-term drop in traffic (and typically no one really knows whether the drop is short or long-term) is to keep flying the routes and paying the bills that mount up (if one can), in the hope that at some point in the near future demand will pick up. Most airlines go one hazardous step further—lowering fare prices in an effort to fill those empty seats. Of course, this will do one of two things, or both: fill the seats in the planes, but with prices that do not cover the cost of flying; and/or spark a fare war with other competing carriers, driving down earnings even further while costs remain relatively static. On a bad day in the airline business—and most of them in the last half-decade have been horrid—there is no way to win—or to make money. The game is lose-lose.

"Most airline boards are not what you might call totally knowledgeable about airline performance," said Fattedad. "Most are highly prestigious business people. Not too many of them are used to an industry where intensive capital investment is required, and the largest operating costs are fuel and labour, so the leverage on your earnings is so high that if you're not on this thing one hundred per cent of the time, it can flip on you overnight.

"What we've seen in North America . . . is that marketing guys keep driving the fares down. And they're driving the fares down because somebody's decided to buy more airplanes, and more expensive airplanes, and the more expensive that orange is to produce, the more you want to sell it—at whatever price. "So what happens is the airlines try to get rid of inventory that would otherwise rot. And that type of marketing in an industry that's so highly leveraged with capital and labour is a formula for disaster."

Added to this cold business reality is the fact that airlines are relatively homogenous—there is really not much to choose among them. Fare price is very often the only differentiating factor. The consumer goes with the airline providing the best price to the preferred destination. Often the only loyalty factor is the lock a frequent flyer program will put on a traveller's business. Without successful product differentiation, the airlines—once again—tend to rely on price competition to lure travellers.

Although many travellers might argue that safety is also a differentiating factor, the whole question of how safe you are flying one airline over another is, for the moment and particularly in North America, almost a moot point. Compared to flying in 1960, today's passenger is twenty times less likely to be killed in a commercial aircraft crash. Thanks to advances in the technological design of modern aircraft and better trained air crews, the fatality rate has fallen over the years to almost negligible levels: 1 death per one hundred million passenger kilometres flown. Worldwide, the year 1993 had the lowest accident rate since 1984.

CAIL was cited in 1993 as one of the top five, safest, midsized airlines in the world. If not for tragic fatalities caused by a washroom fire on board a DC-9 in June 1983, Air Canada would also be in that top five category. If there is a danger for air travellers, it comes when flying on smaller commuter airlines where the fatality rate is about four times that of larger carriers. But overall, flying is safer than almost any mode of transportation—except walking.

Airlines also get locked into costly scheduling, most often by the size and configuration of their aircraft and by the desire to be viewed by the consumer as being competitive. Airlines keep flying half empty largely to be *seen* to be flying. On most Canadian routes the total traffic potential is actually smaller than the capacity of the aircraft servicing those routes. Between Ottawa and Calgary an average of 120 passengers travelled the route nonstop each day in 1991. "Air Canada flew one A320 and Canadian [flew] two 737s daily for a total of 317 seats," the NTA's study noted. "Neither carrier could reduce its flights without significantly harming its market presence, so excess capacity resulted." Excess capacity on major trunk routes in the summer of 1992 averaged more than twenty-six per cent. Toronto-Vancouver was running thirty-one per cent excess capacity and the Montreal-Calgary route was slightly less than forty per cent. The illogical became even more irrational in the summer of 1992: while aircraft seat capacity was far outstripping demand, Air Canada doubled its seat capacity on that Ottawa-Calgary route for "competitive reasons"—just making a bad situation worse, for them and for CAIL.

Alliances and Cost-Cutting Bring New Optimism to Airline Industry
"There seems to be growing confidence in the airline industry that despite continued losses in 1993, there are clearer skies ahead because of new corporate alliances and aircraft that are expected to streamline operations and reduce overall costs . . ."
—*Canadian Travel Press*, April 14, 1994

The truth of the airline industry's survival—in this country as in almost all others—is that governments have always played a strong role in the development, growth and regulation of the industry. Sometimes that role was driven by economic policy goals—like the government's building of canals for transportation in the eighteenth and nineteenth centuries, or the taking over of failed railway operations in the early twentieth century.

With airlines, the role of government probably began as early as 1919 when the French government provided subsidies for domestic pilots miffed that British aviators had started a London-to-Paris service using converted World War I bombers (£42 one-way, not including lunch basket). The British government reacted by forming Imperial Airways, the precursor to British Airways, providing the airline with subsidies and merging smaller airlines to form a single, government-owned and operated airline; in effect, the birth of the national flag-carrier airline.

Governments, Canadian and otherwise, have always had to be there to save the airlines from themselves; save them from what seems an almost blissfully romantic notion that the flying-passenger business is not much more complicated and challenging than running a mom-and-pop grocery store. What was true in 1919 in Britain is still true in 1994 in Canada. The fact is the Canadian airline business has always operated most effectively—*all* factors considered—when government holds the industry's hand.

Canada's air transportation system—the rules and regulations under which it operated, and the events and policies that shaped it—cannot be fully understood without recalling the lessons learned from the development of railways in this country. After the tumult, duplication and massive cost to build and operate a Canadian railway system in the years following Confederation, by the end of World War I the federal government's fixation was on rationalizing the chaotic result of early railway development. Canadian National Railways, one must remember, was formed by government legislation in 1923 out of as many as 400 bankrupt railroads "that couldn't be scrapped without isolating thousands of Canadians," historian Peter C. Newman wrote in the August 30, 1993 issue of *Maclean's*. "They were built by crooked promoters who overcapitalized their projects, squeezed out the profits, and then pleaded bankruptcy. Ottawa had to step in and save the operations through an umbrella amalgamation."

The whole issue of where governments really fit in is a slippery issue we are still, more than seventy years later, trying to come to grips with. But the early examples of overbuilding, huge investment losses—most covered from the taxpayers' pockets—and almost incomprehensible competition between railways led politicians in the late 1930s to think very soberly about how the airline business should be allowed to develop and function in Canada.

Initially, civil aviation was seen as a supplement, not a rival, to railways. In fact, railways would dictate the corporate structure of the domestic airline business, with Canadian National and Canadian Pacific railways becoming the template on which Canadian airline policy would be constructed. Our tempestuous railroad experience had stabilized somewhat by the mid-1930s, although there would still be substantial return visits to the public trough. Canadian National Railways (CNR) had evolved out of the tragic duplication of effort, debt and financial destitution that early railroad competition had given us. Canadian Pacific Railway (CPR) evolved as the "private" carrier, although its success as a free enterprise initiative was achieved through massive, multi-million-dollar public subsidies and grants.

CPR would also, with great fortune, be left holding twenty-five million acres of some of the most valuable land in Canada. From this decidedly unfree enterprise beginning, the CPR would rise (after receiving a few more millions in taxpayer loans during the 1930s) to become the nation's largest nongovernmental company, with holdings in everything from railroads to fine china, from mining to paper and steel making, from trains to planes to boats to hotels and insurance.

The "public" and "private" transportation enterprise camps aligned themselves early on. Liberals and most prairie farmers tended to support CNR, primarily because of the CPR's twenty-year monopoly stranglehold that kept freight rates high and grain prices low. Tories tended to support CPR. When he began cobbling Canada's first airline policy, Mackenzie King and his Liberal government were hoping to learn from the errors of the railroad experience. King sought harmony between the players, not rivalry and mutual animosity. He wanted a national airline for Canada, but he hoped we could avoid the wasteful investment and competition that was the country's earlier experience with railway building.

In the 1920s and 1930s, not unlike today, owning an airline in Canada meant losing your shirt. The whole enterprise "was full of grief and trouble," as businessman and grain scion James Richardson, owner of one of the real pioneer airlines, Western Canada Airways, put it in exasperation in the late 1920s. Despite the rollicking history of our early air pioneers and bush pilots, there was never enough passenger traffic to warrant the capital investment required. Almost all early air carriers relied on government mail or service contracts to survive, and still they could not make money. Figuratively, within moments of starting up operations in the early 1920s, most carriers in the eastern part of the country were failing. By 1929 there were so many casualties in the business they were forced to merge into the Aviation Corporation of Canada, to prevent them from being bought out by Americans.

Richardson would eventually join with Aviation Corporation of Canada to form Canadian Airways in 1930. Richardson admitted the venture at the time—which included CNR and CNR as partners—was "not in a position to make any money in the strict sense of the word," even with government mail contracts.

With the chaotic history of Canadian railroad development fresh in mind, and the threat of the embryonic airline industry being taken over by Americans, the Mackenzie King Liberal government began deliberating over the formation of a trans-Canada airline system. The impetus did not come from any energetic entrepreneurial pressures for profit from flying Canadian skies. It was more prosaic then that. Air service was not in great demand, but some Canadians were already using American air services to make their way from coast to coast, and American operators were petitioning to enter Canadian air space. By 1937 Canada was one of the few industrialized countries in the world without a national air service. They would design one, as Anthony Sampson pointed out in *Empires of the Sky*, in "an ideological muddle."

Under the guidance of C.D. Howe, the Mackenzie King government originally proposed that Canada's transcontinental airline should be twenty-five per cent publicly owned, forty-five per cent privately owned and the remainder in the hands of the two railways, CNR and CPR. Eventually, the percentages worked their way to one-third each. Richardson's Canadian Airways had been eagerly invited by the government to take part. But Richardson, backed by CPR, interpreted his role as putting up one-half the required capital but only retaining one-third of the company's voting power. He ignored the fact that the Canadian government would be compelled to invest substantially more money than his company—to pay for the cost of constructing and maintaining a nation full of airports, for building radio communication and meteorological services across the country, as well as for guaranteeing any deficits the new national airline incurred.

Although Richardson was the only member of the Canadian private sector with suitable air service experience and pockets deep enough to be involved in the national airline venture, he opted out. The only alternative was to structure a major transcontinental carrier owned by CPR. But with smaller air carriers falling like dead flies throughout the 1920s and 1930s, the railway did not have the corporate appetite to be involved in an airline in any but a minority way. Richardson admitted "there was no room for two large aviation companies in Canada." There was no room in 1937, and, it could be argued, there was not much more room in 1994 either. The Liberal government went ahead with the establishment of Trans-Canada Air Lines (TCA) in 1937 as a government owned and regulated national air carrier service, operating as a subsidiary of CNR.

"TCA was, they said, an arrogant monopoly—though in fact it was not a monopoly for very long. Its government backing gave it an unfair advantage and it should be faced with competition—when in fact it had been faced with strenuous competition on many of its routes from the start. Then, when

it did set out to compete, with normal commercial practices and promotions, it was 'wasting the taxpayers' money'—when in fact for all but a few years it more than paid its own way."

  —Philip Smith, *It Seems Like Only Yesterday: Air Canada—The First 50 Years*

By 1942, TCA dominated aviation in this country, holding fifty-four of the fifty-nine air licences issued and accounting for almost eighty per cent of the air miles flown. The CPR had also, by then, reawakened to the business possibilities of air transportation and taken control of nine smaller Canadian air carriers. Along with Canadian Airways, they formed Canadian Pacific Air Lines. In no time at all, CPR was pressing for a merger of CPAL with TCA. Its aim was to do what the Canadian air transportation market told it was the only reasonable way to fly—have one national air carrier, in this case, jointly owned by the federal government and CPR. This move sparked forty years of competition, bitterness and political division between the two carriers. It also formed the basis of an ongoing ideological and partisan debate over the relative effectiveness of the private sector versus public enterprise in the airline business.

CPR's sudden enthusiasm for the transcontinental airline business may have been sparked by the discovery that TCA was becoming a success in less time than anyone had expected. Even with the huge capital development and expansion costs necessary in setting up a national airline service, as well as the costs of acquiring a fleet of new aircraft and of hiring and training air crews, TCA made its first profit in 1940: $539,263. For the next five years TCA would fly without any subsidies from the Canadian government.

Despite the late start, Canadian Pacific Air Lines would never relent in its efforts to unseat TCA. In 1943 it applied to compete directly with TCA on its routes. Even with the early financial success of the national airline, political pressure was building to expand TCA's routes to more communities and to buy more aircraft to service the routes. To meet the growing demand for air transportation and to ease some of TCA's burden, the federal government decided it might invite other carriers to fly "in parts of Canada not at present served" by TCA.

It was therefore not surprising that CPR was now trying to get a piece of the transcontinental airline business. As D.M. Bain noted in *Canadian Pacific Air Lines: Its History and Aircraft*, "There is no doubt that [a monopoly] company would have eliminated costly competition. In addition, the Canadian air traveller might have benefited from the combination of Canadian Pacific's experience and operating acumen with the Government of Canada's control of aviation within the Dominion and its strength in dealing with foreign governments for negotiating international routes."

But a typical Canadian public-private enterprise was not to be in the airline industry. C.D. Howe turned CPR down. Mackenzie King was determined not to give CPAL equal status with TCA. In his 1942 address to the House of Commons, he outlined his vision for TCA and airline transportation in Canada. TCA would be challenged to meet an imposing mandate: to provide Canadians with the benefits of this new mode of civil transportation, at the lowest possible price. TCA would provide the widest possible service, while maintaining both the safety of its passengers and the investment Canadians had made in the airline. TCA was the country's only transcontinental carrier until 1959, when the Diefenbaker government granted Canadian Pacific Air Lines a daily transcontinental flight.

The profits TCA made from its international runs were used to offset losses incurred by flying routes that were inherently unprofitable, but which came under the airline's mandate of "providing the widest possible service" to Canadians. In those days, the airline was free of direct domestic competition and, by legislation, the government's regulatory agency, the Air Transport Board (ATB) , was required to give TCA any licence it required to carry out its contract with the Minister of Transport.

Beginning in 1937, the whole airline policy process was wrapped in the belief that the airline industry had to be regulated by government agency—like early railroads had not been—to protect against the self-destructive urges of competition. Even if TCA had remained a monopoly national carrier, government regulation would be required to protect both the air traveller and the taxpayer. In the mixed scenario the Canadian airline industry was headed into—a quasi-duopoly with two major carriers and a covey of regional pretenders—there had to be, of necessity, some government regulatory influence to protect, not only the traveller and the taxpayer, but the airlines from themselves.

The ATB was responsible for maintaining safety standards, permitting entry and exit of carriers into markets, ruling on fare structures and, by parcelling out licenses and routes, maintaining some sanity in the business. The agency's minimum objective was to prevent the collapse of any air carrier—and the predictable political furore that would ensue. What the ATB could not effectively do was stanch the flow of incessant political lobbying to change the rules in favour of private carriers.

TCA was the nation's flag carrier on all international routes. But in the late 1940s CPAL successfully lobbied for flag carrier status to Japan, Australia and New Zealand—areas not served by TCA—in addition to the domestic routes it had acquired. This success began years of relentlessly lobbying efforts to diminish TCA's national carrier role and to acquire a route structure that would allow CPAL to eventually compete head-to-head. The airline's goal was to get a bigger piece of the pie the Mackenzie King government had served up to TCA. And for decades, CPAL would persist in drawing itself as the free enterprise David up against the state's Goliath.

But Canadian Pacific Air Lines was the air arm of the powerful Canadian Pacific Railway—later Canadian Pacific Limited. Its political strategy was pretty straightforward: get a transcontinental licence to carry passengers, regardless of the restrictions imposed; after that was achieved, fight to have any restrictions removed; then fight to have the government-run airline's special privileges removed. "No concession was ever considered definitive or sufficient," political scientist Garth Stevenson wrote in *The Politics of Canada's Airlines: From Diefenbaker to Mulroney*, "and it was assured that once the process of conceding the carrier's demands had begun, the government would be unable to stop short of eventually conceding the ultimate objective." It would take CPAL roughly two decades to achieve most of its goal.

TCA's objective—the name would change to Air Canada in 1964—would be to fight to hold the dominant position as the public air carrier. "It succeeded in doing so for sixteen years," Stevenson wrote, "a remarkable achievement considering the political and economic power of the Canadian Pacific and the strength of 'free enterprise' ideology in the period of the Cold War." Successful route encroachment by CPAL could mean lower revenues and profits for TCA, which then could be used as evidence by the crown carrier's critics to show that public enterprise was not as effective as the government wished.

CPAL moved its headquarters to Vancouver (CPR headquarters were in Montreal) and was not adverse to using that reality to fuel a continuing West-versus-East challenge. CPAL pushed for and received routes into Latin America, Amsterdam, Lisbon, Madrid, London and Rome. When the Diefenbaker government came to office in 1957, CPAL turned up the political burners and received transcontinental status on the Vancouver-Winnipeg-Toronto-Montreal route, beginning to increase its share of route traffic across the country. After 1959, TCA's objective would simply be to postpone erosion of its transcontinental domination.

The Liberals softened on their traditional support for TCA, now Air Canada, in 1964. The federal government concluded there could also be a "reasonable role" for five regional air carriers: Pacific Western, Transair, Nordair, Quebecair and Eastern Provincial Airways. This new regional air policy was a political initiative that further weakened Air Canada's route structure and revenue potential—and Canadian Pacific's, to a lesser extent. The regional airlines were the flying offspring of a Canadian government policy allowing smaller carriers to act as transportation suppliers during the building in the 1950s of the American's Distant Early Warning system throughout northern Canada. When the lucrative military contracts ran out, the carriers began lining up at the political trough, claiming, with excess aircraft and few places to fly, they would go broke if they did not receive routes in the south, as well as regulatory protection. The Liberals succumbed and established a regional airline policy that carved up portions of the country into five regional monopolies.

Almost predictably, the regional carriers went out and bought the most sophisticated, but largely unnecessary, new jet aircraft their credit could buy. Those unable to make their costs began, of course, lobbying the government for more favourable routes or for merger favours to avoid the hurt and embarrassment of going broke. The shifts and revisions in the federal government's position meant the nation's policy on air carriers was now one that simply would not allow any passable airline to fail.

If you had two Otters, a bunch of outstanding bills, no real cash flow but lots of gung-ho bush pilot energy—and the odd passenger heading for The Pas, Manitoba—you might be allowed to crash, financially. But if you had a couple of route promises, seven Boeing 737s on order, a large loan at the bank and friends in federal caucus, especially if their home riding was where you intended your 737 to drop down occasionally (and maybe perform your aircraft maintenance)—your future was guaranteed. On such science was Canadian aviation policy based.

By the mid-1960s both major carriers had their territories further dissected and were operating under de facto spheres of influence. By this time Canada had, thanks to the quick erosion of its competently regulated monopoly airline, what was potentially the worst of all worlds. We had competition, but not necessarily competition. "[Canadians] were denied the benefits that competition between domestic services might have provided for the consumer," Stevenson wrote of the situation that had evolved in the absence of a strong airline policy, "while on international routes, where Canadian carriers had to compete against foreign carriers in any event, Canada's limited [airline] resources were divided in an irrational and illogical fashion between [Air Canada and Canadian Pacific]. It is thus not surprising that dissatisfaction with the system began to grow and that change, albeit gradual, transformed the system over the next two decades."

Air Canada was, by then, primarily a domestic carrier with international routes, mostly into Europe. CP Air—the name was changed in 1969—was primarily an international carrier with only one-third of its passenger miles accumulated within Canada. At home, they both had to deal with a bunch of lobby-active regional airlines, snapping up routes with every stroking of a local MP with influence in cabinet. The costly and wasteful airline competition that King and others had tried to avoid was now a burgeoning reality.

In 1979, three days before Parliament was dissolved for the federal election, the Liberals announced that CP Air had finally been "freed." The Vancouver-based airline no longer had to remain tied to a fixed share of the transcontinental market with Air Canada. The moved marked, according to Stevenson, "the formal abandonment of the concept of a pre-eminent national carrier, twenty years after the inauguration of CP Air's transcontinental service and thirty years after the beginning of its international service. For Air Canada there was now no real advantage to being owned by the state, and the stage was set for its possible sale to private investors in the years to come."

But for CP Air, victory came too late. The period of rapid passenger growth had passed. Lower discount fares introduced in the 1970s caused some growth, but profit margins were small, shaky or non-existent. Regional carriers such as Pacific Western Airlines were now competing aggressively on many domestic routes. And nothing had changed in the U.S. routes CP Air held. In fact, Air Canada was still the dominant carrier and was operating slightly more profitably than CP Air.

It was also becoming clear to Canadian Pacific Limited that its original goal of competing head-to-head with Air Canada might not be worth the effort. The profit return on CP Air was not encouraging, in comparison to the handsome returns from other business ventures. The federal government's regional air carrier policy had chopped the pie into too many parts, making successful competition difficult if not impossible. CP Air began dropping overseas routes it held. The domestic sky was also getting crowded. It was now beginning to appear that there was probably too much capacity—too many airlines—for the size of the market. From here on in, it would be harder to realize a proper return on investment.

Canada had begun its air transportation policy process in 1937, with the intention of learning from our railroad mistakes and avoiding what was clearly a lesson of history: that competition among large private sector corporations can in some circumstances be inherently costly, ill-advised and predictably wasteful. Our history of competition among large transportation companies inevitably ended up distorting public policy intentions and requirements, causing an immense amount of lost wealth and burdening the taxpayer. Given the mess the Canadian airline industry had evolved into by 1994, it appeared we were actually better off with the old environment of regulated competition we turned our backs on in 1984. When the bottom started falling out of the domestic industry in 1992, the airlines, some shocked lobbyists, even some Tory cabinet ministers, would begin silently praying for a return to the good, old days of a regulated duopoly—even a monopoly.

"It remains to be said . . . that both the policy of monopoly and the policy of regulated competition in their time served Canada well," Stevenson wrote, "providing one of the safest, most comfortable and most convenient of systems of air transport in the world at relatively little cost to the taxpayer." But that would never be good enough for some Canadians.

4 / Coming In on a Wing and a Prayer

"This is an industry that's labour-intensive, capital-intensive, dependent on governments for [air service treaties], subject to taxation like no other industry, leads into a recession and lags out of a recession. Before I say any more I'll get all depressed, but there is no question the industry's going to survive."
    —PWA Corp. vice-president of finance, Drew Fitch, *Globe and Mail*, April 26, 1994, the day before the partnership with AMR was signed

WHEN THE PWA BOARD ANNOUNCED on July 27, 1992 that partnership discussions with AMR had suddenly terminated, it sparked more than just public confusion and sanctimonious monopoly-thrashing from the nation's business editors. It also caused Canadian Airlines International instructor pilot Capt. Bob Weatherley to phone Sid Fattedad, a recently retired CAIL vice-president. Both men were former CP Air senior managers and had survived the 1987 PWA takeover.

"Sid, this thing is happening again," Weatherley told Fattedad. "They're going to sell the damn company. Can't we do something?" Fattedad, like Weatherley, had been part of that rich, West Coast company culture that grew up around Canadian Pacific Air Lines over its fifty year history. Even though CP Air had been subsumed by its smaller Calgary-based competitor, the genealogy of one of Canada's veteran air services still ran strong and deep among former CP Air staff, now working for Canadian Airlines International. And although the first hint of possible merger with Air Canada carried a figure of six thousand lost jobs, most CAIL staffers knew two things: the job loss would be closer to ten thousand and, given the state of federal politics at the time, the first ones on the street would not likely be employees of the Montreal-based Air Canada.

Fattedad could see the only way something could be done was

through the company's unions. A grassroots movement of angry individuals would not work. The unions held the franchise to any quick organization of protest. If the staff were to be mobilized, it would have to be through them. As a former vice-president, Fattedad was already familiar with the financial numbers needed for the airline to survive. He had worked out a rough outline of a possible financial deal involving Canadian's unions and PWA before he called Capt. John Dunlop, head of the airline's pilot's union on the August 1 long weekend.

"John, are you interested in trying to do something about this company?" Fattedad asked him. He was, but did Fattedad have a plan? "I had a plan, one I had worked out and one which at the end of the day looked something like what we're at today," said Fattedad. After walking through the plan in detail, Fattedad's next call was to International Association of Machinists and Aerospace Workers (IAM) representative Bill Farrall. "We've got to do something," Fattedad told Farrall. "We've got to try to save this airline. I need you to call a meeting of all the union leaders. You guys either have to buy into this thing, and in doing so you can save the company, or you don't. It's up to you."

While IAM's Farrall was gathering together other union leaders for a meeting—including representatives of the management group, who now faced the same possible threat to their jobs as staff did—CAIL employees were already pressing their union leaders to come up with a plan to save the airline and their jobs. They had been shocked by their company's sudden reversal on July 27. During the sultry days of early July, the employees, like almost everyone else, had pictured a now-secure future with giant American Airlines owning one-third of CAIL. But now the employees' sense of urgency was strong enough to get all but one union to agree that very day to an agreement in principle. The agreement called for an instant coalition of CAIL employees to work toward a multi-million dollar wage and benefit concession package that might keep CAIL aloft—despite the PWA board's now-stated intention to couple with Air Canada—through a partnership with AMR.

The coalition's first move was simply to go to Canada's banking community for two hundred million in "up front" money, money to keep the airline flying, backed by the unions' guarantee. "We talked with quite a few [banks] and none of them would put up the money on the say-so of the employees," Fattedad recalled. "They would only put up the money if they had [government] guarantees." With the airline's current and long-term debt, and its shortage of cash, the banks were only being prudent. CAIL was looking more and more, to more and more observers, like a financial disaster waiting to happen.

Although beating the bushes for $200 million in the hope of getting PWA back to the table with AMR seemed like spinning a lot of wheels—given that merger talks with Air Canada were now already underway—it did not deter members of the newly formed Council of Canadian Airlines Employees. Veteran airline people like Fattedad had already figured out what the boards of both airlines would eventually discover: a merger was not financially possible. A merged airline could not fly.

"You look at the whole thing and it's not as complex or difficult as some people think," said Fattedad. "You add up two companies and the total debt is $8 billion, and between them they don't have $6 billion in revenue, and you know this ain't going to work. So we always knew that Air Canada had to go and get one-and-a-half to two billion dollars worth of government money to bail out the whole damn thing. We didn't think [that] was going to happen."

The PWA board met on August 6 to weigh Air Canada's first merger offer—effectively a takeover of CAIL. By this time PWA senior officials were aware, as was AMR's executive vice-president Donald J. Carty, of what the employees were planning. Would the two parties entertain a pitch from the employees when the right time came? they had been asked. They would, came the answer. The employees' council would bide its time.

The PWA board rejected Air Canada's first offer but sent out feelers for a sweetened second offer. Considering the tenuous financial position the corporation was in, it seemed, from the sidelines, that the board's coyness was like being picky about who would be your pallbearer. On August 7, as the employees' council waited out the merger charade, CAIL employees demonstrated against a merger with Air Canada. The nation's newspapers, looking left and right for someone to blame for the country's airline mess, had begun mauling the Mulroney government for "killing the AMR deal" that would have saved PWA and its airline. Why were they not trying to fix the problem now? Tory privatization czar Don Mazankowski tried to distance the government from the fray by stating the talks were a "private sector" matter between CAIL and Air Canada, implying that the Mulroney government had kept a healthy arm's length distance from the whole troubled episode all along, in keeping with its natural ideological inclination.

When Minister of Transport Jean Corbeil admitted the home base for a merged airline would have to be Montreal, he stoked more rumour fires in the West about a putsch on Air Canada's behalf by Quebec-based Tory MPs. While the confusion swirled, Air Canada was also still talking to both United and Continental Airlines in the hope of striking an international partnership, almost as if the foundering CAIL wasn't a large enough preoccupation in its greater scheme of things. It probably was not. Right about now Air Canada was certainly in the pilot's seat.

Events came together like a bedroom scene out of a Broadway farce, with actors switching rooms and chasing other partners behind each other's backs. It was getting harder and harder for the Canadian public to make sense of it all. Many assumed the country was now heading full-speed-ahead to a monopoly airline. Others could not see where PWA's board got off turning down an Air Canada offer when CAIL seemed all but dead. It *was* all but dead, wasn't it? How could they turn down a bail-out offer? And what's this bit about Air Canada teaming up with a U.S. partner? And what about the accusation that Air Canada had been practising "predatory pricing" in its battle with CAIL? Wouldn't that put a damper on marriage plans? What about the Mulroney government's talk about deregulation and hands-off open competition? From the press reports leaking out, it was beginning to look like the Mulroney government was forcing PWA into a merger—although Corbeil was quick to deny it.

It was now an issue that had transcended the financial problems of the Vancouver-based CAIL. It was quickly evolving into what appeared to be a major political screw-up. The Toronto *Globe and Mail* was calling it "the merger that wasn't," and the Tories handling of the affair was leaving the political and airline scenes strewn with wreckage. The demand for government action to settle the airline crisis was rising from a number of other quarters. The Tories deregulation plan was now being openly termed a disaster. Travel industry representatives began speculating nervously that an airline merger—which the Tories were now being blamed for forcing on the two airlines—could only mean higher ticket prices and reduced service for consumers. Given CAIL's shaky state, and lingering stories of collapsed charter airlines leaving passengers high and dry in exotic places around the globe, some industry people were cautioning their customers to be careful about travelling on the airline.

To add further to the confusion, rumours about American Airlines returning to the table began circulating by August 8. On August 10, word was out that CAIL employees were pressing the Competition Bureau to stop the Air Canada-CAIL merger talks. On August 11, as investment dealers were arriving in Vancouver to help the employee council prepare a formal proposal to the PWA board, which was hoped to include financial support from some provincial governments, the board announced it intended to review the latest Air Canada merger offer by August 14.

More speculation began circulating about the Tories' involvement. It was now rumoured they had stirred the chaos by trying to force a merger "as a favour to Quebec" in the midst of the Charlottetown Accord national unity discussions. Corbeil's statement about a Montreal home base for Mapleflot seemed proof of Tory intentions. Some cabinet members began wondering out loud if they were not being taken for suckers by a flirtatious PWA board. The board's dismissal of the first Air Canada offer, its coy request for a sweetened proposal and rumours about an employee bail-out plan involving AMR were interpreted as delaying tactics rather than negotiation in good faith.

On August 12, Prime Minister Brian Mulroney stormed onto the scene to defend his government's actions in the July 27 failure of the PWA–AMR negotiations. He claimed the Tories had not used bullying tactics to force merger talks, that it was the PWA board that had come to the federal government asking for financial aid. It was the PWA board, Mulroney said, which informed the government with great alarm that their airline was in imminent danger of crashing. He called for PWA board members to come clean publicly and tell the truth that Ottawa had not forced PWA to Air Canada's table. Corbeil joined in and denied applying political pressure for a merger, and Mazankowski maintained his position that the Tories were seeking a "private sector solution."

On August 13, the Alberta Conservative caucus warned that a merger of the two Canadian carriers would not be in the best interests of Canadians in general. A federal government official admitted that the Tories were, in fact, leaning toward a private sector solution, but that Ottawa civil service bureaucrats might not be so inclined. The Ottawa-based bureaucrats tended to support a merger of the two Canadian airlines, raising the question: Who were the policy bosses in Ottawa these days and who the worker bees?

On August 14, the PWA board met and announced it had considered two proposals: one from the employees' council and a second offer from Air Canada. The board declared that certain provisions of this Air Canada proposal "were unacceptable." The board then instructed management to "pursue both alternatives." Although it looked as if both offers were still being considered—the board playing both ends against the middle, as it were—the nod towards the employees meant that AMR was now effectively back in the running, fronted by the employees' council proposal. The second Air Canada offer was de facto dead. But it was not, really, if Air Canada had a better offer.

On the same day, CAIL reported a semi-annual net loss of $79.1 million. Air Canada had already reported half-year losses of $293 million, and it was still losing $1.5 million a day or more, in part due to the fare price war it had instigated.

The prime minister let it be known how heartened he was by the CAIL employees' initiative, further reinforcing his call for a private sector solution. He blamed media for leaving the impression Ottawa favoured Quebec over the West. Mazankowski went on record as saying a merger between Air Canada and PWA may be the only option. A merger? But wasn't Tory policy in support of competition? Didn't Mulroney just say . . .? Through some phantom twist of supply-side ideology, a monopoly was now palatable to the Conservative government.

Air Canada had also suffered a recent setback in its efforts to woo an American air carrier into an alliance. On July 21, USAir had bailed out of alliance talks with Air Canada and joined with British Airways. On August 18, obviously frantic to find an international partner, Air Canada signed a joint marketing agreement with United Airlines, American Airlines' chief competitor. No equity was swapped with the U.S. giant, but Air Canada had at least now opened the international door they had been knocking on for months. With United's five hundred and fourteen aircraft, flights to thirty-three countries on five continents, and 1991 revenues of US $11.7 billion (more than three times Air Canada's), United seemed to represent that solid global partner Air Canada had been looking for. Given the fact that almost every airline on the continent was losing money, United's 1991 net loss of US $331.9 million did not appear to be a drawback. It was getting to the point in the deregulated North American airline business where you were nobody unless you were losing hundreds of millions of dollars or defying bankruptcy.

While all this was going on, AMR strolled out of one of the bedrooms and announced its old offer—the one spurned on the July 25-26 weekend—was still on the table, in case anyone did not notice. Heads were scratched again. PWA was back talking link-up with AMR. Air Canada was still shopping for more American partners (Houston-based Continental Airlines, currently locked in bankruptcy, for one). Air Canada and CAIL seemed to want a marriage like Bosnian Serbs and Muslims want to kiss and make up.

On August 19, PWA let it be known the company was having "conversations"—as opposed to "negotiations"—with AMR representatives. The next day the federal Competition Bureau said it was investigating allegations of predatory pricing against CAIL by Air Canada. The Canadian Press reported that CAIL employees were willing to raise their offer and buy up as much as forty per cent of the troubled PWA, though that offer would probably sink to twenty-five per cent when AMR came back on board. And in a front page story the *Globe and Mail's* Ross Howard wrote that Air Canada and Jean Corbeil now believed "Canadian Airlines entertained a merger offer from Air Canada last week only as a delaying tactic while it solicited support from its unions and some provinces for an eventual integration into American Airlines."

Air Canada, Howard went on, was "planning to announce more co-ventures with international airlines in rapid succession to restore public confidence in the airline's viability, while behind the scenes it is likely to lobby hard to cripple Canadian," including campaigning hot and heavy for its long-desired routes to Japan. This new political initiative by Air Canada would put to use the airline's full fleet of forty-three registered lobbyists on Parliament Hill. Some airlines do not have that many staff.

At about this moment things were so stormy in the Canadian airline sky, some formerly ardent exponents of deregulation began reversing previous demands to get government out of the regulatory business. On August 20, the Consumers' Association of Canada (CAC) put its latest position on "Competition in the Canadian Airline Industry" together for presentation to the House of Commons Standing Committee on Consumer and Corporate Affairs and Government Operations. The CAC had long been a supporter of deregulation and had maintained the organization "favoured strong competition." But now the CAC was saying the deregulation status quo was "unworkable" and that "something had to give and soon."

The consumer watchdog association now considered the state of the Canadian airline business so intolerable it was apparently prepared to toss the idea of deregulation overboard, at least for a while. A little government regulation might now be in order, the organization's paper seemed to be saying. Not only that, the CAC now considered that a "monopoly situation could be tolerated over the short term." A merger between the two Canadian carriers to form a noncompetitive monopoly, for all its doctrinal warts and ideological blemishes, "is one solution which at least keeps a Canadian owned and operated airline flying," the position paper timidly trumpeted.

> *"When in Montreal, I took up the matter with Mr. Beatty and I mentioned to him that I thought it would be very unfortunate indeed if any action of the Canadian National were to force the Canadian Pacific to spend money in aviation, as I did not need to assure him there was no room for two large aviation companies in Canada."*
> —James A. Richardson, 1929, in *Canadian Pacific Air Lines: Its History and Aircraft*

On August 24, 1992 the *Globe and Mail* helped blow the lid off the merger plans in a lengthy front page story outlining how a PWA board member had, in mid-July, pursued Deputy Prime Minister Mazankowski for federal financial aid and helped spark the midsummer airline confusion. The *Globe* story confirmed the street version of the matter: the Tories had refused financial bridge assistance for PWA, help that would have allowed it to close a deal with AMR. The Tories, it appeared, then allowed the Ottawa bureaucracy to use the possible purchase of the three A310-300 Airbuses by the Department of National Defence (DND) as the stick to get PWA into merger talks with Air Canada.

On August 25, one month to the day since the PWA board was

forced to sit down and consider the federal government's condition—to drop further talks with AMR and head over to talk with Air Canada about merging and we will take the A310-300s off your hands—it was reported PWA–AMR talks had formally resumed in Texas. The next day the DND announced it would purchase the three A310-300s from PWA for $150 million, as "an indication of Ottawa's support for the Calgary company's proposed alliance"—with *American Airlines.*

The plot was now so thick the average citizen-air traveller had no idea what the outcome might be. Urged on by a nervous PWA board, the Tories had evidently responded by pressing for an Air Canada-CAIL merger. To make it happen, the government was prepared to buy CAIL's three A310-300 Airbuses. But PWA was also talking to AMR about a deal. And Air Canada was off talking to its own American suitors. Now the DND strolled into the fray and informed everyone the agreement to purchase CAIL's three Airbuses would help close a deal—between PWA and the Texas-based AMR.

The division between the two Canadian love birds seemed even wider when, on August 28, it was reported that Air Canada was now trolling with Texas-based partners to buy a twenty-four per cent piece of Continental Airlines, the fifth largest airline in the U.S. with forty-two thousand employees. Continental claimed a fleet of three hundred and forty-one aircraft and US $5.1 billion in 1991 revenues. Continental was also at the time in Chapter 11 bankruptcy—for the second time.

On September 1, PWA put the tattered remnants of the wedding party into a further tizzy when it attempted to slide out of its Gemini computerized reservation responsibilities by claiming Gemini had been insolvent since January 1, 1992 and "unable to meet its financial obligations as they become due." Then, PWA turned around and announced, the same day, that *it* was indefinitely suspending dividend payments on its series-A First Preferred Shares until further notice, allowing it to save $4 million a year. PWA officials called the move "prudent."

With the Air Canada-CAIL shotgun marriage now believed by most observers to be a dead issue, the would-be spouses no longer speaking to one another, the previously jilted AMR hovering outside the love nest once again, whistling its own love song, the CAIL employees rounding up cash and promises to keep a deal with AMR flying, and the Mulroney government just hoping that someone—

anyone—would make a deal to save face, let alone a second Canadian airline, Air Canada announced on September 2 that it had presented another merger proposal to the board of directors of PWA.

"This may be the last [offer]," Air Canada president Hollis Harris warned at the press conference. "This is the best offer they are going to get from us." In fact, it would not be the last offer. PWA—although still talking to AMR—announced it was reviewing the offer and would respond "in due course."

Air Canada was now proposing that a new holding company be established (referred to by the NTA as "Airline Holdco") to manage the operations of both Air Canada and Canadian Airlines International. The offer was seen as a "partnership" rather than a "takeover," with both acting as separate airline companies, with their own presidents and chief operating officers. CAIL would maintain its headquarters in Calgary and Air Canada would do the same in Montreal. Shareholders would receive one common share of Airline Holdco for each common share of Air Canada or PWA, giving Air Canada shareholders, by virtue of the number of outstanding shares, sixty per cent control of the company. Duplicate international operations would be eliminated, excess aircraft capacity would be "adjusted" to suit each airline operation, job losses would be less than originally forecast, and there would be equal representation for both companies on Holdco's board of directors. Significantly, Air Canada did not ask for an exclusivity clause that would prevent PWA from talking with other suitors. PWA was given until 11:59 P.M. on September 9 to make up its mind—again.

The CAIL employees' response to this made-in-Canada solution was predictable. Some called it a "desperate move" on Air Canada's part. Many citizens scratched their heads again. The Toronto Stock Exchange reacted accordingly. Air Canada shares fell twenty cents to $4.30 and PWA shares edged up fifteen cents to $3.30.

But more importantly, Air Canada's chairman, Claude Taylor, took advantage of the situation to go public with his airline's position. On September 2, Taylor prepared a comprehensive, eighteen-page statement for the House of Commons Standing Committee on Consumer and Corporate Affairs and Government Operations. It outlined Air Canada's view of the global state of the industry, argued for his airline's future place in it, and tried to answer many of the questions people had been asking about who might be responsible for the deteriorating state of Canada's airline industry, including trying to set the record straight on the involvement of the Mulroney government.

Taylor began by pointing out it had been PWA, all along, that had been looking for a deal, ever since it had approached Air Canada with the request to be bought out as long ago as February 1991. Citing the trend in almost every other country to consolidate airline operations for purposes of survival in the highly competitive international marketplace, Taylor was not sure why Canadians persisted in clinging to a "status quo that is at best outdated, and at worst, a prescription for national failure." Only America and Japan, with dominant economies and their large population bases, could afford the luxury of more than one international carrier. Most other nations had already figured it out, he said, consolidating and marshalling their airline resources in national strategies to remain competitive—internationally and domestically. The Canadian airline industry seemed content to let the participants beat each other up, instead of making domestic peace so they could take on the world together.

Taylor was also blunt about where the current internecine battle was leading: "The Canadian airline business is in serious trouble—you know the numbers as well as I do. Anyone who believes these companies can be restored to profitability in their present form and still offer security for all employees and bargain basement fares for all customers is engaging in self-delusion."

Taylor argued that an Air Canada-CAIL merger would result in a job loss of only six thousand employees, that competition would be maintained in the long term, and that the alternative to merger was two, weak Canadian operators dominated and controlled by American interests. The result would be a $4.6 billion annual loss to the Canadian economy.

He denied Air Canada had indulged in predatory pricing by adding extra capacity in the spring of 1992 with the airline's decision to deploy three new jumbo jets. He defended the move as just good business, given that the planes had been sitting idle since the winter of 1991 and their introduction costs were marginal. (The NTA felt otherwise in its 1992 review, saying Air Canada's capacity increase went beyond "the normal pattern" and bumped up domestic capacity fifteen per cent over 1991, despite the fact that 1992 was the worst year financially in the company's history.)

Taylor stated that a PWA-American deal would leave the giant foreign carrier "calling the shots," and that what PWA was doing was "handing over the operational management of your airline" to American shareholders. And the federal government, whose financial support was being sought for an PWA-American deal, should understand that that was exactly what they might be financing.

He also took the time to clarify what the federal government's role had been all along, at least from his perspective. The government's response to Air Canada's made-in-Canada solution had always been "interested neutrality" as far as he was concerned. They might want to monitor developments but "at no time did [the government] take sides in favouring one airline's position over another." And they made no attempt to direct Air Canada "towards any particular outcome; nor, to my knowledge, did they attempt to do so with anyone else." He had it on good authority that the Mulroney government was seeking a private sector resolution, and only then "would they deal with its public policy consequences."

On September 3, PWA announced the closing of the deal to sell three A310-300 Airbuses to DND. PWA received $150 million, with two-thirds of that figure going to pay down debt. On September 5, the *Globe and Mail* ran a detailed and revealing front page story ("Split revealed in PWA board: Warning of collapse spurred Ottawa to push for merger"), by transportation reporter Geoffrey Rowan. It was Rowan's relentless reporting and analysis that helped shed the most light upon this confusing affair. His September 5 story explained how the Tories got involved in PWA's financial crisis, how deep that crisis really was, and who said what to whom to get PWA to drop its agreement-in-principle with AMR and to begin merger talks with Air Canada.

"The marvel of the modern mixed economy is its potential internal strength and its resulting ability, on frequent occasion, to surmount the inadequacy, error, indifference or grave ignorance of those assumed to be responsible for its performance."
—John Kenneth Galbraith, *The Culture of Contentment*

The *Globe and Mail* front page story focused on one PWA board member, Calgarian Ron Southern. Along with a number of other board members, Southern believed, so Rowan's story went, that "the airline is in worse shape than PWA has publicly revealed." Southern was the driving force for a merger with Air Canada as the solution to PWA's financial ills. As early as that spring, the board had apparently voted on the merger idea. Southern led a group of members, including former Alberta premier Peter Lougheed, Winnipeg businessman Arthur Mauro, Newfoundland publisher Harry Steele and Max Ward, who subsequently left the board. Beyond the bad financial shape of the Calgary-based airline, Southern and others were particularly concerned that board members might be personally liable for millions of dollars in outstanding commitments, primarily wages to staff, if the airline went into bankruptcy. But PWA chairman Rhys Eyton was able to convince a majority of the board that the American Airlines deal was a better option than a merger with Air Canada.

Southern was best known as the head of ATCO Industries. As the company's president and chief executive officer, Southern would earn a reported $1.4 million in 1993, placing him on a salary ladder with Canada's top bankers, probably also making him the highest paid executive of a public company in Alberta. Southern was legendary for his business acumen and his no-nonsense approach to business. As one industry source told the *Globe*: "If Ron Southern believes this company is nearly out of business, then they are nearly out of business." Twice, the board had voted on the merger issue during the summer, and twice Eyton had prevailed.

As the story unfolded, the deal with AMR seemed to be creeping to conclusion by late June 1992. But at a meeting in the first week in July, AMR representatives suddenly upped the ante, saying the American airline giant now would require at least another $150 million on PWA's books before an ironclad agreement could be finalized. AMR had become increasingly concerned PWA would not have enough cash to even make it through the regulatory review process following the eventual closing of the deal—assumed to be about mid-August. "America's new demand launched a frenzy of activity by a core group of PWA directors, spearheaded by Mr. Southern," the *Globe* reported. "American was asking for more cash, and had already been concerned that management and the majority of the board of directors were painting an unduly optimistic picture of the company's financial health.

"Bankruptcy might be weeks away, Mr. Southern thought" and the personal liability issue haunted Southern and the other members.

Although the board would later put aside $40 million against the liability threat, it would be nowhere near enough to cushion a possible $105 million liability total. The board was to later discover that its existing liability insurance would only total $10 million. What board members seemed to be facing by mid-July was a relentless wave of financial setbacks—all during a time when PWA's numbers were growing worse and worse each day.

Earlier in June the board had made a request to the Alberta government for a $100 million line of credit, to be secured against $100 million worth of assets. The request was turned down by Don Getty's Conservative government. A bank check revealed the airline had insufficient unsecured assets at that time. The Getty government was also, no doubt, sensitive about investing in failing businesses after twisting in the wind over their recent Novatel Communications fiasco, a move that saw as much as $600 million in public funds lost on the venture. In addition to Novatel, the Alberta government was stuck with the Gainers Inc. hog and cattle processing business. That barnyard dalliance with Peter Pocklington's former company would end up costing Albertans a further $209 million.

The airline also saw a potential $80 million in new cash drift away when a deal to sell its interest in the Ireland-based aircraft sales and leasing GPA Group Ltd. suddenly fell through. The airline needed at least a $100 million cash and credit backstop to meet payroll commitments through the fall. At the same time, its cash position was being squeezed as the seat sale war with Air Canada continued into the summer, with both airlines losing huge amounts of money. CAIL was still losing as much as $800,000 a day. And then, although first-round negotiations on a deal with AMR concluded on July 9, seemingly with success, in the middle of July AMR suddenly slapped on the $150 million new cash requirement. To make matters even more difficult, a now extra-cautious AMR also requested another two weeks to review service agreements.

"Since nothing had been signed [with AMR]," the *Globe* reported, "PWA directors could only grin, bear it and try to round up the money." At the July 15 meeting—July 15 being one of the "ides" of the year, according to the ancient Roman calendar, and never a time of much goodwill and good luck—the board also discovered PWA had only $70-80 million in cash on hand, or about $150 million less than American had been told. As well, half the cash had already been earmarked for the directors' liability fund. The board seemed trapped. It needed all available cash to pay bills and close the deal with AMR, and it also needed the cash as a possible cushion against personal liability. The board was caught between two equally perilous alternatives, neither of which could be avoided without falling victim to the other.

At this point, some board members became distraught. The AMR deal, which looked so do-able during June, started to take on Sisyphean qualities—every time it looked as if the board had been able to roll the rock to the top of the hill, it broke away and rolled back down again. In addition to the extra $150 million AMR required, there would also be the cost of extricating PWA from the Gemini computer reservation system agreement—a possible minimum $20-30 million a year for the five years remaining on the contract. AMR had also asked for assurances—and PWA had been prepared to give them—that CAIL's unions would not strike and would agree to a wage freeze package for as much as a four-year period—something that had not even been discussed with the workers. It would seem the deal was coming apart. The directors' concern finally boiled over. Southern was made chairman of a board committee to study the AMR deal and given a mandate to seek out financial help from governments. Southern headed for Vegreville, Alberta to meet with Deputy Prime Minister Don Mazankowski, a trip, as the *Globe* later reported, that set in motion events that rattled the Canadian airline industry to its foundation. "The turbulence has left shareholders counting their losses, employees fretting over their jobs and Ottawa trapped in a political maelstrom that [has] further complicated national unity talks."

Southern's mid-July message to Mazankowski was that PWA and CAIL were doomed unless the Mulroney government helped out financially. Mazankowski was "so alarmed by the spectre of PWA failure—including stranded passengers, screaming shareholders and directors on the hook—that he made a 10 P.M. phone call to Mr. Mulroney."

While spasms of political fright sparked across the highest political levels in Ottawa, PWA board members met again with Don Getty on July 16, the day the AMR-PWA agreement was to originally have been announced—only to be turned down by the Alberta government. Unless other provinces anted up, Alberta would not take part in the play. The board was turned down by B.C. Premier Mike Harcourt the next day. On July 18, the board learned of its limit on liability insurance. On July 21, a handful of board members led by Southern met with provincial and federal government officials in Calgary. He outlined how dire PWA's straits were. The company needed at least $150 million in loan guarantees, plus $195 million in government guarantees to cover a badly needed new share issue. It was suggested that without this sort of financial help from government "the company would fail as early as July 25"—four days away.

PWA was asking for $50 million in new equity from the three provinces in attendance—B.C., Alberta and Ontario—and $65 million from Ottawa to "backstop a $200 million equity offering." The provinces balked, pointing out with a fair degree of correctness that PWA's problems stemmed from the Mulroney government's 1988 deregulation of the airline industry. It was up to Ottawa to fix things. But Ottawa was only prepared to assist by closing the outstanding deal to buy PWA's three idle A310-300 Airbuses. The board was apparently devastated. The situation was desperate. The only remaining options were "bankruptcy or some kind of government help in reaching a merger with Air Canada."

The board was backed into a brutal corner. Their lives were in everybody's hands except their own. The merger-monopoly option began growing as the doctrinal tenets of free enterprise, open competition and freedom-to-fail were stuffed, like embarrassing family secrets, out of sight. Federal bureaucrats apparently favoured the idea. The Tories' Mazankowski, the man who helped shepherd deregulation of the airline industry through the House of Commons, with its anticipated increase in competing airlines, was now leaning towards a merger—a monopoly—solution.

As if the stars for a merger were aligned in convergence, on the same day, July 21, British Airways, one of the world's largest international carriers, announced it was joining forces with USAir in a strategic alliance. By itself, the announcement was just more news about major carriers jockeying for position and survival in anticipation of The Big Shake Out in the Sky and the global airline universe of the future. But to Air Canada, which had long been courting USAir for a possible international alliance, the news suddenly left it without a foreign partner. It meant no new international route access on the horizon, making Air Canada almost as vulnerable as PWA–CAIL. Those forty-three Air Canada lobbyists immediately began circling their political wagons.

Two days later on July 23, the *Globe* reported, Mazankowski detailed PWA's troubles over lunch with the prime minister, discussing "the urgency of rethinking the nation's air policy and the effects of deregulation." There was also the matter of Air Canada's reluctance— having been spurned a number of times by PWA—to even be involved in another, useless round of merger talks. But that could be overcome with a little pressure from Ottawa, enough to hurry the merger along and settle this fractious issue.

A few hours later, according to the *Globe* report, Clerk of the Privy Council Glen Shortliffe telephoned Rhys Eyton and told him that the federal government would purchase those idle A310-300s "but only if PWA halted talks with American and began merger discussions with Air Canada." Eyton was reportedly "flabbergasted . . . He did not believe merger was the only option available, and he was stunned to learn the government was interfering in a private business transaction. He didn't understand that most of the government's thinking was a product of Mr. Southern's doomsday scenario."

On Saturday July 25, the PWA board met "to do what it felt it must—break off talks with American and resume negotiations with Air Canada." The board made its announcement on Monday July 27, shocking CAIL employees, angering AMR officials and helping to drive PWA's stock down twenty-five per cent. By Wednesday PWA stock dropped another forty-seven per cent to $1.55, rallying to close at $2.08 for the day. "It's been a while since we've seen this kind of activity on the floor," one Toronto Stock Exchange official was quoted as saying.

"Canadian chose to try and forge an alliance with [American]," Mazankowski told reporters. "That obviously failed. The only other option is merger." His equivocation on the question of whether PWA had approached the government for bridge financing ("These are two private organizations and we had expected that the negotiations that Canadian was having with AMR would have been on a straight commercial basis.") only muddied the waters until July 30, when the *Globe* broke the story, revealing the full extent of the government's involvement. All hell broke loose.

Angry western MPs denounced the merger plans and Ottawa bureaucrats hunkered down into damage control. Air Canada's first "merger" offer was seen as a simple, de facto takeover of CAIL. It gave them sixty-five per cent control of the proposed merged company in any share swap, and the top jobs in the new airline. The accusations flew that the Mulroney government, once again, had favoured Quebec over the West, opting for a solution that helped the Montreal-based Air Canada to the detriment of Calgary's PWA. Coming right in the middle of the government's national unity build-up, many western Canadians simply saw the issue as another sell-out to Quebec.

All that was left was a sudden, angry protest from the prime minister, claiming the PWA board had come to the government, not the other way around. But when Mulroney stretched his story to the point of claiming his government had not "killed" the AMR–PWA deal—waving a copy of a handwritten facsimile message sent from New Zealand by Ron Southern as proof—the country then had to contend with a subsequent letter from PWA chairman Eyton telling Mulroney "that Mr. Southern's version of events was wrong." According to the *Globe*, Eyton's letter asserted "that Ottawa's top civil servant [Shortliffe] had indeed threatened to scotch an essential deal between PWA and the government if the company didn't begin talking with Air Canada."

By the end of the summer of 1992, Canadians were approaching, not a solution to their nagging and messy airline industry dilemma, but even more confusion and ideological contradiction—enough to last another two years. The simple lesson few were learning from this series of events, especially ardent supporters of the laissez-faire world of airline deregulation, was that when human nature and politics are involved, there are no pure theories—of economics, of business performance or of anything else. Trying to stay alive politically and financially was where it was at.

What transpired was the fundamental revelation that, while it was all right to talk about market forces and the theoretical risk-taking associated with competition in a free market system, when reality knocked on the door—and the Grim Reaper of the bottom line announced you and your company would now go down the financial tubes—board members, management, investors, debt holders, Conservative politicians, even job-for-life Ottawa bureaucrats—do the human thing: toss all that neoclassical theory overboard and scrape like Hades to stay alive and avoid the consequences of failure. The theoretical beauty of business—that failure offers opportunity for other investors and more "competition" to improve life for the poor consumer—was something taught in Economics 101 and Commerce 101 courses. The real world did not work that way. So everyone began working to keep CAIL flying beyond the point of reason, all because of politics, which, after all, is what makes this dysfunctional world—including the Canadian airline industry—go 'round.

5 / A Dysfunction in the American Mind

"The irony of deregulation is that the more freedom business is given, the more dependent it becomes upon government as the saviour of last resort."
—John Ralston Saul, *Voltaire's Bastards: The Dictatorship of Reason in the West*

AIRLINE DEREGULATION, like its handmaiden, privatization, was, of course, a gift from our friends to the south. It has proven grievously inappropriate as a public policy and has caused irreparable damage to the industry in both countries, but particularly in Canada. Deregulation was driven by simple neoconservative notions that enjoyed their most novel days during the Carter, Reagan and Bush presidencies. Yet this ill-considered initiative actually ran against the grain of American social and economic history.

Deregulation—or placing the emphasis on market-driven competition, consumer sovereignty and individual private enterprise instead of public purpose and regulation by government—has to be one of this century's most effective swindles, vying historically with the eighteenth-century "South Sea Bubble" share scandal and Holland's seventeenth-century "Tulipomania" frauds.

In fact, if the American capitalist experience is to be admired for its success—and on the whole it has been, to this point, a success—it is primarily the involvement of government, not its absence, that has marked it. Throughout its history, the United States has been more stable, more prosperous and a more equitable place to live, by most economic standards or social measures, when federal and state governments have played the largest role possible in guiding and supporting the activities of business and commerce. When government's role has been diminished in favour of expanded and unrestricted advantage for the individual in a private sector, most of America has been the loser to some degree.

The belief that the U.S. was built on the muscular backs of free, open business competition and private initiative is also an astounding myth. At the very beginning of the Republic, the Founding Fathers sensed their new nation could never enjoy dramatic commercial growth and economic development without the very prominent hand of government in play. Since its struggling inception, American economic success was largely due to astute regulation of, and support for, industry and commerce. The early investment by governments in quasi-public enterprises actually set the commercial tone for the U.S., helped expand international trade and formed the very national infrastructure upon which the private sector could then operate. Government, not business competition alone, was the historic key that ensured growth and prosperity for the nation.

In the U.S., healthy competition between corporations was, and is, a contradiction in terms, one that—when allowed to play itself out in fits of commercial exhaustion—actually reduced, not enhanced, the country's overall economic performance, in 1800 as in 1994. As history reveals, those moments when competition and the influence of the private sector were paramount were the periods of the greatest loss of wealth and capital destruction in the United States of America, not to mention the immense social costs and the massive burden placed on the American taxpayer. The days preceding and im-mediately following October 1929 would provide the most glaring example. The days following deregulation of the nation's savings and loan industry would provide the most recent.

The myths of deregulation and privatization have fed upon a number of issues living within the American belief system. The matter of liberty and the rights of the individual, versus a threatening and encroaching sovereign, are deeply embedded in American political, economic and business thinking. Taken on its own, liberty of the individual is without question a much-respected principle upon which to set the foundations for the nation-state. But even the concept of liberty must have caveats attached. Taken to its extreme, it can be a dangerous and self-destructive notion.

Liberty cannot be properly exercised except within the context of a body politic. Liberty, and the inalienable rights of the individual, are irrevocably entwined within a social compact. As American philosopher Joseph Tussman wrote in *Obligation and the Body Politic*, a trenchant 1960 essay on the individual and his or her relationship to, and within, the state: "It is easy to forget that the consent of the governed, upon which we insist, is consent to be governed . . . A body politic is not a state of anarchy in which sovereign individuals confront each other; it is an organization in which individuals are sovereign neither in theory nor in practice but are related as members or parts of a system."

Membership in the body politic involves not simply a recognition of common, or national, values and good. It also entails recognition that one's own interests constitute only a subordinate part of a broader system of interests. Unfortunately, in their pursuit of wealth creation and consumer advantage, most neoconservative thinkers hope to avoid that part of the responsibility equation. Government, and the regulations it conjures, is not only perceived to impinge upon the individual's rights and hinder the application of market principles, it is also seen as costly and cumbersome, even redundant. Government, neoconservatives say, stops us from improving our lot. But, as Tussman wrote: "It is not the aim of government to give us what we want. Government is not the tool of our impulsiveness but the instrument of our deliberate selves; it is people doing as they think best, and this is not always 'what they want.' "

Neoconservative economic thinking has also relied to some extent on the arcane belief, bred in the late nineteenth and early twentieth centuries, and revived in the 1950s, that equated government involvement in the national economy with the tenets of European socialism. American critics of government and government regulation tend to buttress their defence of the complete effectiveness of private enterprise by equating government-in-the-economy with the despised "command economies" of post-World War II Eastern Europe and the former Soviet Union. These were examples, many physically brutal, where government central planning and the existence of state enterprise barred the door to free and open market competition. Consequently, this perception of the "evils of government," perceived through the cracked ideological glass of America in the 1950s, helped spread a growing doctrinal belief in the value of a less-government-the-better economy.

Using the American historical model, and citing those periods of economic strength associated with the influence of a strong central government (such as during the Jackson and both Roosevelt presidencies), it can be argued that periods of unchecked capital expansion and private sector self-interest could not only be corrupting and wasteful, they also could be decidedly antidemocratic, even constitutionally dangerous. The periods when government was most absent from the economic scene often carried the potential for destabilizing the entire nation. There are many who would argue the U.S. is once again at that dangerous point. A strong central government and active state governments, participants in leading and building a strong economy, have traditionally protected American democracy—while providing the essential foundations for corporate, individual and national wealth.

One of the principal reasons for the growth and maintenance of an affirmative government role in the economy—planning, regulating, checking corporate excesses—is that, as American historian Arthur M. Schlesinger, Jr. wrote in *The Cycles of American History*, "democracy would not endure if private concentrations of wealth were permitted to become more powerful than the democratic state. Ultimate power has to reside somewhere in a democratic polity. If that power is not exerted by the public government, then national policy is seized by self-serving private interests. Government off the back of business means business on the back of government. The attack on federal authority [today] is conducted in the name of the state and local rights but the beneficiary is corporate power."

Although three recent American presidents thought otherwise, government has always been the most effective solution to the U.S.'s economic problems. In fact, all too often it has been government's job to repair the economic and social damage inflicted upon Americans by destructive spasms of laissez-faire competition. Before Jimmy Carter was president, he proclaimed his major goal was "to free the American people from the burden of over-regulation." Ronald Reagan was well known for uttering during his first inaugural address that: "Government is not the solution to our problem. Government is the problem." Both men were wrong, from a contemporary point of view and from the view of past American experience.

The idea that somehow, from the start, American history evolved in the absence of government involvement in the economy, and had only recently gotten "too big," is simply wrong. "The American government from the very beginning willingly implicated itself in business," Lewis Lapham wrote in *Money and Class in America*, "financing toll roads, canals, the first experiment in mass production (of rifles) and whatever else seemed likely to turn a profit." The principal discussions during the 1787 Constitutional Convention were focused on how the federal government could be structured to be the necessary central player in the new nation's finance, commerce and agricultural initiatives. To the Founding Fathers, there was no reasonable mechanism to achieve their nation-building goals other than a strong, interventionist government. As Schlesinger wrote, "The Founding Fathers, in short, had no doctrinal commitment to the unregulated marketplace. They were not proponents of laissez-faire. Their legacy was rather that blend of public and private initiative known in our day as the mixed economy."

The original thirteen American colonies had long been accustomed to government intervention in economic affairs. "Republicanism preferred virtue to commerce, commonwealth to wealth, and feared that uncurbed self-interest would bring social decay," according to Schlesinger.

Alexander Hamilton saw the national government as the grand instrument by which to transform a pastoral economy into a booming industrial nation. He called the notion that the economy could regulate itself a "wild, speculative paradox." When enterprise was "unbridled," Hamilton wrote in the 7th *Federalist*, it led to "outrages, and these to reprisals and wars." Hamilton's national economic program of the 1790s—using the state to "steer wealth to those who would employ it under public guidance"—was the very foundation for the success and growth of the American economic experience throughout much of the nineteenth century. In fact, early American corporations "were quasi-public agencies, chartered individually by statute. They were granted franchises, bounties, bond guarantees, rights of way, immunities and other exclusive privileges to enable them to serve specified public needs," Schlesinger wrote.

But the myth that America was built by private enterprise has, unfortunately, endured. That myth, as Schlesinger pointed out, "both flattered the vanity and served the interests of [nineteenth century] business leaders." And to support their vanity, they would often use—as our modern day neoconservative business thinkers would as well—a flawed interpretation of what the eighteenth-century Scottish economist Adam Smith had written about managing an economy in *An Inquiry into the Nature and Causes of the Wealth of Nations.*

Contemporary free enterprise supporters, particularly acolytes of Ronald Reagan's neoconservative beliefs, the back-to-basics types who once wandered around the White House with Adam Smith neckties, believed religiously that *Wealth of Nations* had played a large part in defining the American Constitution, in effect being an important factor in the foundational thinking of America. Yet Smith's *Wealth of Nations* was not even published in the U.S. until 1789.

Not only were there few proponents of laissez-faire at that time, but Alexander Hamilton and friends were clearly intent on sculpting an economic system based on "the fostering hand of government," as Smith scholar E.A.J. Johnson wrote, the opposite of Smith's "invisible hand" of business self-interest. The truth of the matter is that "modern advocates of free enterprise would find Smith's attack on corporations deeply disconcerting," John Kenneth Galbraith wrote in *The Culture of Contentment.* "It is perhaps unfortunate that few, perhaps none, who so cite Adam Smith had read his great book."

Granted, Adam Smith opposed mercantilism and favoured freer trade. But he was adamant on four significant points that should stick hard in the throat of any modern neoconservative. First, Smith was strongly opposed to corporations or joint stock companies: "The directors of such companies . . . being the managers rather of other people's money than of their own, it cannot well be expected that they should watch over it with the same anxious vigilance with which the partners in a private copartnery frequently watch over their own . . . Negligence and profusion, therefore, must always prevail, more or less, in the management of the affairs of such a company." Second, Smith believed that government and its role in support of commerce was a real and necessary expense. Without it, a nation with aspirations to economic growth and development would be little more than a crowd of "barbarians." Third, Smith advocated proportional wealth taxes—the more money one made from commerce, the more one was required to contribute to the commonwealth. Finally, although Smith did believe there were benefits to be had from self-interest in a free market economy, he couched that belief very strongly in a Christian imperative.

Smith believed that an individual involved in business enterprise had a social and moral contract, not only with the state, but with God. To the extent individuals would be "free" to practise enterprise within the nation's polity, they would be required to follow rules, including the twenty-fourth Psalm. Smith's free enterpriser was only free to pursue his self-interest if the result did not do damage to a fellow citizen—in economic as well as moral terms—and *only* if the result of his labour improved and strengthened the state, and furthered the economic purposes of the government and the state.

Smith was a supporter of cooperation, not destructive market competition. Were Adam Smith able to visit the battleground of today's deregulation of American industry, finance and commerce, he would shake his head in sorrow at the damage done in his name. If he were to cross the 49th Parallel to view what we had done to the Canadian airline industry through deregulation, he would probably weep.

> *"Smith's position on the role of the state in a capitalist society was close to that of a modern twentieth century U.S. liberal Democrat."*
> —Spencer Pack, *Capitalism as a Moral System: Adam Smith's Critique of the Free Market Economy*

Getting government off the backs of business was a misconceived battle cry of the last twenty years throughout North America. Historically, the idea was not even hinted at until more than a hundred years after the U.S.'s formation. All the way into the 1890s, the country had grown strong and prosperous on the back of government. It was only with the rise of large, monopoly corporations and cartels in the latter part of the nineteenth century—brought to their level of business success thanks to government regulations protecting them from competition and from their own destructive inclinations—that the "let-alone theory," as it was termed, began to surface.

Government—state and federal—had been, literally and figuratively, the major stockholder in the developing nineteenth-century American economy, owning controlling interest in successful ventures almost too numerous to mention—in banks, turnpikes, canals, railroads—as well as carrying massive public debt to underwrite the success of industry and ensure orderly growth and development of the American economy. In fact, corporations were considered to be largely "public," and state legislatures regulated them to ensure they operated in the public interest and avoided wasteful competition.

Too many Canadians think regulation of business was, somehow, a Canadian invention, a last-resort policy of a competitively weak nation bent on protecting its fledgling companies and businesses from failure and commercial attack from the south. In fact, regulation of industry was an American idea. Historically, the U.S. raised regulation of industry to one of the nation's most successful art forms. Regulation was and, to the extent that elements of it still exist after the Reagan years, still is largely meant to check the destructive excesses inherent in the free enterprise system. Excessive regulation of American industries would seldom have been required if the corporations and industries in question had performed in a socially responsible manner, working not only for wealth and profit, but to strengthen and enhance the state within which they prospered. If, by the late nineteenth century, regulation was perceived to be an intrusion into, and an impediment within, the free market environment, it was because industry had called their own dogs of war down upon themselves.

Formal U.S. regulation began with controls over a very shaky banking industry in 1864. The nation's banks had been under regulatory scrutiny one way or another since the beginning of the Republic, primarily to prevent failures and the loss of citizens' funds. The fear was well founded, given the erratic tendencies of American investment capital and the resulting frequency of bank failures. But it was especially true after the failures of 1929-1933. After 1933, Congress and numerous administrations were solidly convinced, not at all incorrectly, that the underlying problem contributing to the banks' failures had not had anything to do with regulation. The cause had been "excessive competition."

The first major U.S. transportation regulatory agency was the Interstate Commerce Commission, introduced in 1887. The commission was originally responsible for the orderly operation of the nation's railroads, thanks in large part to the disastrous record of the nineteenth-century "robber barons"—among them, John D. Rockefeller, the man who, when irritated by a congressional committee's question about how he had acquired his wealth, replied: "The Lord gave me my money." These "grand predators" were no believers in free enterprise and open competition. Their goal was monopoly control. Rockefeller told another committee (he was the frequent subject of congressional investigations into his monopoly practices)

that business was like growing roses: "The ga
raise a perfect American beauty rose had no ch
bulbs of the lesser roses intruding on its light." Of ,
social critic Thorstein Veblen once observed: "It
given case—indeed it is at times impossible until
spoken—to say whether [their actions are] an instance ⸲
salesmanship or a penitentiary offense."

Behind every great entrepreneurial fortune of the
century, Lewis Lapham wrote, stood the brooding presenc
crime: "Clearly it was true that capitalism promoted ⸲
encouraged hope, inspired invention and provided the rev
fortune. Unfortunately, it was also true that unless harnessed
principles of moral restraint, capitalism yielded bountiful frui
greed, fraud and crime. It was the darker side of the American mι
that had to be denied."

One form of denial used by the very people accused of criminal
behaviour in their business conduct was to demand that they be "let
alone"—that government and its regulations were only hindering
them in their pursuit of greater wealth. It would be in this strange
economic environment of greed, corruption and corporate impunity
that the call would swell for government, and its regulatory constraints
on competition, to give way to the purer instincts of unbridled
competition in an open, free marketplace. The cry would be listened
to. Regulations would be loosened. The market would be made free.
But this free market would lead the nation, by the fall of 1929, into
the worst depression ever suffered by America.

In the strange and vertiginous environment that began in the late
1880s, the purview of the Interstate Commerce Commission expanded—in sync with the failure of each industry to police itself
properly and to work in the best interests of the citizen—to include
oil pipelines in 1906, telephones in 1910, trucking in 1935 and
interstate water carriers in 1940. In the 1920s, regulation stretched
into the new field of air transportation, when early carriers were
contracted for delivery of the U.S. Mail. Americans were compelled
to apply a regulatory regime over almost anything private enterprise
was involved in—food and drugs, cosmetics, false and misleading
advertising, automobile safety, pollution, industrial safety standards,
mine safety, consumer protection, public security issues, nuclear
energy, utilities, aviation and, until the Reagan administration stripped

policy initiative, deregulation was then pushed to the far reaches of outer space by Reagan's former vice-president, George Bush.

In contemporary terms, if anyone doubted the need for regulation of private enterprise in the U.S., all one had to do was track the deregulation of the American savings and loan industry in the 1980s and add up the costs to a naive and unsuspecting population. Economist John Kenneth Galbraith called the savings and loan deregulation episode "the most feckless and felonious disposition of what, essentially, were public funds in the nation's history, perhaps in any modern nation's history." Thanks to the Reagan administration's complete relaxation of regulatory rules, the American taxpayer would eventually be required to bail out the savings and loans industry to the tune of more than US $300 billion.

By mid-1994, America was still mopping up the slime of that deregulated excess. Among the muck was a report in June that at least one perpetrator—Thomas Billman—had been sentenced to forty years in prison for bilking US $29.5 million from Community Savings and Loan of Bethesda, Maryland. After simply wiring US $22 million to Swiss bank accounts, Billman fled the country in 1988 and lived lavishly on two yachts in the Mediterranean before being arrested in Paris in 1993—where he had been posing as a champagne dealer.

The primary focus of the U.S. deregulation movement was on more than two dozen federal agencies responsible for regulating everything from interstate transportation to the nation's natural resources from policing air, water and noise pollution standards to the safety of consumer products. Although most of the actual intent of the movement was to loosen or eliminate regulations relating to American business, there was also a strong desire to reduce the costs of government by downsizing the regulatory bodies themselves, thus saving tax dollars. Yet between 1980 and 1985—the truly hot years for the regulatory reform movement—the budgets for the twenty-six major U.S. regulatory agencies went *up* from roughly US $2.76 billion to $3.3 billion. If one throws in the estimated eventual cost of the Republicans' savings and loan industry debacle, the regulatory reform movement south of the border has been a costly disaster indeed.

Like so many other elements in our two societies that defy the imprimatur of "democracy," the movement toward regulatory re-form, or deregulation, did not materialize out of any loud public demand for change. There was no plebiscite endorsing the move to deregulate airlines, or any other industry, in either country. There was no collective expression of anguish over the state of regulated industries from the streets of the nation. No crowds of angry citizens picketed. There was no overwhelming letter writing campaign directed towards Parliament or Congress. Those within and around the airline industry—carriers, travel agents, regulators, bureaucrats—were not anywhere near overwhelmingly in favour of wholesale deregulation. In fact, it could be said that the "demand" for deregulation was, if anything, rather underwhelming.

> *"Men, it has been well said, think in herds; it will be seen that they go mad in herds, while they only recover their sense slowly, and one by one."*
> —Charles Mackay, *Extraordinary Popular Delusions and the Madness of Crowds*, 1852

The initial premise for regulation in the field of transportation was to prevent the wholesale collapse of competitive carriers—rail, truck or airline. After World War II, criticism mounted, particularly from shippers, about the cost of doing business when high-cost carriers were protected by regulation from the normal effects of competition. As the University of Wisconsin's Leonard W. Weiss put it in *Regulatory Reform: What Actually Happened*, there was a variety of participants at the genesis of the American experience: "businessmen who found themselves pestered with a flood of reports to file, businessmen who felt that regulations were raising their costs of production or weakening their competitive positions, economists who thought that regulation often reduced competition and increased costs, and political scientists and lawyers who thought that the regulatory agencies were often captured by those they were meant to regulate."

Economists played especially important roles, carrying out most of the critical studies that resulted in regulatory reform. They were also the source of many of the specific proposals for change. "The air, the most visible marketplace filled with identical products, was becoming an economists' playground," Anthony Sampson wrote, "which offered a unique opportunity for bold experiment." The problem for the rest of society would be the zealousness with which many economists would see to their task. Like twentieth-century versions of Inquisitors for the Holy Roman Church, many would push their pedagogical beliefs upon the North American political and business scene with an intensity bordering on "tough love"—always believing whatever damage their ideas caused would be far less than the evils of government regulation.

Much of the economic thinking on regulatory reform was fed by the ideas of American economists such as Milton Friedman. It would be timid to call Friedman a "free market exponent." With all of history facing him, Friedman does not even allow for a debate over what kinds of regulations might be suitable and what regulatory goals are legitimate, as other economists might be prepared to do. Friedman believes that not only should there be no regulatory role for government in a free enterprise economy, he also believes both education and medical care should be in the hands of the private sector.

On a visit to Vancouver in May 1994 to speak to the right-wing Fraser Institute, Friedman claimed the U.S. was moving "towards socialism" with the Clinton administration's intention to imitate Canada's health care system. Medicare, Friedman told reporters, "destroys human freedom and prevents innovation." He also said radical reform is needed in the American economic system so that employers do not have to contribute to their employee's medical care. In response to a question concerning the Las Vegas reputation of the Vancouver Stock Exchange, Friedman replied predictably: "I have yet to meet the problem for which more government regulation is the answer."

In many cases, the statistics and data presented by economists about the benefits of deregulation were compelling. In other cases, their findings seemed almost naive, given the "perfect model" world they often worked toward. Unfortunately, the deregulation work of some economists tended to overlook the reality that humans are not perfect individuals, following logical paths of performance. We are bent out of shape by our desires, our weaknesses, our biases, our experiences, our interactions with others and our doubts. We are unpredictable animals. When pressed, we will choose practicality over doctrine, theory or even science, a behaviour many economists would find hard to factor into their models.

In the December 1993 issue of *The Atlantic Monthly*, James Fallows wrote about how the U.S. was now beginning to rethink the role of government in economic and international trade matters, pointing out that modern economic study had become too precise, and consequently there was a tendency to believe that theories derived in laboratory settings were applicable in real life: "Anglo-American economists devote much of their effort to 'equilibrium studies' and 'constrained optimization'—in essence, laboratory experiments involving economics. In a laboratory you can control many variables . . . so as to focus on the single factor you want to understand. In mathematical economics you can 'control' many variables by taking them for granted, and then focus on what you want to understand." But you cannot do that in politics.

Writing in the November 1993 issue of *Scientific American*, World Bank economist and author Herman E. Daly castigated neoclassical economic thinking that drew on David Ricardo's observations on the logic of "comparative advantage" among nations to support deregulated international commerce and free trade. Daly dismantled the free trade argument, in particular its ignorance of the impact the theory has on the environment. But he was as critical of the methodology of many of today's economists as he was about the impracticality of their conclusions. "[M]y major concern about my profession today is that our disciplinary preference for logically beautiful results over factually grounded policies has reached such fanatical proportions that we economists have become dangerous to the earth and its inhabitants."

By 1992, certainly in the airline industry, some proponents of deregulation would be imploring governments to re-introduce a touch of sanity by "reregulating" the industry. As their computers and graphs filled with massive clumps of new data on airline failures, fare confusion and airline industry unemployment, the ranks of the economists began to split, with a number having second thoughts about the costs and benefits of the application of their professional thinking throughout the 1970s and 1980s.

In 1994, MIT professor—and head of the American Economics Association—Paul Krugman, published *Peddling Prosperity*, a telling indictment of American contemporary economic thought and practice. The book traced how loose some academic thinking had been, on issues such as money supply as a means of steering the economy, and deregulation of certain industries. The result of this thinking has been a misguided debate about the economy. Questionable theorizing by some U.S. economists, along with the biases of partisan think tanks which often employed them, led to "pop economics." Some academics now performed as "policy entrepreneurs," their ideas locked in contractual sync on the payrolls of the various business and lobby organizations bent on seeing their particular policy view turned into legislation.

Krugman's book was an indictment of contemporary economic scholarship carried out by a number of his peers, many of whom would be comfortable in the policy camp of airline deregulation. In some instances, their work belied the axiom that the economist works best by critically weighing and assessing flawed theory—not in forming theory. In the worst cases, their work helped distort public issues and policy formulation.

As Bernard Baruch wrote in 1932: "All economic movements, by their very nature, are motivated by crowd psychology. Graphs and business ratios are, of course, indispensable in our groping efforts to find dependable rules to guide us in our present world of alarms. Yet I never see a brilliant economic thesis expounding, as though they were geometrical theorems, the mathematics of price movements, that I do not recall Schiller's dictum: 'Anyone taken as an individual, is tolerably sensible and reasonable—as a member of a crowd, he at once becomes a blockhead.' "

Although there is still some debate over whether deregulation of the North American airline industry has been a failure or a success, there should be no debate over the fact that what both countries ended up with has little to do with what was originally hoped for by politicians, the business community, even the academics. Airline deregulation in the U.S. has been, if not a failed enterprise, certainly a much-qualified success. Some defenders of deregulation claim that American consumers have saved roughly US $6 billion a year and the airlines about US $2.5 billion a year. But beneath the simple data—like today's price of an air fare between New York and Los Angeles, or the absence of flights in and out of Fargo, North Dakota—a more complex truth, bred of a host of troublesome facts, indicates that deregulation has been a costly experience for the total American economy, certainly for all those people who have lost tens of billions in investment wealth, a struggling airline manufacturing industry, employees who have lost jobs—and governments missing a few tens of billions in tax revenue they would normally recoup from all parties were the industry still stable.

> "Deregulation has not resulted in a fully competitive ideal. In 1992, Canada's [airline] system is a highly concentrated duopoly in which the prospects of a new entrant are questionable at best."
> —National Transportation Act Review Commission, *The Major Canadian Airlines: Past Performance and Future Prospects*

The U.S. *Airline Deregulation Act* of 1978, the legislation that spurred Canadians to act on their own a decade later, was supposed to increase competition among airlines, encourage the growth of new airlines, create more choices for travellers, and drive down the price of air travel by releasing domestic carriers from regulations concerning where and when they could fly, and what prices they could charge. The legislation was the culmination of more than twenty years of irritation with the regulated airline system in the U.S. As early as the 1950s, articles had begun appearing, questioning the cost and usefulness of airline regulation. More articles and a rush of academic research in the 1960s pointed to overregulation as the cause of the airline industry's lack of growth, when compared with other industries. By the early 1970s it seemed clear that, using unregulated intrastate carrier service as a glaring comparative case study, the regulation of the airline industry by the Civil Aeronautics Board (CAB) was hampering industry development, blocking healthy competition, keeping fares high and restricting service. As awkward and slow to respond as the Canadian regulatory system appeared to some minds, its track record never came remotely close to matching the messy trail of America's airline regulator.

The CAB had taken over regulatory responsibility for aviation from the Interstate Commerce Commission in 1938 and was given authority over interstate airline service: mail routes, the awarding of carrier routes, the regulation of fares and the maintenance of airline safety standards. Its primary concern was carrier profitability, using regulation as a means of stimulating industry growth and maintaining the stability of airlines. "The decision to establish the CAB and to grant it broad regulatory powers was rooted in fundamental scepticism of the time about the ability of the free market to function effectively," Daniel P. Kaplan wrote in *Regulatory Reform: What Actually Happened.*

"There was an underlying fear that the unchecked forces of competition would lead to fares that were chronically below costs, which would prevent the fledgling airline industry from growing and prospering."

Over the years the CAB severely limited entry of new carriers into the marketplace, refusing roughly a hundred submissions for major carrier status between 1938 and the mid-1970s, eventually restricting the scope of service to eleven major carriers. It restrained competition and fostered an expensive subsidy program for local service carriers that was covered by keeping fares on long-haul routes higher than the market required. Intentionally or not, the presence of the CAB gave birth to an imperfect form of cartel or trust. More than a little ironically, the lingering smell of the performance of nineteenth century American trusts had been the strongest motivating factor for regulation of transportation in the first place. The CAB would largely create what it was meant to prevent.

Lucrative routes were sometimes awarded to financially weak carriers to strengthen their operations. With carriers unable to compete on the basis of price, many would offer elaborate service amenities, or increase the frequency of flights to levels that simply increased the number of planes flying near-empty—adding to their cost of doing business—and making them even less profitable. But within states where the CAB had no jurisdiction, airlines often operated very successfully, setting their own fares, deciding what routes they wished to fly and going out of business whenever they got the bottom line wrong. Particularly in California and Texas, the intrastate carriers were providing low fares and operating more profitably than interstate trunk carriers protected by the CAB.

This phenomenon did not go unnoticed. The story of the intrastate carriers revealed that the CAB's regulation raised price levels and encouraged price discrimination. The result was the airlines kept their costs high, as well as the fares they charged the travelling public. Instead of an industry being regulated with the more immediate interests of the consumer in mind, the CAB's goal had become the long-term interests of the airlines, including their immutability, their guaranteed returns on investment and their perpetual lack of competition.

Another factor contributing to the movement for loosening air industry regulations was the introduction of wide-bodied aircraft like the Douglas DC-10 and Lockheed L-1011 in the 1960s. The extra capacity these aircraft offered, plus their lower per-seat operating costs, seemed to promise a mass market explosion in international air travel. But when these jumbo jets were introduced, fares on scheduled airlines did not drop as expected. Many scheduled carriers simply replaced their smaller aircraft on regular routes with the new aircraft—driving down their load factors and often flying the expensive wide-body airplanes below fifty per cent capacity. On the other hand, U.S charter carriers also began flying the new aircraft, filling their planes with paying passengers and offering even cheaper fares. The growing disparity in fare prices was not lost on air travellers. The CAB's days were numbered.

The CAB was formally challenged in 1969 over its decision to grant across-the-board fare increases to U.S. carriers. The relationship between the regulator and the large airlines had become the tightest in the regulatory world. Senate hearings were held in the mid-1970s into the CAB's regulatory activities, resulting in bipartisan support for a deregulated airline industry. In October 1978, President Carter signed the *Airline Deregulation Act*. The legislation eliminated domestic airline regulation—and the CAB itself by 1984. The issue of whether airline deregulation in the United States worked, made sense and saved everybody money would become as large a debate as the CAB's operating procedure.

The predicted increase in competition never happened. "Almost from Day 1 of deregulation in 1978 . . . the scenario went awry, full of twists and turns that students of human nature could have predicted but that were completely unexpected by the market theorists," social critic Herschel Hardin wrote in 1987. "The advocates of airline deregulation in the United States painted a rosy picture of lower fares, more carriers and better service. The reality has been almost the opposite. Fares have come down in the most heavily travelled routes, but have shot up for others. Marginal carriers have been forced out or taken over by the larger companies."

Many of the familiar American air carriers were immediately in rough financial straits after deregulation was introduced. Many of the new carrier entrants would fly just long enough to make an advertising name and then crash themselves. Others would park themselves in Chapter 11 protection to avoid the sheriff's knock at the door. And the deserts of southwest America would fill with a new endangered species—"whitetails." It was the name given to hundreds of surplus jet aircraft parked in the dry desert air, their collective tails poking into the sky like tombstones in a cemetery. By the summer of 1994 it would be estimated that one thousand jet liners were parked on U.S. deserts, while the world's remaining ten thousand passenger airplanes were flying thirty to forty per cent "permanently empty."

The introduction of U.S. deregulation was also plagued by bad timing. The cost of jet fuel rose dramatically in 1979. A severe recession followed, leading to a sudden downturn in passenger traffic, just as airlines began adding massive amounts of new aircraft capacity and debt. The price and value of air fares went into a Mixmaster, coming out with some great bargains on busier routes, and some fares on other routes three and four times the price charged under regulation. As expected, new carriers competed aggressively, like People Express which offered fare prices and no-frills service that generally drove ticket prices down in the short term and forced many carriers to fly their planes much below cost. "The airlines would have had to seat passengers on the wings as well as in the cabin to cover expenses," according to Hardin. And many started to crash.

Braniff Airlines went into bankruptcy and ceased operations in 1982. Houston-based Continental first filed for bankruptcy in 1983, went to The Wall and literally "transformed itself into a low-cost carrier" over a weekend—by using Chapter 11 bankruptcy protection to abrogate its labour agreements: firing then rehiring its former employees at lower wages and with more flexible work rules. The Chapter 11 provision of the U.S. bankruptcy proceedings also had some bizarre side applications. In November 1991, four of America's major airlines hiding under the protection of Chapter 11 were also participating in an air fare war—cutting prices in many cases below the cost of flying passengers, even though they were technically bankrupt.

Continental emerged from bankruptcy protection in 1984—only to fly back in 1990-91, despite all the cost trimming it achieved by gaffing its employees. Other swirls of smoke trailed from the clouds to the ground for Pan Am, Eastern, Midway, People Express, New York Air, Frontier, Air Florida, American West, Ozark, National, to name but a few. By 1991, of the one hundred and fifty airlines which started up under deregulation, one hundred and eighteen had failed, filed for bankruptcy protection or merged. Between 1978 and 1993 the number of truly major U.S. carriers shrank from twenty to roughly three—American, Delta and United airlines.

Although many analysts and academics argued that "average" fare prices fell ("average" being a term even some analysts and academics now consider an "imperfect measure"), the drop was only recorded on select—usually the busiest—routes. One detailed analysis carried out in 1985 found that "beneath the churning of fares," as Hardin put it, "the *average* fare in the first six years of deregulation (1978-1984) increased 50%, roughly at the pace of inflation." Real savings in fare prices, it turned out, would be more illusory than real.

According to some studies the price of fully refundable airline tickets between the twenty most-travelled U.S. routes rose forty-five per cent between 1988 and 1991, compared to a rise in the Consumer Price Index of a little better than thirteen per cent. Even the cheapest tickets available on those popular U.S. routes rose thirty-seven per cent in the same period. It got easier and easier with each new release of statistical damage to decide whether U.S. deregulation was a win or a loss.

Service was said to have improved vastly under deregulation, but, again, largely only on the busiest routes. *Consumer Reports* magazine, in its July 1991 assessment, pointed out that, although it might be easier now to fly from one state to another, flying within a state, such as North Dakota, might be merely wishful thinking since "in-state air service has virtually disappeared." The saddest part of the U.S.'s deregulation's legacy was how "advocates didn't foresee how effectively major airlines would use the advantage of size to thwart their smaller rivals." Americans did not end up with greater competition among airlines. They got greater concentration of ownership and control instead. And consumer dissatisfaction.

Major airlines gained a sizable competitive advantage by investing heavily in hub-and-spoke networks. But hub-and-spoke networks often meant pointless, time-consuming connections for travellers— purely for the convenience of the airline. The average trip of under two thousand miles can now take twice as long as it did before deregulation. The delays are estimated to cost Americans US $2 billion a year in lost time alone. By 1994, American, USAir, United and Northwest had added up their hub-and-spoke costs and were jettisoning a number of previously favoured hub locations. One study revealed that American Airlines alone could generate US $900 million in extra revenue if it simply took its short-haul flights off the increasingly expensive hub-and- spoke system. The hub-and-spoke system was aggravating airport flight delays, and driving up operating costs by the millions with aircraft idling and eating up expensive jet fuel. It also gave birth to a standard industry tease that when you died and were on your way to heaven, you now had to change planes in Atlanta.

By forging ownership concentration rather than expanding competition among the airlines, deregulation also did little to check the "cooperative" instincts of the airline cavaliers themselves. Writing in *Empires of the Sky*, Anthony Sampson related the tale of a conversation between Braniff's chairman Howard D. Putnam and American Airline's president Robert Crandall. The conversation between Crandall and Putnam, which reportedly took place in February 1982, four years after deregulation was introduced in the U.S., was recorded by Putnam, whose struggling carrier was locked in deadly competition with American Airlines on some important routes. According to Sampson, Crandall told Putnam the airlines were "dumb as hell" to pound each other on the same routes when neither was "making a _____ dime."

> PUTNAM: *Do you have a suggestion for me?*
> CRANDALL: *Yes, I have a suggestion for you. Raise your goddamn fares twenty per cent. I'll raise mine the next morning.*
> PUTNAM: *Robert, we . . .*
> CRANDALL: *You'll make more money and I will to.*
> PUTNAM: *We can't talk about pricing.*
> CRANDALL: *Oh, _____ Howard. We can talk about any goddamn thing we want to talk about.*

To keep current events in step with their faltering theory, deregulation supporters began speculating that, with the congestion caused by hub-and-spoke systems and the increased number of travellers, perhaps it was time to deregulate and privatize *the entire airline business infrastructure*, not just the airlines themselves. In the passionate interests of proving their competitive models worked, academics and many airline analysts would begin suggesting doing to airports, air traffic control and air safety what deregulation had just done to the air carrier portion of the industry.

They apparently could not see that the issue was not one of more deregulation. It was, and always had been, a matter of *better* regulation of the aviation industry. A revised regulatory regime, free of protective instincts, would also have been capable of dealing with the problems left to the industry by deregulation, such as the fact the major carriers were now more powerful in their control of the marketplace than ever before.

The major carriers that survived deregulation were able to use their preferred positions at airports across the nation to lock up airport landing slots and sublet them—and often their ground crews—to their new competitors at exorbitant rates. They also controlled most of the nation's computer reservations systems (CRS), charging handsome fees to new competitors, who would find their flights and routes listed behind those of the airline owning the system when a travel agent was looking for an available airline to book. This weakness in the CRS was a practice the government "stopped" in 1984, but in the industry's deregulated state, one that was relatively easy to circumvent.

Inside the cabins, those same computer systems allowed the application of a new airline business science called "yield management"—a system of seat pricing that enabled airlines, through systematic management of passenger data, to create several categories of fare prices on the same flight, right up until the last few hours before take-off—keeping the oranges fresh, as it were. Yield management was a creative way for the airlines to maximize revenues and profit (in theory) on each flight. For some passengers, yield management was a boon, especially for time flexible bargain-hunters. For others, like business travellers often caught with few options or little flexibility, the results of yield management could be irritating. It could also provide the business traveller with a Sicilian kind of memory, aimed at an airline that charges her full price while insisting she sit next to the traveller flying at a seventy per cent discount.

In fact, Hardin argued, the price of air fares is not a real measure of effectiveness at all. The cost of operating an airline is the more pure test. And when the test is finally applied, not many pass: "Here we find that deregulation not only has perpetuated the worst of the structural inefficiencies in the U.S. industry—excess [aircraft] capacity—but also has added new structural diseconomies all its own." Airlines became more "productive" by laying off employees, establishing two-tier wage structures (a lower starting wage for new employees) and eventually selling percentages in the airlines back to their employees in exchange for wage and benefit concessions. This "productivity" was not the result of precise economic theories or shrewd management. It was the recognition, as one observer put it, that deregulation was "the largest piece of anti-labour legislation the U.S. Congress has ever passed." And the issue of the social cost of deregulation—in increased unemployment benefit costs, in lost taxes, in social costs to workers and their families—not surprisingly, hardly ever shows up in those neat, clinical tables of facts and figures on reports from economists and analysts proclaiming this very risky deregulation enterprise to be a success.

> *"Maybe it's sex appeal, but there's something about an airplane that drives investors crazy. That's the notion behind regulation. You can't leave it to the free market because it will do crazy things. But that's the purpose of the free market—to let people do crazy things."*
> —Alfred Kahn, economist, deregulation advocate and former chairman of the CAB, in *Empires of the Sky*

If deregulation was not the single, most significant cause of the U.S.'s airline problems, it certainly was a totally inappropriate policy initiative for the times. America did not need a deregulated airline system. They needed a better system of airline regulation.

After the casualty count had been completed and the last of the whitetails rounded up by the bailiff, even airline deregulation supporters were having doubts about the folly. But rather than admit that airline deregulation was a mistake, they most often pointed at the current chaos within the industry and attempted to excuse it as a "paradox."

The state of the American airline industry could only be a paradox to supporters of deregulation because of their conviction that this experiment in twentieth-century business thinking had clearly been a victory of good (market forces and competition prevailing) over evil (old and wasteful government regulation). The data are irrefutable, some of them said. But by limiting deregulation's assessment to a count of angels hovering around the bottom line, the thesis ignored a massive amount of cause-and-effect damage related to deregulation—the social costs of airline collapse and bankruptcies, the copious costs of litigation and idle equipment, the effects of lost jobs or lower paying jobs, the disruptions to state and federal tax revenue, and the increased operating costs of airport congestion—statistical information and noneconomic social impact concerns, much of which could go some distance in enlightening the true believer puzzled by the "paradox."

In the Canadian example, apologists were prepared to argue, as the National Transportation Act Review Commission seemed to do in 1992, that most of the damaging factors involved in the airline deregulation experience were extraneous to the airline deregulation experience. "Economic Regulatory Reform," or deregulation by another term, according to their assessment, did not cause *any* of the problems for the Canadian airline industry. The baby-of-blame was placed at the doorstep of commercial life—higher fuel costs, the Gulf War, recessions, low aircraft load factors, labour costs, high interest rates and taxes. To claim, somehow, that this list of very normal causative business factors were extraneous to the workings of a deregulated airline industry was a bit like trying to pretend the world could be flat if it were not round, and the sky would be black if it were not blue.

By 1993, many observers of the U.S. deregulation and the market-driven competition experiment were beginning to have very serious doubts. More than a decade of Gordon Gekko greed, bills for the savings and loan industry, high individual wealth and investor returns accompanied by deep poverty and high unemployment, the controversy over airline deregulation, and a nagging sense that America's international competitive position was being seriously eroded—not by its competitors but by its own business style—began coalescing into a sort of national economic case study. Many lucid minds were now questioning whether the U.S. had not made a rather large theoretical blunder.

The whole concept of the value of competition was being questioned. There were now more losers than winners. In North America in particular, the poor were getting poorer and the rich, richer. Competition did not always stimulate optimum performance in a nation, and in most circumstances competition seemed to be doing as much damage as benefit to national economies. There was a whole community of thought arguing that the ultimate measure of a society was its level of consumption. Competition was good because it kills off producers whose prices are too high. Yet, many nations outside North America were arguing convincingly that emphasizing consumption and competition would eventually be self-defeating, bringing to mind the thoughts of Sinclair Lewis's *Babbitt*: "You know my business isn't distributing roofing—its principally keeping my competitors from distributing roofing . . . All we do is cut each other's throats and make the public pay for it!"

Since World War II, the message about the value of market principles and consumer sovereignty and competition carried with it a moral certitude that rang with tones more of romance than reality. Corporate America was strong, went the call, because it allowed the individual to compete, win or lose, on the battlefield where only the fittest survived. The benefits of their victory would, somehow, trickle down, they believed, spreading the residual effects of their success and wealth to the rest of American society.

The economic "trickle-down" belief, most prominent during the supply-side days of Ronald Reagan, carried the same scientific validity, as John Kenneth Galbraith pointed out, "as the doctrine that if the horse is fed amply with oats, some will pass through to the road for the sparrows."

What the belief seldom considered was that, ultimately, this style of business competition, as democratic and libertarian as it appeared, could actually destroy things—companies, people, dreams. One result may, in fact, be corporate, investor and individual wealth accumulation, but it also left a legacy of cost, debt and social destitution in the form of decaying urban centres, increases in crime and the accompanying deterioration in social values. The American business ethos could be, in the extended analysis, one which could eventually lead to its own inner destruction.

One of the principal reasons the U.S. is struggling in the global marketplace is because of its belief in the benefits of open and unrestricted industrial and commercial competition—that it is rational to have a marketplace where American companies are encouraged to fight against each other to the death *and* against foreign competitors. And the last thing needed is government, with its rules and regulations.

But there are many observers surveying the casualty-strewn battlefield of deregulation and privatization trying to make sense of the new American paradox: the more the workings and direction of the economy are left primarily to the competitive rules of marketplace, the weaker the nation's economy seems to be (certainly where maintaining employment and creating new jobs is concerned).

Yet those nations now competing most successfully in the international arena have chosen to protect their economic self-interest with government setting the rules and direction for their competing corporations. Government has been the major missing active ingredient in the U.S.'s international competitive strategy. And its absence shows.

"The role of government is often considered an embarrassing afterthought in American and British discussions of how economies should work," James Fallows wrote in *The Atlantic Monthly* in his extensive analysis of America's failure to retain its dominance in international competition. When American industry was doing everything right according to American economic competitive theory, it began to collapse. "When Europe, Japan, and Korean producers broke all the rules of American market rationality [by relying on government guidance and support] they started to pull ahead."

Real economic growth has been severely hindered in the countries which believe so fervently in a diminished role for government—Great Britain under Margaret Thatcher, Canada and the United States of America. Many other nations figured it out long ago—societies function most effectively if they pay less attention to the immediate benefits that might accrue to the individual, consumer or corporate—and more to the welfare of the nation. Canada once seemed to know that rule, used its ideas and benefited from the experience, but then succumbed to the siren call of American market-driven competition ideas wafting across the 49th Parallel in the late 1970s and 1980s.

There is nothing inherently "rational" about market failures: about companies going broke, about unemployment figures three and five times higher than they should be, about high national debt, caused by insufficient tax revenue as much as overspending. It is folly to believe, in a world of international trade and governments, that what is best for the individual is best for the nation. The lessons of history, certainly the lessons from two decades of watching Japan, Taiwan, Korea, Singapore and Thailand in action, prove that proper regulation of the nation's economy results in more winners, overall, than losers. Today, it can be said, an economy left guided by the ether of self-interest contains all the science and risk of a bad game of Russian Roulette.

No nation has achieved acceptable economic growth, prosperity and high social standards by relying on laissez-faire as a guiding economic or business principle. Not even the U.S. On the other hand, no modern economy, such as in Germany, Korea or Japan, has achieved impressive growth without some application of the rules of competition. Rather than a dichotomy, these truisms point to two factors which many neoconservative thinkers wish to avoid. First, no economic system or ideologically-based business belief can ever be simply transplanted, holus bolus, across national borders. Any system or theory must be adjusted to fit the specific cultural settings in which it is to be tested and, if it proves worthy, applied. It must fit the strategic goals set for the economy by government.

Second, competition is only beneficial when it improves products and services to the consumer and when it builds, not destroys. To the extent its practice is meant to enhance and enrich the individual as well as the state, competition must be delicately regulated if either is to prosper. Saying there is beauty, truth and prosperity in allowing Air Canada and Canadian Airlines International to fight it out to the edge of extinction, or until the only option left is ownership of one or both by foreign interests, is ludicrous. More than that, it is, as political economies more successful than ours have proven, a national death wish.

6 / The Revenge of Karl Marx

"For a long time, corporate chairman have been saying that their real assets are their employees, but few of them really mean it and none have gone so far as to put those assets on their balance sheet. That may change. Management theorist Peter Drucker points out that the 'means of production,' the traditional basis of capitalism, are now literally owned by the workers because those means are in their hands and at their fingertips. What Marx once dreamed of has become a reality, but in a way in which he could never have imagined."
—Charles Handy, *The Age of Paradox*

BACK IN RICHMOND, B.C., one of greater Vancouver's southern municipalities and the place most Canadian Airlines International employees called home, many may have been unsettled by the weird events in Ottawa over the summer of 1992, but they had not lost hope. The AMR relief package for their airline seemed a bit remote, to say the least, now that Air Canada had been beckoned back to the table for a possible merger, but the degree of distress felt within the employees' council was not as severe as it might have been.

"We always said to ourselves: we didn't think [the Air Canada-CAIL merger] was going to happen," Sid Fattedad recalled. "We just carried on working with the council. We went underground. Throughout all this we were talking to AMR. We told them: here's what we've got. We're keeping this thing alive. We want you [AMR] to be there [when the merger talks collapse]."

Out of this chaos, a new, engrossing reality of business was beginning to unfold: the airline—what the economists would call "the means of production"—was no longer going to be solely controlled by the people, management and investors, who thought they owned the business. A more radical form of ownership was about to envelop the troubled airline industry—on both sides of the 49th Parallel.

The PWA board now had until 11:59 P.M. on September 9, 1992 to decide whether or not to accept Air Canada's Airline Holdco offer.

But they also now had an equity participation plan from the employees' council. Under this new offer, CAIL employees would put up $150 million in equity through a payroll share purchase plan. They would cajole at least three, if not four, provinces to pony up another $150 million. B.C. and Alberta were naturally making investment noises, considering that most CAIL employees were stationed in those two provinces. Ontario was watching the play with interest but no commitment. Saskatchewan was playing cheerleader: no money but lots of moral support.

The employees' council was also short one CAIL union, the Canadian Auto Workers (CAW), who refused to take part in the bail-out plan for the airline. When the provincial government commitments were finally added up, they were also short on that score. Only B.C. and Alberta were prepared to assist the airline, to the tune of no more than $75 million in total. As one CAIL employee put it: "Everybody was saying what a wonderful thing this was, that the governments fully supported [the employees'] initiative, but when it came to writing a cheque, we didn't have enough." It looked, again, like the PWA princess would be forced to kiss the frog. They would have to agree to Air Canada's "sweetened" merger offer.

"So the company walked away from us," said the IAM's Bill Farrall. "But we never stopped working, because we said at the time they will have to expose themselves. They had no other choice. The combined debt was an impossibility. As soon as Air Canada announced they were junking the deal, we were right there at the table with [financial] agreements ready to go."

Still, on September 9, the PWA board announced it had accepted Air Canada's revised proposal for a merger. Air Canada president Hollis Harris called the decision "an historic day for the Canadian airline industry." Harris extolled the benefits of the merger, claiming that Canadian consumers would enjoy stable, competitive air fares in what might become a deregulated monopoly industry. He did not elaborate on how. The next day Air Canada offered a $100 million line of credit to PWA, to help it through its "troubles" while merger talks were being concluded.

But market and consumer reaction was decidedly negative. No one was kidding anyone. Travellers could look forward to significantly higher air fares and reduced levels of route and frequency service. The number of projected job losses was still at a minimum of six thousand. The two carriers had ended 1991 carrying a combined total of $4.5 billion in debt. Losses for the first six months of the year were mounting—on their way to a combined record of $997 million. It was difficult to see how this was such a great deal.

On October 8, a pre-merger agreement was signed between the two parties. On October 19, the *Financial Times* added up the liabilities for its readers and concluded that Airline Holdco could not fly, something the CAIL employees' council had known for months. The merged entity would, in the end, need at least $1 billion in additional cash, most likely coming from the federal government, if the numbers were to work. The *Financial Times* reported that, with all the necessary commitments added in, the merged entity would have an untenable $29 worth of debt for every $1 of shareholder equity. At the end of June 1992, the combined debt was estimated to be $7.7 billion, with equity of only $937 million. Merger costs were thought to be in the $200 million range. Now, after refusing the earlier request for $195 million in loan guarantees, a "senior government official" opined that the federal government was now "not ruling out government support" for the venture.

On Tuesday October 27, two months to the day after the PWA directors last threw up their hands and agreed with Ottawa to sit down and talk with Air Canada, the two airline boards turned down their merger committee's recommended plan to merge CAIL with Air Canada. The No. 1 problem was the immense debt the union of the two carriers would represent. It added up to the third-highest absolute debt level of any airline in the world and the highest debt-to-revenue ratio, according to one analysis. Who on the financial street would be willing to pick up a few hundreds of millions in a new share issue for a company with numbers like that? The good news was that PWA stock was idling at about $1.93 a share at the time. The bad news was that it would eventually fall even further.

The next day more numbers would be rolled out of the hangar. It was projected Airline Holdco would lose a modest $666.4 million in 1993. Holdco might make a $184.4 million profit in 1994. There would be a $363.9 million one-time merger cost, mostly in salary settlements and downsizing costs. The company would be down to its last $100 million in cash by the end of 1993. And there would be no likely cash or equity infusions on the horizon until at least 1997.

It seemed clear Mapleflot-Airline Holdco could not get off the ground—again.

But there was an up side to all this, as the merger committee saw it, by doing what came naturally. In that nice, neat, tight world of monopoly control of an industry, revenues could be boosted substantially by reducing discounts, raising the price of air fares and by eliminating "dilutionary industry practices"—cut out all that extra aircraft capacity the two airlines had previously bought into under open competition. And almost perversely, thanks to the Liberals and the Conservatives, there was now no regulator to make sure consumers would not be gouged. Airline Holdco would do to a deregulated industry what the Tories had no stomach for: de facto regulatory control over "the industry," through its operation as a monopoly carrier without a watchdog.

The deal cooked up by the merger committee was a nonstarter. Everybody, especially the Mulroney government, was back to square one. That immense, initiative-throttling debt load, partly the result of years of profligate, old-fashioned airline management, hung over the companies, the government and the consumer like the Hindenburg curse. Both the suitor and the prospective bride began edging away from the wedding suite. "Conversations" were reportedly now being held between AMR and PWA–CAIL types once again. It was all beginning to appear a bit surreal.

> "As for competition on the level playing field, a classic demonstration of how it works was provided by airline deregulation in the United States in the 1980s. The promised result was to be more airlines competing to fly to more places at cheaper prices. Instead, fewer airlines are now flying to fewer places at higher prices. Unregulated competition leads to oligopolies at best and monopolies at worst. And both lead to price fixing."
> —John Ralston Saul, *Voltaire's Bastards: The Dictatorship of Reason in the West*

In August 1992, the National Transportation Act Review Commission hired consultants SYPHER:MUELLER International Inc. to review the performance of the nation's airline industry between 1981 and 1992 and "identify factors responsible for its weaknesses." They were asked to see if the objectives of Economic Regulatory Reform (deregulation) had been met and if ERR had been the cause of the industry's ill health. Coming as it did while the issue of "to merge and not to merge" was being battled in Ottawa, Montreal, Calgary and Vancouver, the consultant's mandate extended to examining whether it was even viable to consider an Air Canada-CAIL merger. The findings were tabled in October—*The Major Canadian Airlines: Past Performance and Future Prospects*—just as everyone in this strange tale was seemingly running out of patience, options, money and time.

Of all the objectives set for ERR, according to the study, the only one that had been met was that frequency of flights had increased slightly. More points were being served by the airlines now, but primarily in smaller communities. Other than that, *nada*. Average domestic ticket prices in real terms over ten years had increased slightly—not gone down dramatically as many predicted under a deregulated sky. Yields on international routes had declined for the airlines, as a result of international competition. Domestic travel growth had not been stimulated as expected, or as had happened in the U.S. And airline productivity in Canada—the hoped-for net result of increased competition with smarter planning, lower costs and more shrewd management—did not improve and was "virtually unchanged since 1978." When held up against the debt horror show the industry was suffering, the report's findings would almost make anyone in their right mind ask for a return to the good old days of a crown-owned monopoly carrier being chased by a national pretender like CP Air, both tempered in their excesses by a public regulator looking after the travellers' and the taxpayers' interests.

There were many reasons for this sad state of affairs, according to the study. The airlines had been poorly capitalized at the beginning of deregulation. Air Canada was unquestionably in a better position to compete than CAIL. The Gulf War had a stifling impact on airline travel. Increases in fuel prices and falling consumer demand had not helped. The Canadian airlines had not been able to reduce their costs per available seat kilometre to compete with U.S carriers. The mergers that created CAIL had led to an increase in operating costs and a weakened capital structure, which the airline was unable to absorb before traffic declined in 1991. Both Air Canada and CAIL had undertaken "massive re-equipment programs" that drove debt structures to "unsafe levels." And the two major Canadian carriers had "not delayed or cancelled significant new aircraft deliveries" in the face of declining traffic.

"The factors of weak financial health at the outset of economic regulatory reform, excessive and inflexible investment in new aircraft, absence of labour productivity gains and traffic declines explain the current state of the industry," the study concluded.

Of seven factors, four could be attributed to airline management decision-making: the maintenance of high, uncompetitive costs and continued low productivity; the extraordinary cost of mergers to form CAIL; the dramatic increases in debt due to "buying the iron"; and the reluctance to unload purchase or lease commitments for new aircraft when economic bad times hit.

Playing with the idea of merging the two carriers, the consultants concluded a merged airline would need immediate infusions of cash in 1993 but would be unable to borrow because its equity "will be near zero." It would have to seek government equity assistance to the tune of $1 billion, or to allow investment on that scale from a foreign carrier. As if to make sure readers knew where their findings were leading, the study pointed out that even if you merged the two carriers, it was likely the world airline industry would evolve into a handful of mega-carriers within the next few years, and "it is reasonably obvious that a Canadian-led mega-carrier will not be one of the survivors."

The consultants offered two options. Permit the merger but allow foreign carriers to compete with the merged Canadian entity "under an Investment Canada approach that seeks to maximize benefits to Canada," or refuse the merger and let the two financially beleaguered airlines work things out between them, "with the goal of having two smaller but viable carriers at the end of a two year period." Whichever avenue was taken, the decisions facing the government, the report warned ominously, "are more difficult than they appear on the surface, and there are no soft options." The Mulroney government was once again backed into a political corner of their own construction. They were staring at the ugly inevitable: either a massive financial bail-out or the failure of CAIL, with sixteen thousand angry former employees (the number had shrunk by about one thousand during the fiasco) lining up for UIC.

On November 3, Air Canada called off any idea of a merger with

PWA–CAIL. It was "unachievable." Most CAIL employees were elated. AMR slipped back into the scene. By week's end, talks were on again between AMR and PWA in Dallas. This round of "good news," relatively speaking, was greeted by the Toronto Stock Exchange with a rise in the PWA share price to $1.53.

On November 9, Air Canada and its Texas-based partners agreed to invest US $450 million in Continental Airlines Inc. of Houston, Texas. Air Canada would put up US $235 million to buy twenty-four per cent of the fifth largest US airline. The purchase of a piece of bankruptcy-plagued Continental would provide Air Canada with access to more than 190 destinations Continental flew to. The deal made sense within this strange industry, but on the street it might have seemed like something out of *Twilight Zone*.

Air Canada was investing in a U.S. carrier stuck in Chapter 11 bankruptcy proceedings for the second time in a decade. Continental was, by normal standards, a beat up airline. In fact, it was a composite of five other troubled companies—Texas International, New York Air, People Express, Frontier and Eastern airlines. With the Air Canada partnership, and with approvals forthcoming, Continental could become the first of the major American airlines which filed under Chapter 11 in recent years to emerge successfully from bankruptcy. Other big name carriers—Pan Am, Midway—had either gone in and disappeared or, like TWA and American West, were hanging by their fingernails. In 1990, Continental had headed back into Chapter 11 with US $2.2 billion in debt. It would lose US $340.9 million on US $5.4 billion in operating revenues in 1991, compared to Air Canada's loss of US $218 million on US $3.5 billion in revenues.

To the ordinary citizen watching this latest act unfold, these moves seemed capricious, even deadly, for Canada's premier carrier, especially when one took into account the amassed debt Air Canada was already carrying and its poor track record in getting costs down and its balance sheet in order. When you were deep in debt and prospects for the future looked shaky, you took what cash you had, converted what assets you might still hold into cash, and paid down your debt—according to conventional business wisdom. But this was the airline business. In the airline business, evidently you bought into other troubled carriers.

Despite carrying almost $3 billion in debt, in the midst of the worst financial year in the airline's history and losing as much as $1.4

million a day, Air Canada had built up cash reserves in excess of $500 million. Given the state of the industry—with international compet- itiveness seemingly the key to future financial success—and given the patience of creditors and shareholders, it made sense to expand an airline's marketing and commercial alliances as far as frugality allowed. The working adage was: the more places you could go around the world, the more likely you were to make a profit. You certainly weren't going to make money flying half-empty and head-to-head with CAIL between Calgary and Toronto.

PWA's overtures to American Airlines made survival sense. But it was Air Canada that was one step ahead of its Canadian competitor by jockeying for strategic alliances with a number of foreign carriers, including Air France, United Airlines and Korean Air, in addition to its ownership stake in Continental. Not surprisingly, there was also a down side to the strategy. Presumably bigger was to be better in the global airline world of the future. But, as Tae H. Oum of the University of British Columbia's Centre for Transportation Studies cautioned in *Maclean's*, if both PWA and Air Canada forged strategic alliances with U.S. partners, the result could be the technical survival of two domestic carriers, but with severely curtailed Canadian route structures that fed into U.S. hubs for most international flights. "Not only would you devastate Canada's $7 billion aviation industry [but] domestic travel would become much more inconvenient," Oum said. By the spring of 1994, this seemed to be the flight path on which both domestic carriers would be flying.

At the same time, things began looking up a bit for mateless PWA. On November 11, CAW members announced they were now prepared to join the CAIL employee stock option participation plan by throwing $15 million in wage concessions on the table in support of a CAIL–AMR alliance. B.C.'s Minister of Finance Glen Clark rattled Ottawa's cage by insisting the federal government come up with $200 million in loan guarantees to help close the AMR deal. "You started deregulation. You pay," was the gist of Clark's theme. In return, B.C. would consider throwing in $20 million.

The same day, Gemini Automated Group Distribution Systems Inc., the computer reservation system shared by Air Canada and CAIL, announced it was suing PWA and AMR for $1.5 billion—$1 billion for the latter and $500,000 for the former—for trying to break up Gemini. And Air Canada chairman Claude Taylor publicly "demanded" that

Ottawa refuse to help finance loan guarantees leading to any PWA–AMR deal and reportedly threatened "to sue" if the government offered money to PWA or allowed it to slip out of Gemini. Air Canada should receive equal treatment, the chairman demanded. His airline probably could not survive in the face of a competitive Canadian Airlines-American Airlines alliance. The primary reason for his outburst (which he was said to have clarified for the minister shortly thereafter) was that the day before, PWA chairman Rhys Eyton, along with employees' council representatives, had presented the latest version of the employee share plan to federal Minister of Transport Jean Corbeil. Although no promises of federal support were forthcoming, it was strongly implied that PWA might be forced to seek protection from its creditors if help did not materialize from somewhere soon.

"We met with [Corbeil] to tell him that the employees' group was still there," said Sid Fattedad. "And that all of the conditions that we had to satisfy to get AMR onside were there, and that AMR was prepared to come in [on a deal with PWA]. "We went to see him and said: What we need from the federal government is 'X' millions of dollars in loan guarantees. I think it was a big shock to Mr. Corbeil, because I think there was a general sense that when Air Canada announced there was no deal, Canadian would collapse. We saw him and they agreed to come out to Edmonton [for a subsequent meeting]."

Corbeil coyly avoided criticism for cooking up a deal that would depend on Tory funding by responding that the federal government was not talking money. They were only discussing a "proposal." The semantics were important to a free enterprise government. Although all the parties to the proposed employee bail-out were pressing for substantial financial assistance from the Mulroney government, the Tories were trying everything they could to avoid just that. Shortage of federal funds was one thing. But having to eat free enterprise crow over the sudden disappearance of high-minded principles like the right to allow companies in the marketplace to compete, succeed or fail, was more than they could stomach at the moment.

Corbeil's initial thinking was that Ottawa had done enough in agreeing to purchase the three A310-300 Airbuses from CAIL. But Ottawa now had a first glance at what the employees planned. Their wage concessions in return for shares in the company, added to federal and provincial government loan guarantees, could help keep the airline flying until a deal with AMR could be closed to save CAIL. CAIL would also have to bail out of Gemini and sign a twenty year contract with American Airline's SABRE reservation system. But, theoretically, CAIL would be able to keep flying. The employees had put their cards on the table. To paste together the deal they now needed the federal government guarantees, followed by similar help from the provinces.

Western Progressive Conservative MPs—including some of the most ideologically rigid from Alberta, suddenly began calling for the need for Ottawa to support the package. Bobby Sparrow, an ardent free enterprise Tory MP representing Calgary Southwest, was now on the record as seeking federal financial support on the very practical doctrine that there were "too many jobs at stake in Calgary and Vancouver." If nothing else, this kind of road to Damascus conversion revealed just how deep the free enterprise ideology went in some minds. A private sector solution to this tale was fading about as fast as a Mulroney election promise.

The new package tabled in Edmonton on Friday, November 13, would have AMR putting up $246 million for a twenty-five per cent voting share of CAIL, but receiving thirty-three-and-one-third per cent of the airline. CAIL employees would put up $145 million through wage and salary concessions of roughly five per cent over three years. A public share issue was expected to garner another $125 million. The provinces—which ones and for how much had not yet been established—were expected to put up a total of $100 in loan guarantees. And the federal government, it was hoped, would put forward a total of $190 million, made up of $100 million in bridge financing guarantees and $90 million in loan guarantees.

AMR was not after one-third interest in a losing airline. American wanted to sell PWA access to its SABRE computer reservation system and contract its management services and administrative help to the struggling Canadian airline. AMR had a different perspective on the future of the airline business. Growth for American Airlines was not going to come from flying passengers from point A to point B. It was going to come from selling data network management services to the rest of the struggling international airline industry. American was so sure of its forecast it was willing to get out of the flying side of the business, entirely, as soon as it was financially feasible.

There was a multitude of other benefits for AMR in the deal. It would also receive access to an integrated route system that would expand American Airline's international reach and marketability, especially into the Pacific. And by having CAIL tied into its SABRE computer reservations system, AMR stood to make substantial profits over the twenty-year length of the service contract, a factor which fit neatly into AMR's strategic business plan. "The sooner we can sell [our thirty-three per cent stake in CAIL] the better," AMR executive vice-president Donald J. Carty would candidly tell the federal Competition Tribunal in February 1993.

The strongest airline in the world at the time, with its six hundred and seventy-two aircraft, one hundred and two thousand employees and eighty million annual passenger load, had already seen a future few other airline operators had. Carty told the National Transportation Agency in March 1993: "This transaction by itself is not AMR's future. The business that is an element of this transaction is its future . . . [American] will probably be a smaller airline and probably be a bigger information systems supplier."

AMR had invested US $1.5 billion to develop SABRE into the world's largest and most profitable computer reservation system. SABRE had penetrated more than half the world market and seventeen airlines used its services. Getting other airlines to ride on their sophisticated computer system would make more money for AMR in the future than fighting it out with the rest of the industry to get passengers to ride in its airplanes.

AMR's SABRE system had recently closed deals with France's national railway, *Société Nationale des Chemins de Fer*, and with Eurotunnel, the Channel tunnel operators, for their reservation system, as well as benefiting from the abrupt surge in U.S. travel business sparked by American Airline's decision to cut its leisure fare tickets in half. (Because SABRE's share of the U.S. computer reservation system was so large, the sudden fare war set off by American meant—coincidentally, of course—instant traffic returns on its reservation system side of the business.) The fact that AMR's Carty could smile broadly at SABRE's success while American Airlines was forecasting a US $48 million loss in the July-September 1992 financial quarter—while a fare war was underway—said a mouthful about where AMR's priorities were. What they lost on the shaky air carrier business, they more than made up by running one of the world's most sophisticated computer reservation systems.

For the moment, CAIL belonged to the Gemini computer

reservation system. Gemini was formed in 1987 when CAIL joined with Air Canada to provide both "partners" with an improved computer reservation system. Covia Canada, an arm of United Airlines, was added to the partnership in 1989. The Gemini partnership had improved both Canadian airlines' competitiveness against their major rival—American's SABRE.

Although loud noises were now emanating from Quebec federal and provincial politicians about backing Air Canada and not allowing PWA to escape from Gemini, the issue of all those lost jobs at CAIL—sixteen thousand employees and an annual payroll of some $863 million—was beginning to catch Corbeil's attention. As he and Mazankowski made their way to Edmonton for the meeting with PWA officials and members of the employees' council, the two airlines were still losing as much as $2 million a day. PWA was talking to creditors about not paying its bills in the hope of preserving badly needed cash. At roughly the same time, AMR announced third-quarter losses for American Airlines of US $231 million. It made one wonder whether the disease was catching. It did not make decision making any easier for the now badgered Tory ministers.

On Friday-the-13 of November, the PWA board endorsed the new employees' council proposal "subject to obtaining the necessary government support." But what choice did it have? With daily losses cooking along at about $800,000 a day, and nothing but losses since 1988, industry and financial analysts were leaning toward government guarantees to keep CAIL alive, as opposed to a merger, simply because PWA's implausible debt-to-equity ratio (7:1) was "superior" to that of Air Canada's (9:1).

Coming out of the meeting in Edmonton, PWA's Eyton maintained that, though PWA's cash reserves were depleted and the daily losses were mounting, the airline was not in "imminent danger of collapse." The federal government was not exactly striding boldly to the table to help out. Ottawa had made the PWA board's acceptance of the employees' plan, leading to a possible AMR deal, a precondition for even meeting in Edmonton. "They wanted to see our eyeballs, wanted to see how committed we were," said Fattedad.

In fact, both the federal government and the employees' council wanted to see something else. They wanted to see Canadian Airlines International upper management clean up its act. Both groups were not at all happy with the way the airline was being run. It was a bit embarrassing for the employees to be begging on PWA's behalf for federal cash when at the same time they knew CAIL's financial situation needed a complete overhaul if the airline was going to even get close to operating profitably. Except for AMR, standing in the wings with its hard-nosed negotiating position, CAIL employees had so far been the only party prepared to "invest" in PWA. In fact, right about now there were a number of them who wondered if they weren't being taken for suckers.

One of the most troubling discoveries the employees' council made in August of 1992, when they finally had a chance to see what AMR and PWA had been talking about, were the warranties or contractual promises PWA had unilaterally been prepared to make to AMR. In effect, it was promising to get future costs down by freezing employees' wages for three to four years. As well, PWA was prepared to give guarantees that employees would not grieve the transfer of jobs to AMR. The discovery of PWA's promises by members of the employees' council sparked anger, mistrust and almost enough resentment to cause the employees to turn their backs on CAIL and let the company go down.

"All the union leaders went in thinking: 'If we put some money in we can save this company,' " Fattedad recalled. "But then you peel open the onion and find out: 'Oh, by the way, we also have to freeze wages for three years, and by the way, we also have to do this . . .' You went through all those stages, of getting ticked off, of saying: 'These guys are rats!' to the point of: 'Wait a second. If we put $200 million in, we're part of this thing, right?'

"It went all the way around to saying: 'We are going to tell *them* we are *not* going to take [a freeze in] wages! We're not going to let them tell *us*! We're going to take some control of our lives here.' "

The negotiations "were wild and woolly" according to IAM president Bill Farrall. "You were negotiating with three governments, PWA, AMR and Canadian Airlines, and all the unions, middle management . . . all sitting around the table at the same time. It was a difficult process because the employer came in at this time, seeing an opportunity to gut union contracts with these massive pages of concessions. I said: 'Sit on it. I'm not here to open up the contract . . .' So those agreements were difficult to come by."

Between the looming spectre of unemployment and PWA management's haughtiness, CAIL employees began taking advantage of the moment to carve, not just a tougher bargaining stance, but a stronger sense of camaraderie and concern for each other. They were willing to walk a long road to save this battered airline by taking, in effect, rather large wage cuts, but few people would have guessed that some of them would be willing to take even larger cuts to make sure that everyone shared the burden equally.

Most of the unions in the council had received wage increases in early 1992, except for the six thousand IAM machinists. If wages were frozen, an imminent possibility—with or without PWA's side deals—the IAM members would find themselves stuck three years behind their co-workers. It was the subject of much discussion around the table. The issue was fairness. But they were all in "the lifeboat" together, as Sid Fattedad put it. "So the pilot union leader and the flight attendant leader [left the council meeting], and they were talking, and then they came back in and said: 'We'll pay for the IAM increases.' The pilots took a one-and-a-half per cent permanent wage cut and the flight attendants took a half per cent cut to pay what the IAM needed to catch up, so everybody was on equal terms."

Their bitterness over the warranties aside, the employees also started after CAIL senior management to restructure the company. The employees' biggest problem was that, with the life of CAIL hanging tenuously in the balance, the employees were the only ones at this point prepared to pay a price to keep the airline flying. If somebody didn't do something to get the debt down, fast, there would not be wages for anyone to freeze. Operating bills were still being paid. Some investors were still clipping coupons and aircraft lease contracts were still being honoured. There were costly commitments for *more* new aircraft still on the books—when the airline was less than two weeks away from crashing. The employees were beating the drums for a company that was unravelling, and management did not seem to be getting the message.

While CAIL employees were getting to know each other better in the lifeboat, Air Canada employees in eastern Canada were protesting in support of the airline merger idea and one strong, national carrier. While the federal cabinet met to discuss the CAIL employees' offer, PWA filed a $1 billion predatory pricing lawsuit against Air Canada on November 17, claiming it had increased its seating capacity and charged fares that were "far below the cost of providing service."

THE REVENGE OF KARL MARX

119

Everyone seemed to be edging toward the cliff. An employee-led bail-out had to work or it was lights out for PWA–CAIL. PWA chief Eyton admitted "I've got no rabbits to pull out my hat" if the deal with AMR fell through. There were other skirmishes going on around the outer circles of the wagon train surrounding Eyton's airline. The B.C. government blamed federal deregulation for the airlines' ills and, in consequence, said the Mulroney government should bring back regulation of Canada's airlines. The *Vancouver Sun* informed its readers that after four years of airline deregulation—with all those Tory promises of more competition, cheaper fares and increased service— the cheapest price for a Vancouver-to-Toronto return fare had risen, as many suspected, not fallen. Vancouver social critic Herschel Hardin, in calling for a return to a government-owned monopoly airline, reminded industry watchers that "the biggest factor in transportation economics is passenger load, and a regulated monopoly can put that to optimum use." Hardin was saying a full plane makes money, but two half-empty planes do not. An airline that optimizes profit by keeping its airplanes full can afford to keep fares low. Everybody can win in a properly regulated monopoly.

But that sort of idea, based on Canadian economic history if nothing else, would only stick in the craw of a government and a corporate sector that believed in the benefits of competition.

"Competition, which is the instinct of selfishness, is another word for dissipation of energy, while combination is the secret of efficient production."
—Edward Bellamy, *Looking Backward*, 1888

On November 19, 1992, Minister of Transport Jean Corbeil tabled the report of the Royal Commission on National Passenger Transportation in the House of Commons. The commission's recommendations were, to many, as simplistic as they were thick. The ideological timing could not have been worse. The commission recommended Canada adopt a total "user pay" philosophy where the cost of transportation was concerned. Under the commission's recommendation, government subsidies for transportation would be phased out, and there would be no financial bail-outs for struggling carriers. Let the marketplace decide the service level, who pays and for how much, was what the commission wanted as a "framework for a national transportation policy."

The Royal Commission's recommendations, where the airline business was concerned, could hardly have been more inappropriate for the times. The Mulroney government's *elixir fixée* of privatization and deregulation was in a clear state of collapse. Privatization of Air Canada had contributed less than zero to the airline's functioning and its effectiveness. Deregulation of the industry had not worked. In fact, it weakened it—seriously damaging the airline industry's ability to compete internationally. And now, a Tory commission was trying to convince Canadians that there was no role for government in setting equitable transportation policies.

The Royal Commission on National Passenger Transportation had just taken three years and $23 million of taxpayers' money to reveal how truly thin some neoconservative philosophies were about how nations, governments and economies worked. They would deregulate everything to do with transportation. They were saying that only commerce mattered, and that the ties, trappings and responsibilities of nationhood did not. And the "user pay" philosophy was even more than the Mulroney government could swallow.

Canada had a not-unique experience of building a nation on the symbiosis between public responsibilities and private enterprise. Many other nation states had used a similar formula to ensure their economies grew and prospered. Either that, or like Japan, they discovered that economic strength and growth can develop dramatically, not through unrestricted commercial competition, but through the integration, cooperation and involvement of government with business, investors and labour.

The Royal Commission dismissed the lessons of economic and business success in other international settings and, in its uncomplicated way, decided that Canada now had "a mature system in place"—one that no longer required a government presence. The entire passenger transportation system should be left to the private sector and simple notions about the "forces" of the marketplace. The costs would simply be paid by the users. If there were no users, there would be no service, it was assumed. The estimated aggregate cost to the Canadian transportation user would be an extra seven per cent. It seemed hardly worth mentioning that the process would also mean the termination of countless miles of roadways, railroads, air services and ferry routes deemed inefficient and costly by the free market test.

Opposition MPs and critics called the Royal Commission's

recommendations "vicious" and "cruel." They would turn the "national dream" into the "national nightmare." Having been left to deal with economic and political realities, rather than with market-driven philosophy, transport minister Corbeil went on to ignore the commission's principal recommendation about no bail-outs for struggling transportation companies. He swallowed hard on the ideological lumps and put up $50 million in loan guarantees as Ottawa's contribution to an eventual PWA–AMR partnership. Although the money was there to assist Canadian Airlines meet "current operating requirements" over the next one or two months, it was also what the Tories used to get the PWA board to put its financial house in order. It was the carrot. The stick was not far behind: Don't do something about your huge debt, and no $50 million, went the refrain.

PWA now needed the money more urgently than ever. Its cash reserves were reportedly less than $5 million at the start of November 1992. Without the Tories' $50 million, Canadian Airlines would have been out of business by the following weekend.

"Up until then [the employees' council] was unable to get the company to look at completely restructuring itself," Fattedad said. "There was just too much debt. We said: 'You're not asking any of the creditors and the shareholders to take a bite.' But on November 24, when the government came out to Calgary for another board meeting to announce their $50 million support, they said [to PWA's board]: 'You have to restructure the company.' The federal government had looked at the state of the company and said: 'If you want to have real assurances of survival, you've got to get your debt down. You've got to restructure.' "

The Mulroney government was motivated partly by expediency, partly by their own ideological confusion, partly by the overriding issue of national unity—and by a lot of primal political fear. Brian Mulroney had already led his party to the basement of public opinion polls and voter appreciation. Christmas was coming. The thought of sixteen thousand very angry CAIL employees—out of work and blaming the federal government for sparking this industry chaos in the first place and then lacking the compassion to help when crisis struck—girded what few loins were left in the Progressive Conservative cabinet. Free market dogma or no dogma, the Royal Commission and its user pay tome notwithstanding, the Tories would assist PWA, finally, with seed money to keep CAIL flying.

In return for the cash, Corbeil had a lot of conditions for PWA's board. He had gone a long way out on an ideological wing in offering to provide what some critics saw as federal "subsidies" for the airline. Although the money was actually in the form of loan guarantees, there still would be a tough list of reparations for Mr. Eyton and Co. As the *Toronto Star* reported, Corbeil wanted Canadian Airlines to stop paying its creditors until its cash situation improved—or as one CAIL supporter put it: "The creditors had to look in their pants, too."

CAIL would be required to immediately restructure the company with an emphasis on getting costs down. The government also wanted one of their officials attached to the PWA board to monitor the airline's operations during the period covered by the $50 million. In fact, the $50 million might not even be $50 million. The money was ladled out in two installments, with the first being $20 million. If conditions were not met by the airline, it might not see the second, $30 million, installment. Also, the $50 million was not to be used for paying outstanding bills. It was a temporary loan guarantee, bridge funding meant to see the company through December and allow it an opportunity "to explore with all interested parties, including provinces and employees, the actions necessary to minimize taxpayers' financial exposure and to support a viable, competitive airline system."

Corbeil must have known PWA was just one symptom of a very sick industry that clearly required, to use his diplomatic phrase, "recalibration." Tory deregulation of the airline industry, coupled with the management track record of the two airlines, had resulted in monumental failure. Some form of reregulation of airline transportation would have to be considered. Even then it was probably too late.

Things were so bad in the Mulroney government's ideological backyard that Corbeil was reportedly now suggesting PWA should begin talking with Air Canada about how to get profitable—while working together. He was not only saying the neoconservative days of wholesale deregulation were being relegated to the dust bin. He was, to be charitable, within a hair's breadth of instructing the two carriers to break the laws prohibiting companies from conspiring to lessen competition. The Tories seemed to have gone from "open competition" to no-competition-if-we-can-help-it in only two sessions in government.

Even more ironically, no one seemed to notice that all the

players—the Mulroney government, PWA's board, the provinces, even AMR Corporation of Fort Worth, Texas—were riding any survival of Canadian Airlines International on the backs of the CAIL workers. The employees—not the government, not investment bankers, not PWA board members, certainly not AMR—were the ones forced to raise their investment in the company each time more money was required. The employees had been the first to put a cash offer on the table—$140 million covered by wage concessions over three years. Then that figure became $150 million. It would not stop there. The provinces, for all their braggadocio and sniping had, at this point, put nothing on the table.

When it was learned during the November 21-22 weekend that Ottawa would not put up the $190 million in loan guarantees requested (instead, only the $50 million announced a few days later), it was the employees' council that "squeezed" another $60 million out of their own hides to bring their contribution to more than $200 million—backed by their collective willingness to take a ten per cent wage cut over four years.

On November 29, PWA announced its new restructuring plan. It would "temporarily cease payments to all lenders, major equipment lessors and certain facility lessors" as the first step in the business plan Ottawa had encouraged—and the employees had advocated since September. The move would be for four to six months and would provide the airline with drastically needed cash flow. By the end of December, the amount in arrears in stalled dividend payments, deferrals of principal, interest and operating lease payments would total $41 million for that one month alone. But even with the stop-payment announcement, the airline was still expected to lose more than $1 million a day through December. And even if the provinces eventually kicked in an extra $70 million in loan guarantees, the airline would be in a negative cash position again on March 1.

The airline would now ask its creditors to trade $722 million in debt for equity. The move to wipe almost a quarter of its $3.2 billion in financial obligations off the books would strengthen its balance sheet, but at the cost of dramatically diluting the value of current share holdings. PWA stock would continue to nose-dive, plummeting to fifty-eight cents.

On December 3, the airline announced it intended to reduce seat capacity by as much as fifteen per cent (they would only achieve about twelve per cent). Domestic fare prices began going up effective December 1. More restructuring came on December 8 with the announcement that CAIL had reached "an amicable agreement" with one of its aircraft leasing companies to terminate three A320 leases. A fourth leased A320 would be returned in January and two more due for delivery in March would have the agreements switched to leases. Delivery of a further ten A320s would eventually be deferred to 1996 through 1999. As happy as this news must have been to Ottawa and the employees' council, the moves to cancel or defer deliveries of this new "iron" would cost CAIL $60 million.

On December 14, a letter of understanding was signed between PWA and the unions and associations representing staff and operating under the Council of Canadian Airlines Employees. The total employee investment would be $200 million (it would eventually edge up to $210 million) in wage and salary reductions in return for a quarter of the company. Senior management salaries would be cut twenty per cent. On December 18, the province of British Columbia came on board with $20 million and Alberta put up $50 million.

On December 19, PWA's draft of its restructuring plan was sent to creditors and lessors with the offer to convert as much as $756 million debt to equity in the form of common shares. A final plan was due for February, but in the meantime, the reason any right-minded creditor or supplier would want to accept this offer from PWA was simple: With the comparatively thin government backing that was in place, and the employees, in effect, helping to eat a large chunk out of the airline's operating costs, they had very little to lose in accepting the debt-for-equity switch.

"A lot of the creditors would have got nothing if they had walked," Fattedad pointed out. "And some of the creditors figured, 'What the hell, if the iron is flying, we're getting paid . . .' [but] if it weren't for the fact you had all these employees out there waving banners and flags and marching in the streets and saying: 'We're putting our money up,' if it wasn't for that, I think [Canadian] would've gone down."

Finally, on December 29, PWA announced that a "comprehensive agreement" had finally been signed with AMR. It was expected, a bit too enthusiastically, that the deal would be closed by mid-1993. American Airlines would invest (Cdn) $246 million for a third of the economic interest in Canadian Airlines International and twenty-five per cent of the voting interest, thanks to federal legislation restricting foreign carriers to a maximum of one-quarter control. In addition, AMR would sell a wide array of information and management services to PWA, including putting PWA on the SABRE computer reservation system. A marketing agreement would allow each airline to participate in the other's frequent flyer program. The AMR–PWA agreement would eventually cost Canadian employees about one thousand jobs, versus the ten thousand expected from a merger with Air Canada. PWA shares on the TSE responded by edging up twelve cents to eighty-two cents.

The news that the PWA–AMR deal had been signed, subject to final closing conditions, was a telling case study in market principles and business takeovers. Like relationships between the herds and predators on the African veld, the big guy always devours the little guy. For (Cdn) $246 million, or less than US $185 million at 75 Canadian cents to a U.S. dollar, AMR got one-third of Canadian Airlines International. When Canadian moved its reservation system from Gemini to American's SABRE, AMR stood to benefit to the tune of $2 billion in services provided to CAIL over the twenty-year course of the contract. AMR expected their computer, management and technology services would generate, in the first year alone, US $115 million in new revenue. At that rate, their investment in CAIL would be paid off in a couple of years—and AMR would effectively control Canada's No. 2 airline. The deal was, to be kind, a major steal.

Despite the twenty-five per cent voting restriction placed on foreign ownership by federal legislation, there were two overriding realities that had to be taken into account. At twenty-five per cent, American Airlines would not just have a major say in how CAIL was run. The extra conditions set by AMR would effectively give AMR control of the most important elements of the PWA board's decision making.

As PWA board member Max Ward predicted in January 1992: "Certainly if we tied up with American, they're going to be the dominant carrier, aren't they? They've got the resources and the markets and their costs are better than ours."

More significant than its two seats on the PWA board were the rights AMR also received—"rights normally afforded a substantial minority equity investor," according to PWA's 1992 Annual Report. They included AMR's approval of: "(1) the annual business plan when a loss is projected; (2) the annual capital and financing plan; (3) capital spending over a threshold amount [$50 million]; (4) mergers, acquisitions, equity issues and asset sales over a threshold amount; (5) dividends over a threshold amount; and (6) liquidation, winding up or reorganization of Canadian Airlines."

It was not a bad business deal at all for AMR. It would acquire a sizeable interest in another airline, with valuable new routes, plus a veto over most of the important issues a board would deliberate over—for a fire-sale price. And it would recoup its investment in probably less time than it would take to get a piece of controversial legislation passed through Parliament.

Not only that, if CAIL continued to founder and if American eventually took its holdings in convertible preferred stock as was suggested, it would, as the *Globe and Mail* put it, "move ahead of some other creditors in the lineup for assets should the company eventually fail." There seemed no down side to the deal for AMR. No wonder it exhibited such patience as Canadian airline executives, politicians, employees, provincial and federal governments wrung hands and negotiated with each other for more than six frantic months. It was win-win all along for the patient American.

The persistent CAIL employees had, it seemed, their 1992 Christmas present. As everyone geared up to celebrate the end of the bloodiest year in Canadian airline history, thoughts began turning to a possible denouement for this tragedy. The warfare and the losses had been so devastating in this *annus horribilus* that 1993 could not possibly turn out as badly. But the AMR "alliance agreement" was still not a done deal. AMR had more hard conditions on the table for the PWA board to wrestle with. The debt restructuring plan still had to be completed before any strategic alliance was struck. Canadian Airlines had to obtain all the required regulatory, lender and third-party consents and approvals to effect the transaction. All of CAIL's foreign routes had to be in "full force and effect." And, the biggest hurdle of them all: CAIL had to get out of the Gemini computer reservation system agreement—to be able to sign on SABRE—and satisfy AMR "that neither Canadian, AMR nor any of their affiliates is or will become liable in connection with the Gemini group for any material losses as a result of entering into the services agreement [with AMR]."

These hurdles would largely escape notice during the celebrations over the end of PWA's Year of Living Dangerously. There was still the matter of those multi-million-dollar lawsuits—Gemini suing PWA–AMR and PWA suing Air Canada—floating into 1993. If the actors on the stage had trouble getting their roles straight and their lines right in this tragedy about the effects of airline deregulation, it was easy to understand how the audience felt. Like 1992, the 1993 version of this play would make it even harder to figure out who was doing what to whom, without a program.

7 / An Age of Damaging Innocence

"Clearly the modern organized economy was designed with a perverse hand. For how, otherwise, could so many needs seeming so inescapable conspire to make a system which still rejoices in the name of free enterprise in truth be so dependent on government? The industrial system, in fact, is inextricably associated with the state. In notable respects the mature corporation is an arm of the state. And the state, in important matters, is an instrument of the industrial system."
—John Kenneth Galbraith, *The New Industrial State*

THE AMERICAN EXPERIENCE WITH AIRLINE DEREGULATION in 1978 did not, of course, go totally unnoticed in Canada. It would take six years before Canadian politicians were prepared to make the first moves to deregulate our industry. It would be a decade before they would go all the way. Unfortunately, by that time the American air deregulation experiment was going sour. Calls were being made for some form of reregulation in the U.S. Complaints were building over deterioration in services, inequities in fare pricing, aircraft safety and dismay over the bizarre wave of airline takeovers, which lessened competition— the exact opposite of what deregulation proselytes had predicted.

One should not confuse the time lag with any assumptions about superior study and reflection on deregulation's impact in this country. For a host of historic, domestic and political reasons, Canadians proved even less prepared than Americans to deal with the upheavals associated with airline deregulation. Liberal and Conservative politicians would time and again profess that they rejected the idea of a U.S.-style deregulation model, protesting that they preferred instead a "made-in-Canada" solution. They would deliberate over it in task force, report on it to House of Commons committees, and debate it in first, second and third reading in Parliament. And a decade after the U.S. introduced its legislation, they would still not be capable of getting it right. They should have left well enough alone.

Canadians had sat front-row-centre to the American deregulation experience. U.S. newspaper stories, magazines and television—those ubiquitous cultural levelers—carried stories about deregulation from south of the border. Everyone seemed aware of how much cheaper it was to fly the U.S. skies. Thousands of Canadians had been taking advantage of their proximity to the 49th Parallel to cross over and buy cheap airline tickets on U.S. carriers between U.S. and international destinations, even between Canadian destinations. At the same time, pressure for deregulation of the Canadian airline industry was being applied at the federal political level by various lobby groups.

The 1970s had been a confusing crucible for the development of any new airline policy in Canada. Changes in air transportation policy in the early years of the decade delivered travellers the lowest economy class air fares in the industry's history. That advantage would be marred by the increases in air fares caused by the 1973 world energy crisis, and by added consumer irritants like the 1974 federal air transportation tax—in effect, a sales tax on air travel. The rate of growth in Canadian air travel would begin to arc downward by mid-decade. But the news for consumers on fares was actually quite good. Relaxation of regulations opened the door for affinity charters and price competition in the 1960s and early 1970s, followed by advanced-booking charters, followed in 1977 by new excursion or charter-class fares. Not unexpectedly, these cheaper fares only made some Canadian air travellers more surly than before.

Excursion fares made it cheaper in some cases to fly across the Atlantic Ocean than to fly across the country. It was inevitable that the travelling public would soon demand similar fares for domestic travel. Another, more activating factor was the irritation suffered by business travellers who had little to rejoice over when it came to lower ticket prices. As fares dropped dramatically for excursion and charter-class vacation travellers, and occasional travellers with flexible schedules, fully refundable economy and first-class fares remained relatively high in price, something business travellers could fix their anger on. The longer the inequity continued, the angrier and more vocal they became.

The history of government regulation of the airlines in Canada differed fundamentally from the U.S. experience. For one thing, the Canadian regulatory body had a much tighter relationship to the political process—in a noncolluding way—and therefore was already much more sensitive to public opinion and its responsibility to work in the public interest. There was less chance for a body regulating Canadian airlines to be "captured" by the carriers, as happened with the American regulator, the Civil Aeronautics Board. It was true that Canadian airlines were well looked after by regulation, but the Canadian air regulatory experience was much more sensitive, as it evolved, to the interests of the citizen and consumer, overall, than the CAB seemed to have been.

As much as anything, decision by cabinet—elected parliamentarians—not unilateral decision making by a politically appointed body, had typified the Canada airline regulatory process. This made for a slightly more responsive pattern of regulation. Political sensitivity to public opinion ensured a regulatory environment in this country that was more fair for all concerned, even for the air traveller, and the results were much more effective than the American experience. In Canada, the Air Transport Board (ATB) acted until 1967 as regulator, overseeing the growth of the industry to maturity with limited authority, and with only partial jurisdiction over the single, most important element—Trans-Canada Air Lines (TCA), later Air Canada.

In fact, the national airline and any other applicant for a licence, was answerable to cabinet more than to any regulator. According to the *Aeronautics Act*, licensing powers held by the ATB were "subject to the approval of the Minister." Any board decision could be appealed to the minister. In any number of cases concerning licensing, the ATB was subordinate to instructions from the governor-in-council as protection "in the public interest." Even licenses required by TCA to maintain its mandate as the national airline were subject to the approval of the Minister of Transport, without reference to the ATB. So, at the fundamental political level, there was no comparison between the way the CAB and the ATB, and its successor, the Air Transport Committee of the Canadian Transport Commission, functioned as regulators.

Granted, if there were differences in substance between the two regulatory systems, there were also a few troubling similarities. The Air Transport Committee of the Canadian Transport Commission, for instance, had a "minimum objective" not unlike that of the CAB when it came to regulating the business—"to prevent the collapse of any air carrier and the disruption of services that would result, with predictable unwelcome political consequences for the federal government," according to political scientist Garth Stevenson. "This fundamental imperative took precedence over all other considerations."

Operatively, the two regulatory styles would be much different. But from a public appearance point of view, after a quick glance to the south, the systems could probably have been seen as having roughly the same results—keeping the price of air fares to the consumer too high, while ensuring airlines did not fall from the sky. So when the Progressive Conservatives under Joe Clark were elected in 1979, carrying with them a decidedly neoconservative policy approach to both the economy and to government, and with forty years of criticism ringing in their heads about big, fat and indifferent Air Canada, too-high ticket prices and the benefits of airline competition washing across the U.S.-Canada border every night at evening news time, the new government set the wheels in motion for a Canadian version of U.S. airline deregulation.

> "The Anglo-American system is long on theories. It is easy to pick any English-language textbook and find theories proving that whatever gives more to the consumer is best for everyone . . . The Asian system is not so explicitly theoretical . . . Its goal is to develop the productive base of the country . . . When it comes to a choice between the consumer's welfare and the producer's, it's really no choice at all."
> —James Fallows, The Atlantic Monthly, January 1994

Canadian airline deregulation was a Conservative, then a Liberal, and then a Conservative initiative. Canadian airline deregulation was supposed to increase competition. Instead, it increased concentration of airline ownership and lessened competition. Deregulation was supposed to result in lower air fares for airline travellers. Average domestic ticket prices increased in real terms over the period 1981-1991. After a brief fare war, ticket prices headed up again in 1992 by an average five per cent. By 1994, both major carriers expected to raise their fares fifteen to twenty per cent over the next two years.

Airline deregulation was supposed to spur domestic travel growth. Although revenue-passenger kilometres grew marginally between 1981 and 1989, by 1991 the numbers had crashed back to 1986 levels. Deregulation was supposed to increase airline productivity and efficiency. By 1992, productivity figures for the two carriers were virtually unchanged. Any change that did occur since then came from laying off airline staff and management.

Deregulation was supposed to stop passenger "leakage" to U.S. destinations or gateways, a problem estimated to have cost the airlines $100 million annually. By 1992, more Canadians than ever were driving to U.S. airports and flying on cheaper American air fares.

Deregulation was supposed to provide the Canadian business traveller, the paying backbone of regular air service, with substantially lower fares. It did not. On average, and in real terms, the Canadian business traveller still pays about the same full-fare economy price for an airline ticket he or she did in 1984.

Deregulation was supposed to provide Canadians with greater frequency of flights and to serve more points with more routes. But unless you live in certain, small communities where frequency of flights did increase somewhat—but with turbo-prop, not jet, air- craft—there was no appreciable increase in service.

Canada once had a regulated aviation regime that provided the nation with one of the safest and most economical air transportation systems in the world—at surprisingly little cost to the taxpayer. The regulatory machine was primarily dedicated to maintaining stability in a growing industry so that Canadians would always have a nationwide air transportation service, at reasonable prices. As awkward as regulation for struggling Canadian air carriers became, particularly the smaller airlines, regulation did bring a certain order to the business. When a carrier overstepped itself with too much or too expensive aircraft for the routes it had been awarded, the regulatory judgement handed down usually allowed the carrier to be merged with a stronger one, avoiding costly bankruptcy and wholesale layoffs while main- taining service for its customers at reasonable prices. The last thing a sane government wanted was mass chaos and unnecessary costs in such an important industry. Particularly if the majority of voters were not opposed to the existing regulatory system.

In May 1984, the Liberal government introduced the New Canadian Air Policy, the first major step toward ultimate deregulation of the Canadian airline industry. The march had begun in 1979 with the Clark government's short-lived efforts to deregulate transporta- tion. The 1984 effort to "Liberalize" air regulations gave carriers more freedom to decide where they wanted to fly, with what type of aircraft and what frequency, and, within certain limits, to charge what the market would bear. The philosophy was: Relaxed rules will increase competition and competition will reduce air fares.

The Liberals' ideological impulses about deregulation did not run very deep. Their new policy was like having half an idea—or half a theoretical conviction. This first policy stab at deregulation did not apply to airlines flying north of the 50th parallel. There the old regulations would apply. But in southern Canada, relaxation of regulations was the order of the day. One could only assume that "healthy competition," "consumer sovereignty" and "market principles" therefore had geographic, rather than philosophical, limitations.

In introducing the new policy, Minister of Transport Lloyd Axworthy believed the regulated air transportation system had led, as *Canadian Business* magazine put it, "to high fares, inflexible service, inefficient management and unsatisfactory earnings for the industry as a whole"—a list of shortcomings not unlike the environment that would exist under a deregulated Canadian sky ten years later.

Axworthy introduced a measure that "totally repudiated the entire legacy of Canadian air transportation policy," according to Stevenson, "contrasting its alleged drawbacks with what it called the 'many important benefits of deregulation in the United States.' " And although Axworthy promised a unique made-in-Canada approach, including the possible sale of Air Canada to the private sector, his new policy appeared all but indistinguishable from American deregulation.

The reason for such haste, for trying to run to catch a place in the American deregulation parade, was that the Liberals were worried about losing more voters, especially in the West, and losing more support among the influential business community—which could mean both lost votes and, perhaps, lost contributions to the party. Canada was now riding its very own neoconservative "let-alone" wave. Many newspapers and magazines were editorializing about "wasteful and arrogant government departments," "being swamped with government regulations" and getting government off the backs of the citizen and business community. Many newspapers, particularly the Toronto *Globe and Mail* and its *Report on Business*, continuously bad-mouthed Air Canada, its "dominance" of the marketplace, and equated regulation and ownership of airlines as "state ownership." It was no surprise, then, that both federal parties had found promises to deregulate the industry and privatize Air Canada particularly suitable for political purposes. It would cost the government nothing and the lower air fares expected would make everyone happier.

The irony, of course, was that fares had already started dropping by 1980, when restrictions were eased on advanced-booking charters following their introduction in 1979. But these fares mostly applied to holiday and flexible travellers. Business travellers got little more than irritation. They were not just angry at the airlines for keeping their fares high. They now had to sit next to a traveller who was probably flying to the same destination for two-thirds off the price the business traveller paid. As far as going further with airline deregulation was concerned, the largest mass of Canadian voters did not seem to give a care one way or the other. If they flew at all, it was usually on discount fares. They had only two concerns: safety and cheap air fares, and they were already getting both. They received the benefit of cheaper fares whether the airlines were deregulated or not.

If anything, most Canadians were ambivalent about regulatory control of airlines and were in favour of maintaining public ownership of public enterprises such as Air Canada. Polls conducted in the early 1980s indicated that as many as seventy per cent of Canadians were content with the degree of public ownership that existed at the time. But the political agenda that deregulated the Canadian airline industry was in the hands of primarily Anglophone *petite bourgeoisie*—an influential stratum of relatively affluent business, corporate and government managers.

All were relatively heavy users of airplanes for business purposes. Many had a preference for CAIL, the private sector airline. Dissatisfaction over the price of air fares was *the* simmering issue for business people paying full price for air fares, and for Liberal politicians hanging on to their seats by the thin skin of their last election promise.

Included in the airline deregulation and privatization support group were organizations such as the Economic Council of Canada, the Business Council on National Issues (BCNI) and the Conference Board of Canada. The Economic Council of Canada, "a tireless proponent of the American way of life since its establishment by the Pearson government in 1963," according to Stevenson, produced a report in 1981 advocating that Canada's airline industry be deregulated. Established in 1976, the BCNI consisted of the CEOs of the 100 largest companies in the country "dedicated to the development of public policy in the national interest." Among their diverse interests, the BCNI would champion free trade, NAFTA, the Charlottetown Accord and lower federal deficits—though, as one author noted, they were silent on the issue of achieving this goal by making corporations pay a fairer share of taxes.

The Conference Board of Canada, a veritable Who's Who of Canadian business, consisted of representatives of a number of provincial and federal government departments as well. The Conference Board prided itself on its private sector perspective—despite deriving a substantial portion of its funding from government sources.

Leading the charge from the government side would be federal bureaucrats in the Department of Consumer and Corporate Affairs and groups such as the Consumers' Association of Canada, always eager to go to bat for the consumer but tied tight in policy terms with its "patron," the Department of Consumer and Corporate Affairs. The CAC lobbied for both deregulation and privatization of public corporations in the belief that privatization could be used to get rid of inefficient public corporations, or those whose mandates were now irrelevant, and that competition under deregulation, of course, would lead to lower costs and lower prices for the consumer.

However, by the time the Canadian deregulation experience was petering out in 1992, it would be discovered that business fares had not gone down since 1984 when the first deregulation initiative was introduced. The group who benefited most from the fare turbulence of the 1980s and early 1990s was the relatively silent vacation traveller, and the occasional traveller who could afford to wait until special fares hit the market before they decided to fly to Toronto to visit Aunt Maude. The average business or government traveller was still paying top dollar. Canadian airline deregulation had delivered them little more than an increase in stomach acidity as they read *The Financial Post* each morning and tracked the terror of the two domestic airlines' share prices and debt problems.

But in 1984 it was hard not to notice the consumer euphoria going on south of the border. All anyone seemed to hear was that air fares between New York and L.A. had been cut in half, or more. In their scurry to showcase the success of the most recent U.S. model of competitive advantage, most Canadian media did not bother to focus on the real issues—fare increases on many shorter routes, a flurry of airline bankruptcies, massive layoffs, labour disputes, enforced wage rollbacks and the end of air service to a host of smaller American communities.

In fact, by 1984, as Canadians were preparing to drastically revamp their air transportation policy, the U.S deregulation experience was already starting to come apart. The moment called for sober second thought. What many proponents overlooked. in their rush to be as American as they could be without crossing the border and taking up citizenship, was that fare prices—except for the double-breasted suit fuming next to the excursion fare traveller in blue jeans—were not the issue in Canada that they were in the U.S. The problem was the *perception* by a minority of Canadians that our fares were too high.

The Canadian Transport Commission (CTC) in Canada had always regulated fares more flexibly than the U.S.'s CAB; not as flexibly as some would like, but certainly not as rigidly—or expensively—as south of the border. Control of entry to and exit from markets were the CTC's primary concerns. Canadian fares were generally set by the air carriers, not exclusively by the government's regulatory agency. The carriers submitted their proposals to the CTC and, by and large, the CTC agreed. Its job was to protect the public against fares getting too high and to protect the carrier against fares going too low. Industry stability was the CTC's primary goal.

To the deregulationists, it really was a matter of who owned the ox, rather than which one got gored. In 1981, the *Globe and Mail*—one of the loudest tub thumpers for open competition, privatization of Air Canada and deregulation U.S.-style—demanded more competition among airlines. Conveniently, this was the opposite position on the issue of open competition the Toronto newspaper took, as Garth Stevenson pointed out, when the 1980-81 Kent Royal Commission recommended more competition—among newspapers. The demand for airline deregulation—from the Economic Council of Canada to the CAC, from the *Globe and Mail* to government lobbyists and business associations—was more emotionally and ideologically motivated than driven by facts or a proper interpretation of history. There was little evidence that complete deregulation promoted airline efficiency or productivity—lots of theories and econometric models, but not much in the way of hard data based on experience that included politics and human nature. There was no evidence that all fare prices would drop under deregulation. As much as anything, that was wishful thinking.

In fact, at the very time the hue and cry to copy the Americans was picking up tempo in the mid-1980s, Canada had more aircraft flying to more destinations per capita in the world, and had fares—the nub of the argument—*lower* than any fare structure existing outside Communist countries. In fact, except for deep discount fares, the price of many fares on large American airlines was still often higher than Canadian fares when converted into Canadian dollars.

What Canada needed was not deregulation of its airline industry, but wise regulation. What consumer or citizen would benefit from an industry with too many airlines with too many airplanes, using up expensive and increasingly scarce fuel, and habitually laying off workers because it could not make the bottom line work? "Regulation protected the weak, not the strong. Deregulation's proponents did not seem to understand this," Stevenson wrote. They were too busy equating airline regulation and government ownership of an airline as evil symptoms of state ownership. But the weak do not get to chat with federal policy makers and cabinet ministers, or to compose their own editorials.

Perhaps the short-lived 1979 Clark government understood what some deregulation proponents did not, or would not. It was a ticklish and highly volatile initiative. The Clark government moved cautiously on deregulation, promising to relax some restrictions and encourage some competition in fare setting. But it was opposed to any policy that would cause a drop in service to smaller communities—a trend that had started immediately in the U.S.. Fare regulation was relaxed appreciably by the Tories, and Wardair was allowed to enter the domestic transcontinental market, increasing competition, though the airline was still frozen out of the busy Toronto-Montreal-Ottawa market.

The net effect was that passenger traffic increased somewhat, but because of the various new reduced fares, revenue for the major carriers did not increase dramatically—and this was in one of the industry's best years. Traffic also began to level off quickly. So did revenue. In Air Canada's case, while operating income for 1979 went up more than nineteen per cent from the previous year, net income rose only fourteen per cent, compared to 135 per cent the year before. Still, political pressure began to open more deregulatory doors, even though the early signs of a tragedy-in-the-making were building.

The most vocal airline supporter of deregulation, Max Ward, the entrepreneur who tried to single-handedly take on both Air Canada and CP Air, warned the Clark government that unless more rules were relaxed, he would be out of business as early in 1980. When the barn doors were finally thrown open to deregulation and open competition, Ward would be one of the first to take advantage. Wardair would expand services exponentially—increasing fleet size, seating capacity, routes and debt—until the airline could no longer get off the ground.

The greener air fare grass across the border blinded deregulation proponents to what should have been a sobering reality. On heavy traffic routes such as Montreal-Toronto and on many transcontinental routes, Canadian travellers were already flying on bargain fares and still had an impressive number of flights to choose from. In 1979, CP Air introduced "Skybus" discount fares which were both low in price and applied to one-way travel as well. By 1982, "Skybus" fares were available on regular CP Air flights to most destinations. Air Canada responded with seat sales and improved cabin service for discount passengers. Canadians were enjoying the benefits of cheaper air travel without either complete regulation or the cost and chaos of deregulation.

By 1982, two years before the Liberals would take the first deregulation leap, it was clear, from the industry's performance under even the most modest relaxation of the rules, that the last thing this country could take would be complete deregulation and U.S.-style open competition. By that year, with its lower fares and relatively polite competition between Canadian carriers, all three major airlines—Air Canada, CP Air and Wardair—were operating at a loss, the result of increasing competition during a recession.

Concerned over the airlines' mounting losses from fare competition, the Air Transport Committee (ATC) of the Canadian Transport Commission held hearings in July 1982 over the issue of deep-discount fares and what conditions should be placed upon them. The CAC, along with the Department of Consumer and Corporate Affairs, opposed any conditions. But the ATC slapped some requirements on in any case, though there were still plenty of fare bargains to be had. That did not stop the demand for deregulation from growing. If anything, it probably fuelled the battle cry.

When Lloyd Axworthy became the Liberal's Minister of Transport in August 1983, the deregulationists' time had finally come.

Axworthy and his Liberal colleagues, suffering in the polls, were particularly partial to the cry of "airline deregulation!" With the knowledge that this policy move would not cost them a cent, or so it seemed, they would begin to bend to its echo.

> "But airline passengers today are not only flying more, they're flying in more-crowded airplanes and sitting in more-cramped spaces. They're waiting in more congested airports, for more delayed flights, and visiting cities they have no desire to go to, simply to change planes. In short, the product they're buying today is a shadow of the product they could have bought 13 years ago."
> —Consumer Reports, July 1991

Because of the speed with which the Liberals were evidently willing to travel to change a highly complex airline regulation policy, there were doubts raised about whether Lloyd Axworthy and his cabinet colleagues truly understood the implications of what they were bent on doing. In *The Financial Post* in January 1984, Axworthy made it clear his was not a Quaker's approach to deregulation ("Perform every task as if you had a thousand years to live . . ."). He was on his way to restructuring, as soon as possible, the entire airline industry, turning forty-seven years of relatively effective regulatory authority and air service on its head. He said he was upset by the fact there was "a mentality of defeatism in the industry" and found it ironic that people in the airline industry were the ones always "giving speeches to chambers of commerce about the joys of the free enterprise system" and were "the ones who are most reserved about it." He dismissed the strong resistance coming from most air carriers and called the fear, generated from the American experience, that low fares on high-density routes would be offset by high fares and poor service in more isolated communities, a "mythology." "That's certainly not what's happening in the U.S.," he said, not quite totally in line with events in the U.S.

Axworthy had instructed the CTC to hold cross-country public hearings on air fares. As the hearings began in February 1984, the question of deregulation was now uppermost in people's minds. A parallel interdepartmental task force, working out of the minister's office, was also preparing a preliminary report on U.S.-style deregulation for the end of February. The ATC heard from a multitude of interested parties—carriers, provincial governments, proponents for and critics of deregulation, and in May the ATC tabled an interim report to a fair degree of anticipation, though the speed at which the Axworthy initiative was travelling caused some observers to refer to the hearings as a sham. "As for the minister, the committee need not have worried about him, for he made up his own mind already," according to political scientist, Garth Stevenson. "His policy statement, decorated with his photograph and a reproduction of his signature, was published in both official languages just twenty-four hours after the ATC submitted its 'advice.' There was little in common with the two documents."

Axworthy's New Canadian Air Policy said, in effect, that Canada was running its airline industry all wrong. Axworthy concluded that the status quo was "not acceptable to anyone." He declared in the House of Commons that the air transportation industry was "in decline," though that was a bit questionable. Although the three largest carriers were beginning to struggle, operating revenues had been climbing, particularly Air Canada's. He opened the door to privatization of Air Canada, controlled sixty per cent of domestic traffic, citing the carrier's operating losses as an indication of the trouble the airline was in. This, despite the fact Air Canada enjoyed its second highest annual operating revenues in 1983, had only lost money in one of the previous seven years, and would make $21 million in 1984.

Axworthy contrasted Canada's policy shortcomings with what he called the "many important benefits" of deregulation in the United States. He claimed the air carriers had been abandoning services and that regulation had kept competition "to the bare minimum."

Almost total deregulation would eventually take place, he asserted, though it would be with a made-in-Canada stamp. And although he wanted change to come in stages so everyone could adapt to the new regime, it was pretty clear the ultimate goal was a deregulated system almost indistinguishable from that which existed in the U.S.

The New Canadian Air Policy was de facto deregulation. It eased entry conditions for carriers into new markets and allowed them greater route and pricing flexibility. Given its dominant position in the marketplace, Air Canada was restricted from anti-competitive pricing and scheduling practices. The airline was also told it would no longer receive funds from the federal government, unless it met certain financial tests. With its traditional capital pipeline effectively closed down, the crown carrier's move into private shareholder hands would be sped up. The deregulation ball was really rolling now.

Axworthy's biggest mistake would be to equate deregulation with low fares. In fact, between 1986 and 1990, average one-way domestic ticket prices would increase forty-two per cent. Economy, business and first-class fares would increase at a rate greater than inflation. The only ticket price that would drop substantially would be discount fares—the fares vacation and recreation travellers had been enjoying for years, benefiting from the more liberal pricing rules in place since the late 1960s. For these people, who probably never cast a vote one way or the other for deregulation, things just got a little better.

If that had been the extent of the Liberal government's efforts at re-engineering the airline business, Canadians could have perhaps considered themselves fortunate. But the full impact of the deregulation forces Axworthy put in motion—on the industry, on its employees, on investors and creditors, on the nation's future prospects for at least one major competing international air carrier—would do significantly more damage than just keep fares roughly where they had always been—or higher. All one had to do was look south.

> *"Everyone does not benefit when we struggle against each other for private gain. It is a simple matter of examining the evidence. To distinguish between what is rational for the individual and what is rational for the group is not rational, period. It is damaging not to the group, but to the individual."*
> —Alfie Kohn, *No Contest: The Case Against Competition*

This was the environment within which the Liberal government would confidently launch Canadian airline deregulation. Instead of the benefits of competition, Canadians got almost instant moves toward concentration by the carriers and an eventual duopoly—but without the full regulatory protection consumers needed to check corporate excess.

A highly leveraged Wardair sped down the runway on the lift of deregulation and was a crash statistic by 1989. Wardair was a serious example of competition at work within the airline industry. But open competition in such a thinly margined and highly leveraged business made little sense. Wardair's short-term presence had increased flight options on major routes and pushed down business fare prices. But

Wardair had no effective computer reservation system and was forced to rely on its competitors. The airline was late into a frequent flyer program and it had limited access to airports. But these sorts of barriers to effective entry were there all along. There should have been no surprise in anyone's mind.

Given human instincts for corporate survival—this was, after all, what competition was all about—the two major carriers did not sit back and let Wardair's presence eat into their profits. They did the natural thing: they worked diligently and quickly, buying into every available regional airline they could to establish a "feeder system" to fill their hub-and-spoke dreams. Both began taking on huge debt. Air Canada's long-term debt would more than triple in the decade following 1983.

Before the Liberals could do any more damage, they were voted from office on September 4, 1984, suffering the worst electoral defeat in their history. It was said at the time that Lloyd Axworthy was considering writing a book about his government's deregulation efforts. The policy march toward full deregulation slowed a bit with Axworthy's successor, Don Mazankowski, in the transport minister's pilot seat. Mazankowski was a supporter of deregulation in principle but was cautious about what impact the policy might have on rural communities. He talked about cutting a deal for the "must-go traveller." As he told *Canadian Aviation* in June 1985: "The poor guy who *has* to fly to Edmonton because of illness or an accident in the family finds he has to pay $600, then hears his neighbour say he went there for $200. He is understandably unhappy." To make his poor guy happy—the type of traveller who probably would only find himself in that must-go position once, maybe twice, in his entire life, the Conservatives were prepared to complete the deregulation job the Liberals started.

Mazankowski wanted fares overhauled but was not specific. He dare not be, because by that time the marketplace, not the CTC, was now the effective regulator of fare prices. Given the still-high operating costs both airlines had saddled themselves with and the debt they were carrying, the only way full-economy fares could drop would be for the cheaper, discounted fares to rise. And if complaints about fare prices from the business lobby had been somewhat muted, albeit very effective, the Tories knew how loud the howl of rage would be from the vacation traveller.

Mazankowski's go-slow approach was being tested by political reality. The Mulroney government had gone public with its intentions to reduce the role of government. Mazankowski had to do something about furthering the move to complete airline deregulation or be caught being out-right-winged on policy by the Liberals. On July 15, 1985, Mazankowski issued a Freedom to Move white paper on transportation reform. The proposed policy framework would "virtually complete deregulation of the airline industry." The old market entry rule of "public convenience and necessity" would be replaced with a "fit, willing and able" test for carriers. Carriers would be free to enter and to exit a market and there would be no regulation of fares. The CTC would be abolished and all transportation legislation would be overhauled.

Although politicians like Mazankowski and Axworthy might have believed, deep down, that what they were doing would increase competition in the airline business and bring fare prices down, they were running against the fundamental survival instincts of the North American business community.

Canada's two major airlines would do what they had to do—market competition theory or no market competition theory. CP Air would finish absorbing Eastern Provincial Airways (EPA). Air Canada and PWA each bought roughly one-quarter equity shares in Air Ontario. PWA would later sell its shares to Air Canada. Air Canada abandoned its competition with PWA on the lucrative Edmonton-Calgary route and CP Air allied itself in an operating agreement with West Coast competitor, Air BC. Air Canada would then buy 100 per cent of Air BC. CP Air, renamed Canadian Pacific Air Lines, took control of Nordair in 1986 and was bought out by PWA for $300 million in 1987. PWA Corp. then integrated CPAL, PWA, Nordair and Eastern Provincial Airways into Canadian Airlines International Ltd. By year-end 1987, either Air Canada or CAIL controlled the nation's most important connector airlines.

CAIL would finish this concentration banquet with a satiated burp, by gobbling up a competition-battered Wardair in 1989 for just under $250 million, or $17.25 a share. This takeover would add to PWA's debt (now $1.8 billion) and would stick in its corporate throat like an undigested boar in the esophagus of a boa constrictor. There are moments when even the predator begins to prey upon itself.

If someone witnessing this had been able to keep track of all the players, and whose team they finally ended up on, there were still two very simple questions to be asked: What ever happened to the basics of open and healthy competition? And what ever happened to the idea of an entrepreneur seeing a market opportunity, investing in a couple of planes, some staff and equipment and starting out fresh in competition with those already in the game? The answer is that the airline business does not—cannot—work that way.

There never was any possibility that airline deregulation would increase competition. Beneath all the ideological jargon about deregulation lies a basic flaw: the assumption that the freedom an entrepreneur has to enter the marketplace eliminates any urge or tendency to merge, or absorb other carriers, as a means of getting into or staying in that marketplace. By this reasoning—and based on any number of econometric models—Air Canada and CP Air should have stood still while Nordair or EPA began flying competitively on their routes. Either that or CP Air would start up new services in competition with EPA and Nordair. Or an unlimited number of completely new airline entrants would just appear on the tarmac of Pearson International Airport one morning, revving their new jet engines and eager to do commercial battle against Wardair.

This fractured logic ignores the fact, among a host of harsher realities, that by buying out regional carriers rather than competing with them, CP Air, for instance, instantly acquired a fleet of aircraft, the clientele and the goodwill of the regional carrier. This is particularly enticing on route systems where traffic volumes are not high enough to warrant competition or where Air Canada is already a competitor. Perhaps in some dream world it works differently, but competition is no more a natural result of deregulation than winning millions is the inevitable consequence of buying a lottery ticket.

Tory dreams notwithstanding, average air fare prices would not go down as anticipated and the confusion over fare structure would blind all but computer systems analysts to what was a good price and what was a bad price for a trip to Toronto. By 1987 Air Canada was offering as many as twenty-eight different fare packages with twenty-eight different prices—between only two destinations, Toronto and Vancouver. To make it all work, Air Canada and the newly minted but heavily indebted Canadian Airlines International Ltd. would begin buying even more new aircraft, increasing seat capacity while their planes were already flying almost half empty, and dropping employees like a Lancaster bomber dropping ordnance over Hamburg in 1944.

On January 1, 1988, the *National Transportation Act* came into effect. Full deregulation had landed in Canada. "Finally," supporters of airline deregulation must have sighed, "we are now going to receive all the benefits of deregulation Americans had been enjoying." But the American experience had been neither smooth nor beneficial to all concerned. And there was a host of reasons for that, most of them not even applicable to the Canadian experience. From a business point of view, the U.S. fundamentals were wildly different. From a cultural point of view, it was as if we had gazed across at the former Yugoslavia, and because, at the time, there existed no evident ethnic rifts—and no one seemed to be shooting one another—we assumed blithely that Canadians could use Yugoslavia as a model for peaceful, multi-ethnic nationhood.

After the short flurry of competitive activity bent on attracting the consumer—the fare wars caused by Wardair, introduction of special offerings like CP Air's "Attaché" service, devoted exclusively to the business traveller (which did not make fares cheaper, just offered more frills and more leg room)—the industry environment settled into a predictable pattern. The simple reality was that, by virtue of size, geography and population density, Canada cannot support two major, competing air carriers. This is a country, like it or not, with a small market size and capital pools not large enough to start major, competitive carriers flying. Even if they do exist, there are far better ways for investors to optimize their returns then by betting on an airline. If service, stability, safety and reasonable air fare prices are common consumer goals, they can more readily be achieved within a properly supervised regulatory regime than by believing in fairy tales about healthy competition and the virtue of something called market forces.

8 / The Era of the Policy Entrepreneur

Canada riding on U.S. economic teeter-totter
"The strong U.S. economy holds the promise of continued growth in Canada. Just ask any economist. It also poses one of the greatest threats to growth. Just ask any economist . . ."
—Eric Beauchesne, *Southam News*, May 7, 1994

BY THE TIME THE SKY BEGAN TO FALL for everyone in the summer of 1992, it was harder to find a supporter of pure airline deregulation than it was to stumble across a Toronto Argonaut football fan. Most of those who had lobbied hard for deregulation were off whistling in laissez-faire graveyards, pretending it was not *their* idea. The Mulroney government was claiming their deregulation policies were working just fine, thank you very much, in the face of massive public confusion, mounting airline losses and statistics to the contrary. Lobby groups such as the Consumers Association of Canada, once loudly and actively in favour of strong competition within the airline industry, were now speculating about it being time for a "regulated monopoly."

Both major carriers were pretending they were not corporate basket cases, and were putting out feelers for partnerships or looking to see whether "reregulation" or "limited deregulation" might be introduced to help save their financial hides. Airline analysts and consultants across the country found themselves in a lucrative growth industry. Their services were being commissioned by all the players—the federal government, the airlines, the business community—to try to figure out what really had gone wrong and how best to get out of this mess. Everyone blamed everyone else for the fiasco.

The Mulroney government blamed lack of competition, rising fuel prices, the Gulf War, the history of Air Canada, the Liberals, greedy regional air carriers and the management of the two major air carriers. Airline management blamed competition, rising fuel prices, the Gulf War, their employees (for negotiating those exorbitant labour agreements with them), fickle consumers, the government (for starting deregulation, but also for having the audacity to charge taxes on the operation of their business) and very, very occasionally themselves— for buying and trying to fly too many expensive airplanes when there were not enough passengers to go around. Among critics of deregulation this position was referred to as "the-devil-made-me-do-it" defence.

Most airline analysts and academics were worshippers at the altar of economic deregulation. They tended to blame both government *and* the airlines. The government got it for not deregulating quickly or widely enough, for not privatizing Air Canada fast enough, and for not deregulating and privatizing everything—from the airlines to airports, from air traffic control to airport parking lots to peanut vendors, shoeshine kiosks and taxi porters. The airlines got it for not cutting their costs more quickly (by laying off more workers), for buying all those unneeded aircraft, and for not paying more attention to all the advice the analysts had provided them.

The defence of airline deregulation and, of course, the reason for its seeming difficulties, often carried a touch of Lewis Carroll. Most assessments treated the idea of airline deregulation as if it had not really been given a proper test since 1984; that once all those intervening social, political, economic and human behavioural factors were straightened out, consumers would be singing loud and joyous paeans to the beauty of its theoretical foundations. But deregulation was never truly subjected to the most deliberate, most scientific analysis of its possibilities *before* implementation. By the late 1980s the consultants were scurrying to apply rationale after-the-fact.

With few exceptions, they began their appraisal of Canadian airline deregulation bolstered by their belief in the American theory of business competition and in the superior performance of the marketplace over government regulation. Consequently, try as they might, there was no way they could properly assess Canadian deregulation's chances with a factor that stood out as awkwardly as the presence of a government-owned airline. That fact alone would be enough to crack the veneer of their moral certitude.

It would be admitted that the presence of the publicly owned Air Canada made country-to-country comparisons of deregulation difficult, and that as a consequence deregulation could not be imported wholesale into Canada. Air Canada was not just an airline. It had been used as a public policy instrument for more than four decades. It claimed about sixty per cent of the market at the time deregulation was introduced. All American air carriers were privately owned and none could claim more than twenty per cent of the market. And so, when it came time to wrap the rationalizations around this troubled initiative called Canadian airline deregulation, the logical thing to do was extend the argument for the purity of the marketplace one step further and recommend Air Canada simply be privatized.

Flipping the pages of assessment of airline deregulation and reading the prognosis for success after the removal of all entry, exit and fare controls (including the test of "public convenience and necessity") one is struck by the realization that this experience might not have been based entirely on reality. It read more like a badly controlled lab experiment. As deadly imposing as the numbers and the conclusions were—and they were very impressive—everything projected within each of the scenarios was premised on the belief that everyone—airline management, competitors, government, consumers, lobbyists, even players on the global scene—would act rationally.

Industry costs were expected to fall by significant numbers under deregulation. They did not. Carriers were expected to improve their bottom lines by shedding excess capital. Instead, they bought more airplanes. Those illusory falling costs would translate into lower air fares. Fares stayed the same or went up. Traffic was to grow by at least ten per cent, stimulating employment. Layoffs began after deregulation. Air Canada was expected to lose significant amounts of traffic because of the restraints of being a crown carrier. The airline's traffic losses were marginal. Other carriers were expected to capture the growth in the market, including Wardair and perhaps a new jet air carrier or two. Instead, they were eaten up by PWA or Air Canada. Canada's air carriers, set loose in the healing balm of the free marketplace and healthy competition, were expected to earn normal profits as in other industries. Enough said.

The important part of the equation that seemed to be overlooked was that we were talking about economic models and tendencies applied to formulation of public policy. Public policy cannot be pieced together in a vacuum consisting of a theory and a certain set of statistics derived from a single discipline, such as economics, commerce or business management. Policy comes out of the meat grinder of "politics"—federal and local, corporate and the individual, business and labour—and functions in an environment consisting of a multitude of human factors: dreams, aspirations and the manipulation of them leading to compromises no one expected. No philosophy or theory ever makes it through the real-world jungle of politics intact.

Unfortunately, many deregulation supporters would have their theories legitimized by a Canadian academic community that had, since the early 1960s, become attuned to the American way of thinking about the place and role of government in the world of business and the economy. It is no exaggeration to say that over the past thirty years, this nation's university departments of economics, its business administration and management schools, and its commerce faculties have been increasingly stocked with professors, assistant and associate professors, even administrators, trained in the American business enterprise experience. Many were born and grew up in the United States. Most received their university training there.

It is also no exaggeration to say that many Canadian-born academics working in these three disciplines were taught at the undergraduate level by American-trained scholars. More significantly, perhaps a majority of them went on to study and receive their postgraduate degrees from American universities. Of the one hundred and two academic members listed in the University of British Columbia's 1993-94 calendar for the faculty of commerce and business administration, only seven carried Ph.D. or MBA qualifications from a Canadian university. Thirty-one of thirty-eight members of UBC's department of economics received their postgraduate degrees in American universities. Three-quarters of the faculty and administration at McGill's school of business and graduate studies in management were trained in American universities. Only forty per cent of the faculty at the University of Western Ontario's business school are Canadian-trained.

Of course, there is nothing inherently improper or technically incorrect in availing yourself of one of the world's most advanced and most effective systems of graduate study. But to argue that there is little or no relationship between what and where one studies, and what doctrines remain locked within the political scope of one's thinking is, it would seem, almost to deny cause-and-effect. Universities exist to harden the belief systems within which they operate, forging those theories and beliefs into the mind of the successful student like flies in ideological amber. As French philosopher Simone

Weil wrote: "[C]ulture is an instrument wielded by professors to manufacture professors, who when their turn comes, will manufacture professors." And they inevitably become disciples for the catechism they ingested.

One of the major structural flaws of contemporary business and economic teaching in North America is its belief in the singular advantage of a smoothly-functioning marketplace, where consumers and investors inevitably "win" as business and corporations fight it out to meet the consumers' demand with lower prices and more innovative products or services. It is a belief that rests on the innocent assumption that trade, particularly international trade, is a game of winners and losers, with no need for a referee. As many are now realizing, after a decade of U.S. Republican supply-side thinking about the evils of regulation versus the mythical benefits of free enterprise and market-driven competition, loose economic thinking can be dangerous to the state of the economy and, ultimately, to the national welfare.

The market's impact on the individual is as old as humankind and the first halting steps to trade an earthen pot full of glowing embers for the left shank of a freshly slain sabre-toothed tiger. As Anacharsis, the sixth century Greek put it: "A market is a place set apart for men to deceive and get the better of one another."

Airline deregulation is a good case study for testing the efficacy of prevailing market theory. One thing seems to stand out when reading the various analyses of airline deregulation in Canada: too many of deregulation's supporters tried too hard to absolve the free market doctrine from blame. Like the mythical robber Procrustes, who stretched or amputated the limbs of his captive travellers to make them conform to the exact size of his bed, the eager supporters of airline deregulation cut and hacked and bent their versions of the Canadian experience to fit their theory; not, as it should have been, the other way around.

Many deregulation supporters were, as early as the 1970s, exceptionally quick to declare that Air Canada had outlived its public policy purposes and should be privatized. This was heartening news for many federal politicians and business leaders, particularly those from western Canada who had been critical of the airline for decades. The idea fit well with dogma that conveniently saw Air Canada as the "state airline." Privatization supporters dipped deep into their bag of rationalizations and discovered, so they said, that Canadians no longer wanted or needed a public air carrier. The airline industry had matured since the days that required Air Canada as a policy vehicle and industry stabilizer.

By the time the privatization and get-the-government-off-our-backs pot had boiled for more than a decade, we landed at 1992 and the Mulroney government's Royal Commission on National Passenger Transportation. Rife with Reaganomic notions, the commission tabled a set of conceptually simple recommendations. It dismissed a role for public involvement in the industry. More importantly, it also supported the belief that the whimsical and erratic ways of the consumer—the user—would be a sufficient enough foundation upon which to build a new transportation policy that would help strengthen and stabilize the nation's economy.

> *"[Managers in government and industry] have been comforted by a seemingly endless parade of business school professors and economists who spend large parts of their lives on contract to corporations in one way or another. These men have provided an intellectual rationale for economic masochism. At the heart of their analyses one inevitably finds the marketplace."*
> —John Ralston Saul, *Voltaire's Bastards*

The study of economics, as experience and events have proven frequently enough, is not a pure or exact science. Too often it has lived marvellously up to its name as "the dismal science." Nor is it a precise or reliable predictor of the future. At its best, economics is a rough measure of probabilities, a system of forecasting based on past performance. The one measure it always seems to miss is human behaviour—the good, the bad, the indifferent—the unpredictable essence of real life.

One of the nagging complications for the economist is their creed of "all things being equal"—economic and business performance can be predicted accurately if all factors remain constant. The term is interchangeable with "all else constant." Those caveats have always sounded as if profits and social benefits can be maximized for all citizens if the world would just stand still for a moment. Human motivations, such as the compromises of politics, are seldom factored into the equation. How else to explain the motivating fear of political defeat, or the sudden feeling of compassion right-wing Tory caucus members, particularly from Alberta and British Columbia, might have for the plight of sixteen thousand CAIL employees facing unemployment before Christmas, 1992?

As one uncomfortable airline observer put it, when questioned whether events in the Canadian airline industry to 1994 did not argue convincingly for Canada to have one successful major airline rather than two crippled ones, "I think that's an argument that only holds water retrospectively." In effect, he dismissed much of history and myriad events as if they had been so many bothersome pebbles in the deregulationists' shoe on their march to market purity. "Of course, if you look at things retrospectively, realizing the depths of the recessions we faced, the collapse of load factors, the impact of fuel prices, etc.—under *those* conditions there is only room for one large carrier. But under healthy, growing vibrant conditions, I would disagree . . ."

He believed, as many deregulation supporters do, that natural intervening factors of human interaction—recessions (which have plagued people since trade was invented), changes in consumer performance (largely due to recessionary factors such as lost employment, high interest rates or a drop in business), and the effects of war (which have been with us since the possessor of the sabre-toothed tiger shank could not get the number of embers in trade he or she felt was fair)—are generally extraneous to current theories about marketplace economics!

On the other hand, when Canadian airline deregulation, as a public policy initiative, was in need of political and economic defence, supporters argued exactly the reverse—that the policy's failure was not due to its inappropriateness, but to all the other previously extraneous factors. Even American conservative William F. Buckley, Jr. once said: "Idealism is fine, but as it approaches reality the cost becomes prohibitive."

In market theory, Canadian Airlines International should have been allowed to go bankrupt. Its costs were greater than its revenue. Its debt greatly exceeded the value of its assets. Its earnings potential was limited. It was insolvent. The employees should have been handed pink slips and the company should have been wrapped up, thereby making room for a replacement competitor, with superior capital, less debt and more manageable operating costs to move in and begin competition with Air Canada. But it did not happen, for all sorts of very human reasons that the study of economics or business can never factor into equations and theories. The move to save CAIL made no theoretical or business sense. It just happened—and it defied Procrustes.

When the cold winds of reality broke across their wings in July 1992, both airline management groups would beseech the federal government to climb back on board and help save them—if not with loan guarantees, then with regulations restricting their own capacity. These were the inevitabilities of the Canadian airline business that most proponents of deregulation had overlooked.

Airlines are not mom-and-pop grocery stores. There are few major industries as nonvertically structured for operation as the airline business. The airline business is shockingly volatile and the participants extremely vulnerable to institutions and circumstances beyond their control. Their day-to-day operations depend on a nationwide infrastructure of airports, traffic control and meterological systems no airline could provide for itself. They also rely on what is perhaps one of the most highly skilled and specialized workforces in the economy to keep their planes aloft. They rely on a complex web of international financial institutions to lend them money to buy planes, and on the manufacturers to produce the right planes at a price they can afford and deliver them on time. They are constantly at the mercy of the economy and the whims of the consumer.

Consequently, it is not at all surprising that the airline industry depends heavily on government to provide certainty, stability and the necessary edge needed to compete successfully in the domestic as well as international marketplace. Regulations serve those very purposes— keeping the industry sane, fare prices reasonable and providing investors with a satisfactory return on their efforts.

> *"Americans persist in thinking that Adam Smith's rules for free trade are the only legitimate ones. But today's fastest-growing economies are using a different set of rules. Once, we knew them—knew them so well that we played by them, and won. Now we seem to have forgotten."*
> —James Fallows, *The Atlantic Monthly*, December 1993

The National Transportation Act Review Commission's 1992 analysis of the Canadian airline industry's performance since 1981 did not just conclude that the important deregulation goal—to increase competition in the domestic market, which would in turn reduce the price of air fares—had not been achieved. It also pointed out any number of negative results.

The review commission trotted out a host of contributing factors, focusing most clearly on questionable management of the two major Canadian carriers. Air Canada had been better positioned to compete because of its market dominance. The airlines had been poorly capitalized at the outset. Both Air Canada and Canadian Airlines International purchased more expensive aircraft that drove their debt "to unsafe levels." More importantly, the management of both airlines did not delay or cancel significant new aircraft deliveries "in the face of declining traffic." The Canadian airlines had not gotten their costs down as most U.S. carriers had done. CAIL's string of post-deregulation mergers (one must remember that instead of competing, PWA decided to buy out its competitors) increased operating costs, weakened its capital structure, and did not allow it to digest these large, and avoidable, debt lumps before traffic began to decline in 1991. And then, in a sort of grab bag of other factors, the report pointed the remaining fingers of blame at the Gulf War, the recession and the introduction of the GST.

Again, the report seemed to be saying that, if it had not been for all those events—wars, recessions, taxes, human weaknesses, management foibles and misperception, not to mention special interest lobbying, politics and hasty policy change decisions by government—the deregulation of the airline industry would have worked nicely. These were all real and compelling factors, but the report, as academically impressive as it was, blaming myriad circumstances of that nature was a bit like saying you could have gotten a great suntan if only it had not been raining.

The report also played down the significance of Trans-Canada Air Lines/Air Canada as an effective government policy venture. In doing so it chose to sidestep some significant historic facts: Air Canada had once provided Canadians with an extremely wide range of service and a very high level of safety at very reasonable cost to the consumer/traveller overall. By largely dismissing the benefits Canadians had long enjoyed with a public enterprise carrier, the report was able to imply that the struggle that Canadian Pacific Air Lines/CP Air went through over the decades was largely a matter of unfair competition.

Using terms like Air Canada's "privileged role," "faced few governmental restrictions" and enjoyed a "massive 'head start'," it was easy to state that CP Air "had long faced onerous 'capacity and routing restrictions on the trans-Canada market'." Of course it did. The men behind CP had even been reluctant to get into the transcontinental race. Of course that gave Air Canada its "head start." That was part of the history of the development of air transportation policy at the time—and, using TCA/Air Canada as the principal tool, it was not necessarily a bad one.

The history of the Canadian airline business, and the competitive development between the two largest carriers, was guided by the federal government's continued support—until John Diefenbaker came along—for a national airline policy that provided Canadians, not with brazen and damaging competition for bums-on-seats, but with the orderly provision of safe and reasonably priced air transportation for the whole country. All things considered, these were hardly inappropriate social or industrial goals for a nation. Considering the airline business we had now been bequeathed through an airline deregulation policy, competition and a stint of questionable airline management, goals like that might have made most Canadians very thankful.

Competition from Canadian Pacific Air Lines/CP Air was always a nagging issue in the overall national air transportation policy, one that was most often remedied by giving the second carrier route concessions, eroding with each gift the original intent of the policy underlining TCA's, then Air Canada's existence. By keeping CP Air and its supporters satisfied with a steady stream of concessions—and then providing the same for an inept host of regional airlines—the federal government also began to lay the foundation for a misguided belief that the policy intention had all along been for a fully competitive environment to exist between the carriers. From that revised assumption, it was easy to conclude that CP Air was therefore not receiving "equal treatment" to Air Canada.

The issue was also surrounded by the myth that CP Air had been, as much as anything, a struggling little airline made up of a bunch of patched-up Ford Tri-Motors flying on a wing and a prayer out of Moosomin, Saskatchewan, fighting tooth-and-nail with the fat, state-owned airline, Air Canada. In fact, CP Air was a very well-heeled airline, owned and operated by the nation's largest private sector conglomerate at the time—Canadian Pacific Ltd. CP Air did not even have to go to private capital markets when it needed money to make major aircraft purchases or expand operations. It just went to Canadian Pacific Ltd. for the cash, just as Air Canada went to the federal government.

In fact, in early 1986, representatives of CP Air held discussions with PWA, not to sell their airline to PWA, but to acquire the Calgary-based carrier. The initiative collapsed when Canadian Pacific Ltd. refused to allow their airline to "go public" to acquire the cash it needed to swallow PWA. When CP Air's parent company balked at the equity plan, it became clear to both airlines that tiny PWA would have to purchase the venerable CP Air because, as one source involved in the discussions said, "We knew we had to merge the two [airlines] in order to stay alive" in any future fight with Air Canada.

But nowhere in the bible of Canadian air transportation did it say the only reasonable thing to do was to grow big enough to compete with Air Canada. Neither airline management seemed to consider that it might make business sense to select a market niche and operate effectively and profitably within it. Pretending the only goal was to get big enough to duke it out with Air Canada was a business plan for disaster.

For starters, both had their handicaps, particularly CP Air. Despite enjoying a slightly better productivity factor than Air Canada, CP Air was never the hugely profitable private sector operation supporters liked to herald. Its return on investment or growth never compared, in the best of years, to what Canadian Pacific Ltd. enjoyed from its many other business ventures. After realizing its best operating profit of $43.8 million in 1978, CP Air's numbers declined annually until costs exceeded revenues in 1981. As fine an airline as it was, CP Air had a history, again not unlike Air Canada, of being slightly overweight, slow to react to market pressures, and not particularly innovative or efficient, though it enjoyed a word-of-mouth reputation for preparing a better meal than the crown carrier was noted for. And its cabin crews were said to be more friendly than Air Canada's.

There was no question that when the Liberals first unleashed deregulation in 1984, Air Canada enjoyed a decided corporate advantage—as it should have, being the nation's major instrument of air transportation policy. It was more than twice the size of CP Air. It had a larger and more appropriate aircraft fleet. It held a better domestic route system, had a virtual strangle hold on transborder routes into the U.S., and was in a better financial position than any other competitor.

CP Air, on the other hand, had a mix of aircraft most suitable for international long-haul traffic (from which it derived better operating profit numbers). To compete effectively with Air Canada on high-frequency, long-and-medium-haul domestic routes, either CP Air—or Pacific Western Airlines, the most effective regional carrier at the time—would be forced to invest in a large parcel of new aircraft and facilities. What deregulation did in 1984, more than anything, was put CP Air on the spot. To make it under the Liberals' liberalized regulatory regime, CP Air would either have to expand operations, at no small expense, to meet the challenges from the larger Air Canada, or to develop small, distinctive markets of its own. It could do so by expanding its existing system structure and operations, or by buying out other, smaller airlines.

What CP Air needed more than anything else to make either strategy evolve successfully was a strong expansion of the economy and an accompanying increase in consumer demand for air travel. If either were missing, the competitive aspect of deregulation, for CP Air in particular, would be a complete nonstarter. "Traffic would have to expand not only to absorb its own augmented share [of capacity], but increases from any countermoves by Air Canada," the NTA Review Commission's report noted. "These problems thus set the stage for the current crisis."

> "[Airlines] are a low-end commodity. They're capital-intensive, labour-intensive, fuel-intensive. You can't sell the seats with sex or caviar. The highest value is price."
>
> —Donald Burr, founder of People Express in *Empires of the Sky*

It is a fallacy that an airline must be big to survive in a competitive environment. Since the mid-1970s CP Air management had been committed to making their airline as large as Air Canada. The feeling was they would "get killed" by The Big Guy if they did not. They began their expansion by ordering new aircraft. That did not work. Then came the merger route. They almost "had" Wardair in a possible purchase in 1982. They then set their sights on Eastern Provincial

For a host of factors, some of them simply beyond the ability of Wardair management to overcome, the airline for some time had seemed headed for failure. In the fall of 1988 it was being squeezed between the weight of its long-term debt, the effects of a fare war and the impending delivery of more new aircraft.

Wardair's balance sheet, according to the Solvency Analysis Corporation's Ross Healy, was absolutely grim. "Therefore, to take a really grim balance sheet into an already failing balance sheet, and then use debt leverage [to finance the take-over] was really stupid."

Wardair had just received the last of twelve A310 Airbuses in 1988, at a cost of US $650 million with spare parts. It had also rattled Bay Street by signing deals for sixteen McDonnell Douglas MD-88s, the first eight to cost $300 million with delivery beginning in 1989, and agreed to buy twenty-four Fokker 100s. The chances of Wardair's survival past 1989 were problematic to say the least. And so the question then arose for PWA: Why would PWA pay for an airline whose assets—all those shiny new Wardair aircraft—would be on the auction block in a few months? Especially a PWA that was watching its operating profits decline by $88 million from 1988, was in the process of losing $56 million for 1989, had a negative capital balance on December 31 of $410 million, and still had firm delivery orders outstanding for new aircraft totalling $1.6 billion? The answer still lies, to a great extent, in the perceived need to be big enough to compete head-to-head with Air Canada.

"The critics were right," said Healy. "You should have just let the damn thing go and nobody would have picked it up anyway—and [Wardair] would have disappeared. But that's operating on 20-20 hindsight."

It was that industry wisdom again—that the only way to survive was to be a large, scheduled air carrier—regardless of the price. As a consequence, when Wardair began to founder seriously in 1988, the idea of sweeping up a mass of aircraft, facilities, staff and new routes was just too attractive an opportunity for PWA to pass up. To not grab the brass ring Wardair's demise offered would have left too much uncertainty in the industry, according to PWA's defenders. Perhaps Air Canada, with its slightly deeper pockets, might have been inclined to cherry-pick Wardair assets, effectively blocking any other domestic carrier from building the critical mass thought required to take them on. A move by Air Canada in 1989 on what remained of Wardair

Airways for acquisition and bought control of Nordair in 1985. But the strategy to go big to survive would not work. It just meant more unmanageable debt and made the airline susceptible to a takeover, which Pacific Western Airlines did in 1987.

"There is nothing in the history of the airline industry that says size is a necessary or sufficient condition for success," said former York University professor, William Jordan, author in 1970 of *Airline Regulation in America: Effects and Imperfections*, a much-respected publication questioning the benefits of airline deregulation in the U.S. The big-is-better belief is "folklore" according to Jordan. "The evidence of successful carriers is that the large carriers have not been terribly successful."

The merger wave of 1985 to 1989 was based to a great degree on the misconception that big was good and bigger was even better. Large airlines, so the thesis went, enjoyed "economies of scale" smaller ones did not—a bigger airplane would deliver lower costs while the airline enjoyed larger revenues. These beliefs, like so many others in this industry with its gaze-to-the-heavens business approach, defied two further facts of airline life.

"One, there are no economies of scale in the airline industry," William Jordan points out. "Two, there are large costs in being big." The marketing advantages of size are contrasted with increased operating disadvantages. "Low-cost carriers are not the big carriers. PWA went the bigness route. Wardair went the same way—thought they had to be big fast, and again, it broke them. The small carriers who are content to grow slowly, by and large, have been relatively successful—Southwest, Midwest Express, Alaska Airlines.

If the extra business demand was not there to pay for the large increased costs of competing—buying new aircraft, expanding operations or buying other carriers—for either CP Air or PWA or Wardair, or any other aspiring carrier for that matter, deregulation would crash as surely as an airplane does when the motors stall. When Canadian Pacific Ltd. fretted over the price it would have to pay for CP Air to play in the new regulatory environment, PWA moved in and bought them out, beginning the inevitable test of whether more or less competition would be a result of deregulation. Canadian Pacific was content to be out of what looked like a no-win business, while PWA itself was headed for trouble.

PWA was now heavily burdened with the debt accumulated from

the spate of takeovers and buy-outs. There were other indigestion problems as well. The task faced by PWA's management of blending five different companies and their cultures, so quickly, was almost unprecedented in the airline business. First, there would now be a multitude of different aircraft styles and types. Many of the aircraft would be surplus to needs, one of the uglier realities of airline takeovers. And then, there would be the problems of integrating different labour forces and instilling a common culture. Pan Am had choked on National Airlines for similar reasons. USAir had great trouble digesting Piedmont and Pacific Southwest. And of course, perennial casualty Continental Airlines struggled to carry the remnants of Texas International, New York Air, People Express, Frontier and Eastern airlines. Together, the impact of mergers has "been one of the greatest problems the world airline industry has faced in the last decade," according to the NTA Review Commission report.

At the beginning of 1984, Canada's four largest carriers—Air Canada, CP Air, PWA and Wardair—were already moving into structural difficulties. Combined, they had a negative working capital balance of minus $348 million, a tiny amount of cash ($177 million between them, on $3.6 billion in combined operating revenues) and a debt-to-equity ratio of 2:1. And now, to compete, they either had to go out and spend a few billion in new aircraft purchases, or find the cash to begin buying each other up so competition under deregulation would make sense—if it made any sense at all.

Although the mid-to-late 1980s were a period of relative growth in traffic and profits for world airlines, including modest operating profit increases for Canada's air carriers, by 1989 PWA had not only absorbed its partners and competitors (and was now Canadian Airlines International Ltd.) at huge cost (in addition to the $300 million paid for CP Air, Wardair cost PWA $146 million in cash, plus $105 million in its own common stock) but it was shopping around—not unlike Air Canada—for new aircraft. By the end of 1989, Air Canada had committed to buying 47 new aircraft for $3.8 billion over the next five years. During 1988, PWA placed $1.6 billion in orders for new aircraft to be delivered before 1994.

In the June 1992 edition of *Airfinance Journal*, William Jordan wrote a finely detailed analysis of what had transpired in five periods since World War II—during both regulation and deregulation—when North American airlines went on worldwide spending binges for new

aircraft. Jordan's cause-and-effect analysis revealed major los incurred by the carriers one or two years after placing above orders for new aircraft. Jordan's data show that losses co predicted based on the date of the spending splurge, as "possession costs" (equipment, depreciation, lease amortization, expenses, interest on debt and leases, etc.) eventually, and inevi showed up on the airline's books. Jordan went on to point out the new costs resulting from the arrival of these acquisitions coul handled during stable economic times. But if the economy sudde turned soft, the bills for these mammoth aircraft purchases remain on the books for years. The new costs lived like a deadly virus insi the company's system as profit prospects, in one of the world's mo volatile industries, spiked up and down "in amplitudes considerabl greater than the economy in general," as the review commission report stated.

The cost of excess capacity cannot be avoided by an airline once the decision to buy is made. The delivery of the cost of unneeded aircraft cannot be escaped, whether they are used half empty or are parked in the desert. "Airlines need at least 15 years to recoup the investment in new planes, yet management often make huge 'life risking' commitments for new deliveries based on two, three, or four years of reasonable profits. This phenomenon is not unique to Canada's airlines: it is endemic to the industry worldwide . . . It is clear that part of the crisis now facing Air Canada and CAIL," the review commission report stated, "is the purchase of too many aircraft in a relatively brief time period." Why? In the belief they would have to be big enough to compete. "Air Canada and PWA Corp. ordered vast quantities of new aircraft in the 1988-1989 boom period. So did the rest of the world's airline industry. However, with extraordinary losses in 1990, 1991 and 1992, all of the major U.S. carriers and many other foreign airlines have cancelled orders/or deferred deliveries in order to preserve cash (and borrowing capacity) and to hopefully survive the current crisis. The two Canadian airlines have continued with an aggressive program of fleet expansion."

The report also dealt with the puzzling purchase of Wardair by PWA in 1989. Wardair had been an airline which had shifted from charter to schedule flights in 1988. It had been in shaky financial shape since 1979, operating with a negative equity base for most years and generally operating close to the edge of bankruptcy more than once.

could have ended the whole issue of competition under deregulation once and for all. No survivor would have the capital to take on Air Canada.

The up side of the PWA-Wardair venture would theoretically mean that Canadian Airlines International would be in a position to compete, finally, on roughly equal terms with Air Canada. After welcoming Wardair into the family, CAIL would have one hundred and one aircraft compared to Air Canada's one hundred and eleven aircraft, roughly $2.2 billion in revenue compared to Air Canada's $2.6 billion (for the first nine months of 1988), higher passenger/miles than Air Canada (13.1 million to 12.3 million for the same nine-month period) and higher productivity (eighteen thousand employees compared to twenty-two thousand). Without running any fingers over the acquired debt, it looked as if Canada now had the airline "competition" CP Air and its supporters had been after for decades.

The down side was pretty clear, too. Not one of Wardair's twelve A310s were being operated by CAIL in 1994, demonstrating that few of Wardair's assets were necessary for CAIL's operations.

"Mergers are costly," said Jordan. "Mergers increase your operating expenses. And in a period when you want to lower operating expenses, you don't want to merge . . . To me, the decision [to buy Wardair] broke the back of CAIL, and it was absolutely unnecessary. "Wardair was going out [of business] anyhow. Why lay out one-half billion dollars to take over twelve planes you don't need? To decrease competition [is the answer]. Air Canada didn't do that, but Air Canada made its own mistakes. Canadian made two serious errors: the Wardair merger and buying too many airplanes. Air Canada made it errors in buying too many airplanes."

The effort to absolve "economic regulatory reform"—Canadian airline deregulation—as even a minor contributing cause of the widespread devastation in the airline industry was an admirable effort on the NTA Review Commission's part, but pretty thin in substance. Canadians had been preached to by two federal governments, lobbyists, business support groups and a pocket of well-commissioned consultants that regulation stymied competition and contributed to higher costs of airline operation, lower productivity, inefficient use of capital and higher air fares than necessary. But deregulation and competition brought almost instant cost, concentration, waste and consumer bewilderment. There were times, it seemed to many

Canadians, when competition in the airline industry made absolutely no sense at all.

Since 1986, many Canadians watched in wonder as Air Canada fed Hong Kong-bound travellers to a *foreign carrier*—Cathay Pacific—at Vancouver, while CP Air struggled to fill its own aircraft with passengers to—you, guessed it—Hong Kong. It would be extremely difficult to argue that this sort of competition made sense or was even remotely in the national interest. It was becoming evident, even to proponents, that deregulation and the kind of mad, twisted competitive forces it spawned, was not working. The solution? Make it even worse. Privatize Air Canada.

"Air Canada is the immediate issue and the case is overwhelmingly for its sale, preferably through a wide public share offering."
—The *Globe and Mail* editorial, July 10, 1987

Most deregulation apologists were quick to protest that the problems were not with deregulation. Many pointed to the government-owned Air Canada as a large part of the overall problem. It had too much of the market from the start. It was, to them, an inefficient, publicly run airline that blocked the success of regulatory reform theory. It was an "unnatural" impediment in a "natural" competition environment. The final argument declared that Air Canada no longer had major policy responsibilities as our national airline, so why not just let it compete like a true, private sector carrier.

The manoeuvre or plan to privatize Air Canada was, according to Herschel Hardin in *The Privatization Putsch*, "most breathtaking for being executed upside down." The move to "make Air Canada more efficient through healthy competition" and thus save deregulation, was just another stumbling step in the attempt to make the real world of the airline business fit theory. But privatization would not make the theories work, nor would it make the ailing Canadian airline industry well again. If anything, it just made the situation worse.

Perhaps the smarter thing would have been to privatize Air Canada before the airline deregulation ball began rolling, not after. Although there would have been no guarantee of deregulation's success had Air Canada been privatized before its introduction, the biggest single factor working against success between 1984 and 1988 was the status of Air Canada. The crown carrier enjoyed domination of more than half the airline business in the country and access to capital funding through the federal government, though the Liberals had limited that access to some extent in 1984. Consequently, it took no time at all for deregulation supporters, battered by the very early deterioration of their catechism, to become privatization supporters. But the move was too late.

Despite its many successes and its impressive record of public service, Air Canada's history seemed marked by persistent criticism. It always stood in somebody's way of making money. It was a monopoly. It was big. It was inefficient. It was protected by the federal government. It was part of an eastern Canadian political manipulative elite, etc., etc. But when the history of the nation's No. 1 airline is tracked properly, and not selectively, the Air Canada story is really quite a success story.

Trans-Canada Air Lines, and then Air Canada, introduced a level of service and technological expertise in air travel to a sparsely populated country that was difficult even for airlines south of the border to match. TCA was one of the safest airlines in the world, at a time when airplanes had an annoying tendency to drop from the sky. Air fares on TCA and Air Canada were often cheaper than comparable flights in the United States. Service, especially to smaller communities, was often far superior than what U.S. carriers could provide for their customers in similar-sized communities. Air Canada's balance sheet since 1938 revealed consistent operating revenue increases, stable net income performance (especially impressive, given the airline's responsibility to constantly increase its routes and service to the public), consistent working capital and growing assets—until we get to the privatized version of Air Canada, where the carrier's year-end numbers suddenly begin to resemble a Vietnamese rice paddy after a B-52 bombing raid.

One of the most persistent accusations thrown at the airline by its detractors was the fact that it did not make enough money, that it was not managed efficiently enough and was therefore never able to maximize returns on investment. It was also said that if the same advantages were placed in the hands of private sector operators, the profits would pour in. But one of the historical anomalies surrounding Air Canada was the strange tension that existed between the airline and its Ottawa bosses; strange enough, in fact, to prompt management to operate the airline for years with the intention of avoiding large year-end profits—profits that the politicians would only take away. Consequently, management was often devoted to providing a broad array of national air services while aiming for break-even—or the smaller the profit the better.

TCA/Air Canada can proudly claim a number of firsts. It was the first airline in North America to introduce an all turbo-prop aircraft fleet, bringing speed, comfort, increased productivity and lower costs to Canadian airline travel. Air Canada was among the world's pioneers in black box flight recorder technology. It introduced a world first in 1961 with its RESERVEC computerized reservation system, pioneered aircraft de-icing technology and developed technology for engine-failure warnings. Air Canada was the first North American airline to introduce nonsmoking flights—American Airlines was still wrestling with them in 1994. Air Canada received international awards for excellence in customer in-flight service, aircraft maintenance and safety, fuel conservation and for on-time performance, ranking among the highest of all airlines in North America despite facing some of the most severe weather conditions on the continent.

Although Air Canada operated largely as a government-owned transcontinental monopoly up until the late 1950s, strict fare management and the practice of cross-subsidizing more expensive routes with revenue from high-traffic, high-density routes meant Canadians as a whole received their national air service at very competitive prices. Air Canada fares were, when all the facts about the airline's huge service and routing responsibilities were considered, a bargain for Canadians as a whole.

The crown-owned airline was also able to maintain one of the most modern aircraft fleets in the world. Critics were quick to point out that the airline did this using public funds from the taxpayer's pocket. But Air Canada's holdings also sat on the public books as an impressive asset. And the vast bulk of Air Canada's indebtedness to the Government of Canada was looked after by a debt-for-equity share issue in 1978. Technically, this was not unlike PWA's 1992 lifesaving debt-for-equity swap proposal with its many private sector creditors. The only difference is that the Government of Canada would put the Air Canada common shares it held from 1978 on the market in 1988 and 1989, and the proceeds from the 1989 sale would go some way toward offsetting any earlier indebtedness.

Before the Mulroney government introduced legislation to privatize Air Canada, the company reported over $3 billion in total assets, revenues of $3 billion and a much-too-modest book value of about $330 million. Despite a March 1988 Angus Reid-Southam poll indicating that a substantial majority of Canadians did not favour selling Air Canada, when the airline was privatized, Air Canada shares sold on the open market like hot cakes. The first sale of forty-three per cent of Air Canada's shares—30.8 million offered in October 1988 at $8 per share—grossed $246 million for the airline. Market dealers considered the $8 figure cheap, compared to any U.S. airline stocks.

Demand was so strong that none of the thirty million shares had to be allocated for foreign sale. The entire issue was gobbled up by Canadians. When the Tories put the government's remaining forty-one million Air Canada shares up for sale in July 1989, the airline's stock price had risen to $12. Salomon Brothers of New York considered the stock at $12 to be "highly undervalued." The price would reach $14.83 by August.

The proceeds of the final sale of forty-one million common shares meant the Canadian government received roughly one-half billion dollars from its portion of the sale of Air Canada. Considering that the 1978 recapitalization of the airline's long-term debt had totalled roughly $324 million—the debt figures critics liked to point out to as an example of the kind of subsidy Air Canada enjoyed as a crown carrier—it was clear that not only had Canadians benefited from the service the airline had provided the country, but Canadian taxpayers seemed to have done quite nicely by their collective foray into the public enterprise airline business.

Air Canada had not just been a very effective and efficient public airline. It had also been, in the minds of many Canadians, a national public enterprise that helped bind the country together. It provided Canadians with one of a number of working models of how public enterprise in Canada could be efficient and profitable for the Canadian taxpayer. "If Air Canada had been just half the airline it was," Hardin wrote, "it would still have been not too bad, but the performance of public enterprise has to be superb to avoid the slings and arrows of privatization doctrine's wrath. Air Canada happened to be such a case."

"Like a lazy dog howling in one yard, and another picking up the howl,
and another dog responding, and another, until there is a motley and comic

barking everywhere in the neighbourhood, privatization advocates have been howling to the sky about 'competitive market situations.' They try to use mere barking of the phrase to get rid of public ownership."
—Herschel Hardin, *The Privatization Putsch*

One reason the *National Transportation Act*—introducing full deregulation in Canada in 1988—did not deal with the issue of privatization of Air Canada was confusion in the ranks of the Mulroney government. Air Canada had been a marked public corporation for some time, going back to Pierre Trudeau and Joe Clark. The Trudeau administration had earmarked the airline for privatization in the late 1970s. From then on, whether or not successive governments moved on the required policy change, the idea would continue to receive working support at the deputy ministerial level at both Treasury Board and the Department of Finance. It was kept alive by federal bureaucrats as Liberals and Progressive Conservatives changed seats in the House of Commons between 1979 and 1984.

Within weeks of taking office in 1984, the Mulroney government went on a privatization binge, unloading government-run enterprises at going-out-of-business sale prices. Among a number of rash ideological moves, the Tories pushed an ailing de Havilland aircraft manufacturer on Seattle-based Boeing Co.—leaving the taxpayers with $400 million in de Havilland's debt. The hasty way the Tories went about this public enterprise "cleansing" caused the process to be referred to in Ottawa bureaucracy circles as "Act First, Think Later," and generated a fair degree of public criticism. But only enough to make the Tories pause.

Symbolically at least, the Mulroney government's eleventh-hour effort to pass control of Toronto's lucrative Pearson International Airport to a private sector operators caught the most public attention. The Tories argued the deal would spare taxpayers the cost of millions worth of future improvements, even generate jobs. But at its heart, this was just another old-fashioned chunk out of the pork barrel.

There really was no advantage to the Canadian public in the proposed Pearson sell-off. Pearson International Airport had always been profitable for the federal government, bringing in about $24 million a year from the two public terminals, money that was used to subsidize other operations across the country. And the overly optimistic estimates about future air traffic growth through Pearson made by the partners awarded the contract signalled that users—airlines and passengers—could expect that if the new owners did not make their profit projections, fees and charges would go up.

Although the Chrétien government would sanctimoniously leap on the Pearson airport issue and cancel the deal, the Liberals would continue the march of privatization by later introducing a commercialization policy aimed at Canada's airport system. In the name of getting government out of the airport business and reducing the cost to taxpayers, the Liberals, like the Conservatives, were prepared to lease the government's airports so the Canadian taxpayer could "benefit" from the superior operating performance of private sector management—in the form of nonprofit "local airport authorities." This politely obscure term meant airports would be passed into the hands of the local business community, no doubt on the assumption it was more capable than government employees of operating the facilities efficiently.

Canadians were not just losing control of public assets with the privatization or commercialization of airports. These important public transportation assets were passing into private monopoly hands.

If, as a traveller, you were dissatisfied with the airport service or the user fees charged, you had no recourse, no other airport to use. But you would no longer be held captive by inefficient Transport Canada management. You would now be held to ransom by largely unaccountable private or local monopoly operators. And it was taxpayers' money which built the airports in the first place.

Added to this development was the other part of the double-barrel private sector philosophy: You could bet the cost to the traveller and the airlines for using the airport were now going up. In some cases in rural areas, the traveller might even lose the airport service they had previously paid for.

Under the Mulroney Tories, control of the profitable Vancouver International Airport was passed over to a local airport authority made up largely of local business people. Together, they would be allowed to operate what was still a public facility with no effective mechanism to make the authority accountable to the public. The authority's conflict-of-interest guidelines were nowhere near as stringent as those that would apply if the airport were still in government hands. In the Vancouver case, an airport authority member's firm was allowed to do business with the airport—something that would not have been allowed if the federal government were running the airport. The member did not personally do the work for the airport, but had been actively involved in the negotiations with the Mulroney government to privatize the airport in the first place, according to the *Globe and Mail.*

The Vancouver local authority also did not call tenders on all contracts related to its $400 million airport expansion program, did not reveal what it pays on specific contracts and, to much criticism, increased airport fees for travellers—introducing, in effect, double taxation for Vancouver air travellers.

In typical user-pay fashion, these additional travel fees ($5 per trip inside B.C., $10 for Canadian destinations and $15 for international travel) were said to cover the cost of the airport's new expansion program. But at the same time, travellers would still be paying a federal transportation tax of as much as $50 on each airline ticket purchased. The purpose of this transportation tax? It was originally meant to pay for airport improvements and maintenance.

Evidently, this was how Tory privatization and Liberal commercialization were superior to public enterprise. Partisan appointees or lessors took control of what was still essentially a public asset and operated it as a private monopoly—without competition and with less accountability then before. The authority then raised the cost of doing business. Their operations would be largely closed to public scrutiny. And the Conservatives and Liberals would continue to preach that these initiatives were superior and more cost efficient than that of any public enterprise.

When Don Mazankowski became the minister in charge of privatization in 1988, he was strongly committed to privatizing Air Canada, reportedly making the sale of the airline a condition of accepting the portfolio. In April 1988, less than two weeks after assuming his new post, Mazankowski announced Air Canada would be sold "as market conditions permit."

Two of the key players pressing the government to privatize Air Canada were the airline's president and chairman—Pierre Jeanniot and Claude Taylor. Taylor had long been an advocate of selling preferred shares in Air Canada as a means of accessing more cash—added capital infusions the airline would need if it was to grow and compete successfully in the international marketplace. He first raised the issue as early as 1977 with the Liberals but was refused.

With deregulation under way, Taylor approached the Tories in early 1988 requesting $300 million in government assistance to allow Air Canada to pay down debt, enabling it to acquire new aircraft. Rather than invest more money in the airline, the Tories announced that shares in Air Canada would be sold in two issues, one in October and a second in 1989.

In an October 1989 *Canadian Business* article, the success of Taylor's personal quest to privatize Air Canada was termed "the cap to his career" with the crown carrier. "We are entering a different world as a new Air Canada," Taylor told the magazine. "It is all coming together as planned in the Great Book somewhere."

When the "public sector" Air Canada books were closed off for 1989, with the investment benefits of an oversubscribed share issue jingling in the airline's pockets, the airline reported a handsome working capital pot of $602 million, debt of a little over $1 billion and an impressive debt-to-equity ration of 1.7:1. At the end of 1992, the third full year as a privatized airline competitor, Air Canada's working capital pot had almost disappeared, dwindling to a precarious $74 million, debt had jumped to $3.75 billion and the debt-to-equity ratio rested at a very, very uncomfortable 10.68:1.

"So, the problem isn't, and never has been, public ownership or public financing which are, indeed, advantageous ways of underwriting enterprise," according to Hardin. "The problem is the [Mulroney] government's privatization ideology. Trying to pass off the [Air Canada] financing argument was much like choking a person while at the same time complaining that the person doesn't know how to breathe."

The same Mulroney government, which would refuse to provide Air Canada with one of its traditional sources of capital, would have no trouble doling out an estimated $11 billion a year in tax concessions, grants and interest-free loans to business. In March 1994, it would be reported that the highly profitable Bombardier Inc. of Montreal would receive $24 million in interest-free loans from Ottawa and Quebec to help finance a plant modernization. Bombardier had a solid reputation for making money and had just reported a nine-month profit of $117 million before it received the $24 million in federal and provincial interest-free loans. (Bombardier would later report a $106.9 million profit on $2.3 billion in sales for the first six months of the 1994 fiscal year.) In an earlier privatization move, the

Mulroney government would sell Canadair to Bombardier in 1986 for $123 million (Bombardier paid the money in cash) while leaving the Canadian taxpayer to absorb Canadair's more than $1.2 billion debt.

The plaintive howl for privatizing Air Canada had been picked up by the nation's trade and business press on the standard assumption that anything that gets the feds out of the domestic air transport business was going to make things—competition, fares, service—better than it had been. The idea of privatizing Air Canada, as *Canadian Aviation* put it in 1987, was "the best thing that could happen in a deregulated environment." The Toronto *Globe and Mail* told its readers in the spring of 1987, in an epiphanous declaration: "It's time to sell Air Canada . . . the case is overwhelming for its sale."

One would be correct in suspecting there were a few million Canadians who might not have agreed with the Toronto publication's push to privatize. The Angus Reid-Southam poll a year later—after four years of Tory drum beating about the benefits from deregulation of transportation and privatization of public enterprises—had a mere thirty-five per cent of Canadians favouring privatization while fifty-three per cent of Canada's person-in-the-streets still were dead set against what the *Globe* was trying to sell. The *Globe* painted those citizens as "sentimental" defenders of Air Canada.

The case against Air Canada as a public carrier was not just badly made. It relied as much on traditional biases and emotion than fact. The analysis was simple: Air Canada kept prices high and quality low. Some critics saw that a publicly-owned air carrier would thwart deregulation. They saw Air Canada as inefficient and costly. The investors who trampled each other in an unprecedented fashion to buy shares in Air Canada in 1988 and 1989 should have proved a pretty strong argument against those points.

One analysis rolled out a list of "favours" the crown carrier had traditionally enjoyed, as if the fruits of being the national carrier should have been equally distributed among all competitors. Certain policies were "designed to benefit Air Canada." Air Canada had "complete monopoly on international routes" until 1948. Air Canada was "favoured in its dealings with the federal government." It was "closely involved in the formation of commercial aviation policy." Its "top executives had access to the minister and other members of cabinet."

Air Canada was "closely consulted on the design and construction of major airports." Air Canada "obtained the lion's share" of federal air travel and they "benefited greatly from the implicit guarantees of its debt by the federal government." But all the favours cited were only to be expected with a public enterprise corporation responsible for carrying out the nation's air transportation and, to a lesser extent, social policy.

As public opinion polls have shown since the early 1980s, a majority of Canadians have been favourably disposed to crown corporations and their public interest goals. But privatization does have the support of certain special interest groups. The strongest support for privatization, according to John W. Langford of the University of Victoria's public administration faculty, in a 1985 paper written for the Institute for Research on Public Policy, comes from "people in professional, managerial and supervisory positions and those earning more than $50,000 annually. This helps explain why privatization—despite its lack of mass support—has made it on the political agenda at all . . . the anti-privatization forces appear to have a majority of the electorate behind them, while the pro-privatization groups are better connected to the decision making process."

The argument for privatization follows the strain that if we privatize, consumers will get a better deal—better products, improved service and cheaper prices, while the privatized company will start earning a normal rate of return on equity. In this neoclassical interpretation of economic interaction, public enterprise gets no points for maintaining employment stability, overseeing steady growth, assuring security of something like national oil and gas supply, keeping utility prices low so private companies can compete internationally, or saving the private sector from itself by avoiding massive surges of lost investment wealth and the collapse of businesses.

The argument that privatization leads to new jobs, new investment, a revitalized private sector and more competition has never been proven—and is highly doubtful. In fact, the opposite is probably true. In the most active era of privatization ever, profits for Canada's entire 1,000 largest companies soared almost twenty per cent in the last year, while Canada's real unemployment rate hovered between eleven and twelve per cent—almost twice that of the U.S. and four times that of Japan. A cruel paradox in the Canadian economy is that, though it has been "growing" over the last three years, unemployment has held relatively steady. Jobs are the first target for cost control in an unregulated and privatized marketplace.

If anything, privatization contributes to increased concentration of industry, not competition. Langford concluded: "There is virtually no evidence in support of the relationship between privatization, jobs and investments."

9 / The Five Horsemen of the Apocalypse

"The Canadian airline business is in serious trouble—you know the numbers as well as I do. Anyone who believes these companies can be restored to profitability in their present form and still offer security for all employees and bargain basement fares for all customers is engaging in self delusion."
—former Air Canada chairman Claude Taylor, speech prepared for the House of Commons Standing Committee, September 1992

THE YEAR 1993 BROUGHT LITTLE RELIEF for either of Canada's two battered air carriers, or for the world industry as a whole. At home, all 365 days would be stalked by the December 31 deadline for final signing of the PWA–AMR agreement. As the clock ticked, the days would fill with court battles, increased public confusion about the financial stability of the two airlines, the faces of embarrassed politicians, and Air Canada's relentless tactics to block the impending agreement in any way it could. There seemed to be more lawyers competing in the courts than there were passengers in planes in Canada's sky.

The central legal issue was Canadian Airlines International's effort to extricate itself from the Gemini computer reservation system partnership so it could join American Airlines' SABRE system. The secondary issue concerned the fact that neither airline could unilaterally stop the suicidal effects of competitive behaviour.

Both airlines had substantially more aircraft and seating capacity than the scope of the business required. CAIL was still bleeding dollars and Air Canada was bound with grinding debt. Both were losing money on every flight and both were still watching load factors fall into the mid-fifty per cent range—meaning their planes were flying almost half empty. CAIL had just suffered its worst financial year ever and would be kept alive on employee concession promises and government loan guarantee carrots all year—and would again come very close to running out of cash. Parent company PWA's shares were trading as low as forty-eight cents. For Air Canada, 1993 would carry two large disappointments: the airline would table numbers showing the previous year had been the worst in its history ($454 million in net losses) and it would go on to record a further net loss of $326 million in 1993.

Both airlines were crying, in their own way, for a return to some sort of reregulation of the industry. The two were tied in a competition death-lock. Like two Mexican knife-fighters in a duel that would end with no winners—unless someone else intervened to untie the knots in the bandanna that held their wrists together—they could slash to the death. The scene brought to mind AMR chairman Robert Crandall's barb that the airline business was as close to "legalized warfare" as you could get. By the end of the year CAIL would be kept alive, virtually, by the nickels and dimes hesitantly nudged at it by a Mulroney government in its own death-throes, the shrinking offerings of two provincial governments and the promise of the collective contributions of its employees.

The world airline situation was not much better than Canada's. The industry had not seen an operating profit since 1990, had accumulated losses of almost US $11.5 billion in just three years, and was headed in 1993 for another US $4.1 billion in accumulated losses—for a four-year total of US $15.6 billion. In the same period, the world's airlines would "shed" more than one hundred thousand airline workers, according to the International Air Transport Association, and still the airlines could not keep their costs low enough to make a dime. The future seemed no better than the recent past.

There were now five apocalyptic horsemen galloping after the world's airline industry—Traffic and Yields that were too low, Capacity and Costs that were too high, and Interest Charges that rose geometrically with every bad year-end. The worst hit were the U.S. airlines. Fifteen years of deregulation might have made the odd fare cheaper but had severely damaged the nation's airline industry. Some international airline observers speculated that if trends continued, and the growing encroachment from international competition continued, there might not even be an American airline industry in two decades. So much for the results of healthy competition.

The No. 1 U.S. carrier, American Airlines, had suffered a sizeable

US $200 million loss in the fourth quarter of 1992. By the time it added up all the bad numbers for the year, American would lose US $935 million. In 1993, the industry giant would speed up its "transitional planning" to get it out of the airline business in the long-term and be shoved out of its No. 1 position by United Airlines—in more categories than one. United would finally fly more revenue-passenger miles than American in 1992, but it would lose US $957 million doing it. By the end of the year, United would be on its way to being fifty-five per cent owned by its employees.

Foreign airlines were beginning to consider buying in to some major U.S carriers to boost their own mega-carrier status. Some turned down the opportunity because the American airlines were too weak financially. Except for the U.S. and Japan, almost every country in the world was consolidating its international airline efforts into single flag carriers, not allowing competing domestic carriers to bash each other's brains out. In all this airline industry turmoil—domestic and international—*Canadian Business* magazine published what perhaps could be considered as one of the most ideologically extravagant editorials on the airline business to ever pass before the eyes of the nation's business community.

The magazine's January 1993 editorial questioned the very need for national air carriers. Entitled "Sacred Cows of Nationhood," the editorial claimed national airlines made "hollow symbols at best." The "central villain" in the airlines' problem was "lack of competition," it claimed, and Canada should be the first nation to simply open its entire sky to a takeover by international airlines in the name of maximizing competition and lowering air fares. Not even free enterprise Americans would agree with *that much* free enterprise competition.

With all the evidence available about the industry's inherent huge capital and operating costs problems, its traditionally narrow margins of profit, its market volatility, its fundamental dependence on government support and direction, and its natural tendency toward concentration rather than competition, *Canadian Business* was saying that it made sense to believe that *more*, not less, competition should prevail in this blue-sky world of Canadian air travel.

Canadian Business saw a future in which Canada's sky would be full of international carriers competing for the Canadian travel dollar, beating down prices for the appreciative consumer. "We wouldn't lose all airline jobs, however, nor would we lose all airlines," it went on. Smaller regional carriers such as Time Air and Air BC would "conceivably continue to operate," feeding passengers to the likes of Lufthansa or JAL, who would then fly them from Vancouver to Toronto.

Perhaps they were joking, but the magazine's editorial seemed to miss the essential point: in that surreal, competitive world, Lufthansa and JAL would not pause seconds before they devoured Time Air and Air BC, doing what airlines tend to do—monopolize or, at the very least, split the market into a controlled oligopoly, running their operations, administration and maintenance from their facilities, not in Canada, but on home-nation soil.

"The sooner we abandon vainglorious national symbolism," the editorial ended loftily, "the sooner we'll be back to the business of not only creating wealth, but enjoying it."

For a nationalist, this was embarrassing stuff. It was the kind of intemperate laissez-faire woolgathering that occasionally popped up when globalism's evangelists forgot they still had to have a country to bed down in at night, after they finished clipping the coupons of their day's bond market successes.

If it had been April 1 rather than January 1, *Canadian Business* magazine's ideas might have had some merit. But this was open competition mentality taken to absurdity. The reasoning ran against the facts and evidence of what happens when human beings interact in a highly volatile industry like the airline business. And this editorial extremism was appearing in one of the nation's business bibles, reinforcing for many those North American fundamentalist beliefs in the superior benefits of market forces, the sovereignty of the consumer and completely unfettered private sector competition.

Mickey gets his wings
"Japan Air Lines said it will paint Disney characters on three of its Boeing planes as part of a one-year family travel campaign to lift sagging sales. Mickey Mouse and Donald Duck will be taking off on Aug. 1 "
—The Globe and Mail, *July 2, 1994*

Most Canadians probably assumed the December 29, 1992 agreement by AMR to buy a one-third stake in Canadian Airlines International meant the turmoil in Canada's airline industry was now over. Not only would the deal not be consummated by the December 31, 1993 deadline, but the path to a signed contract would be marked by a bitter legal fight to remove PWA from its three-way partnership in the Gemini computer reservation system with Air Canada and United Airline's Covia. Getting out of Gemini and signing on to American's SABRE reservation system was the *quid pro quo* for AMR to hand over its $246 million to PWA. And Air Canada was not at all prepared to stand by and let that happen, at least not without a protracted legal fight.

Air Canada began its scorched earth strategy on February 4 when it filed a formal objection to the PWA–AMR agreement with the National Transportation Agency, arguing that American's one-third holding would mean control of the airline would reside south of the border, and that both CAIL and Air Canada would eventually end up being minor feeder carriers for dominant American carriers. In spite of the initialling of the PWA–AMR agreement, Air Canada also let it be known it was still interested in a merger with CAIL and was working on restructuring the massive aggregate debt problem that had blocked merger possibilities the previous fall.

On February 19, PWA chairman Rhys Eyton triggered the call for his own version of reregulation (he would refrain from calling it that) by telling the House of Commons transportation committee that the federal government "must force the country's two leading airlines to ground some planes or both firms may go broke." The competing airlines "were slowly driving one another out of business" and "needed a nudge or a bang on the head" from the likes of transport minister Jean Corbeil—who had already told the airlines the previous fall to cut their capacity—to end the insanity. Four days later Corbeil would warn the airlines that if they did not cut capacity "we could legislate [minimum passenger loads on certain routes] within weeks."

This stutter-step arabesque was necessary for two reasons. First, the dyed-in-the-wool Tories had no appetite for legislating regulations back into an industry it had loudly pronounced did not need regulating. Second, all three dancers must have been aware they were stepping very close to a potential violation of competition law. Slicing into the ethos of competition could result in fares going up for the consumer. Added to the difficult swirl of their heel-and-toe shuffle was the lurking reality of another carrier—Montreal-based Nation-air—offering deep-discount fares between Toronto and Montreal.

Nationair was undercutting both Air Canada and CAIL fares at the time, hanging on to its business life while lobbying Corbeil and the Tories for some breathing space on payment of federal airport fees and taxes. Nationair was cash-strapped, charging fares below cost and asking for federal relief to avoid bankruptcy. Lumbering along with $87 million in debt, Nationair would crash by early April. This was free market competition in the Canadian airline business circa 1993.

A few weeks later, the NTA Review Commission would publish a call for more, not less deregulation of airlines; the privatization of CN Railway; and the raising of permissible foreign ownership levels in domestic airlines to forty-nine per cent from the existing twenty-five per cent level. NDP transportation critic Iain Angus pointed out Tory deregulation had already destroyed the Canadian transportation system and now "all the government's hired guns can do is recommend that we dig the hole even deeper."

On February 25, PWA announced its net loss for 1992 was a record-smashing $543 million. On February 28, it would send a revised restructuring plan to its many creditors, whom it had stopped paying the previous November. By April 2, PWA would suffer another setback. An Ontario court denied CAIL's bid to have Gemini declared insolvent, throwing up the first in a number of roadblocks preventing the easy closing of the PWA–AMR deal. PWA had argued Gemini had all but broken down, thanks to its poor financial performance, and the tension and lack of cooperation among its partners. The court thought otherwise. Although PWA stated it intended to appeal the ruling, the courts were already looking unfavourably at their case, citing PWA's clear intent to see Gemini unravel, freeing it to move to SABRE.

Air Canada's Hollis Harris went public again, warning that a consummated deal to join CAIL with the giant American Airlines (the deal was apparently code named "Iceberg" by the participants, perhaps an unwitting reference to the sinking of the *Titanic*) would strike a "death blow" at Air Canada, making the once-proud crown carrier "as weak as Canadian Airlines is today."

In April, the federal Competition Tribunal refused to allow PWA's request that CAIL be permitted to cut its partnership ties in Gemini, sparking a ping-pong effect of law suits, appeals and further confusion. The tribunal ruled it did not have the authority to free CAIL from

Gemini, but if it had, it would have allowed CAIL to bail out of the three-way computer reservation partnership. PWA announced it would appeal the tribunal's ruling. In effect, both PWA and CAIL now had their fate in the hands of the NTA.

By the first week in May, Hollis Harris was in Houston, Texas being thanked and feted for orchestrating Air Canada's life-saving involvement in the consortium purchase of Continental. In early May, Harris also called upon Ottawa to reregulate the domestic airline business because "nothing else will solve the industry's problems." The No. 1 problem was overcapacity, and a CAIL-AMR partnership would just make things worse. Harris again claimed he was eager to talk merger with CAIL, having reworked those horrid Airline Holdco debt numbers into something that would be more palatable to investors. There were no takers from PWA's side of the table.

The euphoria in Houston, where seventeen thousand Continental employees took part in the "Thanks to Air Canada" celebration on Harris's arrival, would dim quickly when Air Canada announced its highest quarterly loss ever—$293 million for the first quarter of 1993. The airline was well on its way to over a billion dollar in losses in the four years since it had been privatized.

Internationally, the International Air Transport Association discovered that the industry's mergers and continued financial troubles—most of them centred in the United States—were having an impact on future prospects. Almost a third of businesses surveyed were saying they were drastically paring travel budgets and investigating other technology-based means of communicating among themselves, and with customers, rather than flying on airplanes. In American skies, Northwest would spark a summer fare war in May with up to thirty per cent off regular fares. Northwest would be followed down the below-cost pricing path by American Airlines, United, Delta, USAir and Continental, none of whom made money in 1992. Some of them had not been in the black for a long, long time.

Some airlines were so into this "healthy competition" thing, they were even undercutting themselves. In Canada and other countries, desperate air carriers were now working with ticket "bucket shops"—wholesalers of cheap airline seat tickets. Bucket shops are ticket scalpers. They make money by buying blocks of empty airline seats at very low prices and selling them at what the market will bear.

Now, it was discovered, the airlines were selling those cheap seats, on their own planes, to wholesalers, some of whom were even discounting first-class tickets.

Worse still, the airlines were referring potential passengers to bucket shop dealers, thus ensuring their own tickets—at regular prices—would be undersold. The airlines' marvellous system of "yield management" would certainly not yield any profits playing that game.

"Once you get hooked on the airline business, it's worse than dope."
—Ed Acker, former chairman of Air Florida and Pan Am

Mid-May brought the news of a "significant decline in business travel" for the two Canadian air carriers. One of the three Gemini partners, Covia, filed a court motion to add the names of PWA officers to Gemini's $1.5 billion lawsuit, filed the previous December against PWA. On May 21, the *Globe and Mail* reported that the NTA was expected to say "no" to AMR's plan to buy into Canadian Airlines International because the deal would move control of CAIL outside the country. NTA sources were said to have provided Corbeil with a draft copy of their decision. The *Globe* reported the transport minister was apparently "unhappy" with the imminent ruling and had requested NTA staff to provide him with "several options." Corbeil's department vehemently denied the report.

An NTA ruling of that kind could be the kiss-of-death for CAIL, which was once more rapidly running out of cash. The issue centred on a powerful clause AMR had negotiated into the deal, giving it veto power over capital expenditures in excess of $50 million. Such a clause would provide the American partner with substantially more power and control over CAIL decision making than its one-third percentage of the airline would normally buy. Air Canada had also trotted out figures, refuted by PWA, that seemed to indicate that AMR's holdings in CAIL could eventually reach as high as fifty-six per cent, giving it clear control of the Canadian carrier.

Even if all the NTA decision did was force a change in the amount AMR might invest, the entire package would have to be renegotiated and restructured, and each of the other contributing parties forced to up its portion of the airline-saving ante. PWA representatives called the release of the NTA's intentions "premature and designed to create confusion and uncertainty in the marketplace." It was also reported that, as a contingency, the troubled airline was now preparing to file for protection from its creditors, as it had been before winning last-minute loan guarantees from the federal and provincial governments.

On May 27, the NTA announced that a purchase of one-third of CAIL by AMR would now *not* give control of the airline to the American partner, that a PWA–AMR deal would now be "in the public interest" and it was okay for the parties to proceed and close the deal. An NTA spokesperson said the agency's decision "demonstrated support for the principle of competition in the domestic airline industry." He did not say that turning down the PWA–AMR deal, allowing CAIL to go bankrupt and opening up the industry to the introduction of carriers other than the wobbly CAIL could also have been "support for the principle of competition." Air Canada announced it would appeal the NTA's decision to the federal cabinet.

Pragmatism was once again aloft in the Canadian sky. On June 15, Air Canada announced, with some gusto, it had signed a letter of intent with American airplane manufacturer McDonnell Douglas that would lead to the modernizing of Air Canada's aging fleet of DC-9 airplanes. At a cost of about $10 million each, or about one-third the price of a new plane, Air Canada would extend the life of its DC-9 fleet by fifteen years, create more than seven hundred jobs over three years (with another seven hundred jobs derived from subcontracting), put to use underutilized maintenance crews and facilities, and get the 100-seat aircraft it needed without incurring a huge new capital investment estimated at more than one billion dollars.

On June 17, PWA's Rhys Eyton publicly called for Ottawa to appoint a mediator to resolve the stalemate over CAIL's release from Gemini. His airline needed to be set free from the computer reservation partnership by the end of 1993 or "we are a well-cooked goose," he was reported as saying. PWA had the NTA on side now, but Air Canada had stretched out the process by appealing the NTA decision.

On June 23, a fast-fading Mulroney government announced it was backing the NTA in its decision favouring approval of a PWA–AMR deal. According to Corbeil, the government concluded that: "consistent with our policy of fostering a strong, viable and competitive airline industry," it should not overturn the NTA decision. Behind the scenes, it was said the decision contained a quiet rider that would probably give Air Canada a half a loaf—the new route access to the Asia Pacific the airline had been lobbying for.

But what the Mulroney government's decision left out was an answer to the nagging question about whether the country could realistically support two competing, major airlines. The government's decision just prolonged this costly charade. In the simple light of their reasoning, it was awfully hard to see how the government's decisions were "fostering a strong, viable and competitive airline industry."

On July 30, the Federal Court of Appeal ruled the federal Competition Tribunal *did* have the jurisdiction to rule on the Gemini partnership. The court ruling turned everything around again and meant the case was being sent back to the tribunal for reconsideration. As CAIL's financial clock ticked down, the legal wrangle between the airlines was now becoming so complicated, newspapers began printing sidebar charts to domestic airline stories, showing the key dates and decisions made about the Gemini partnership.

Less than two weeks later, the Ontario Court of Appeal rejected PWA's effort to declare Gemini insolvent. With the year-end deadline coming closer and continuing cash problems, PWA's Eyton now called for Ottawa to step in and force a negotiated settlement on the Gemini issue. Air Canada management had refused to negotiate, maintaining CAIL had no real problems. Air Canada's solution was simple: just sell those lucrative international routes to it as originally proposed. Eyton admitted again that CAIL was probably dead by the end of the year unless something was done. He now hoped, perhaps at the very least, that AMR would extend its deadline into 1994.

In mid-August, Air Canada ran full-page newspaper advertisements, estimated to cost $250,000, proclaiming that what the country needed was one, strong national air carrier, geared for future competition with international airlines. The ads claimed the Mulroney government's policy "mandates fight-to-the-death domestic competition" that virtually guaranteed Canada's inability to compete internationally. The Mulroney government's inconsistent policies were tying the hands of both carriers, resulting in "duplicate domestic flights flying to the same destinations half empty" and suffering massive losses. To allow AMR to buy into CAIL would "send thousands of Canadian jobs south of the border," ultimately meaning Canada's two major carriers would be "relegated to the status of being feeders to U.S.-based mega-carriers." The solution, the ads concluded, was an

Air Canada-CAIL merger and a revised airline policy that would help create jobs, rebuild the aviation industry and guarantee a place for Canada in the international marketplace.

"Air Canada: Are You Confused?" asked CAIL's rebuttal advertisements—which ran only as half-page ads and cost an estimated $70,000, in keeping with the airline's more frugal policies. The CAIL ads pointed out that Air Canada's board had been responsible for killing the last merger talks. The ads argued that AMR was not buying "control" of CAIL; that Air Canada was really talking about forming a monopoly airline; and that by resolving the Gemini issue, the two airlines could go on to provide their customers with more service— which was what competition was all about.

The ads were all part of everyone's federal pre-election strategy. Both airlines had hired well-placed lobbyists—and there were many of them, perhaps more of them than lawyers arguing myriad points of law on the airlines' behalf—with very close working and political ties to the fading Mulroney government—now transformed into Kim Campbell's personal sea of troubles.

All bets were off in this strange political atmosphere. The PWA–AMR deal was no sure thing at all. There was less than five months left to shape the deal or it might dissolve. On August 18, barely a week before PWA would face its creditors and shareholders to vote on PWA's complex financial restructuring plan, Air Canada muddied the waters again with a billion dollar bid for CAIL's overseas routes.

The Montreal-based airline offered $200 million for all CAIL's international routes, allowing CAIL to retain its domestic and U.S. routes, but potentially reducing the Calgary-based carrier by one-third its size. Air Canada would also throw in roughly $800 million to cover the cost of eight jumbo jets it would buy, including debts, leases and crews.

Air Canada's latest pitch was a "diabolical plot to destroy Canadian Airlines," Eyton responded. The offer "minimizes job losses, saves Gemini and creates a single international carrier for Canada that can compete on a world scale," Hollis Harris replied. Stripped of its lucrative overseas runs, Eyton said such a deal would be "the beginning of the end for Canadian Airlines." He called the pitch a "public relations strategy" and Harris, a Georgia "gunslinger," here to "tell us how to organize our Canadian [airline] structure." Later in September, Harris would refer to Don Carty and his Fort Worth,

Texas friends as "AMR gunslingers." The slashing was getting personal as the bandanna tightened around their wrists.

On August 24, the PWA board turned down Air Canada's offer flat. They saw no merit "whatsoever" in the offer. The proposal would have huge transition costs, result in surplus aircraft, strip CAIL of much of its revenue, cost about six thousand jobs (Air Canada said thirty-five hundred) and simply lead to the collapse of PWA's financial restructuring plan. On August 27, the PWA board met with its creditors over the plan. The board required a simple "yes" or "no" to a proposal that essentially turned approximately $722 million (according to the PWA's annual report) in debt into equity in their airline, pushing up PWA's shares in number from about forty-eight million to more than one billion. Despite some grumbling, the creditors and shareholders agreed overwhelmingly to the proposal. They had no other choice. It was either hold a share at roughly fifty cents or hold a bag of air where an airline used to be.

> *"Major change is again sweeping through the nation's airline industry . . . But unlike the labour-management fights that contributed to the disappearance of the oldest names in U.S. aviation history . . . unions at some of the bigger carriers are taking an active role in trying to reshape the industry by pressing for an ownership stake. By the end of the decade . . . half of the ownership of the nation's major airlines will be in the hands of their employees."*
> —*The Washington Post National Weekly*, September 1993

The same month, after six weeks of hearings, President Clinton's specially appointed commission (the National Committee to Ensure a Strong Competitive Airline Industry) to investigate the U.S. airline industry's spectacular three-year slump, released its report. It effectively said there was no big problem at all. Despite the US $10 billion the airlines had lost in three years and their US $35 billion in total debt, the tens of thousands of employees out of work, the devastation caused by an endless string of airline failures, the continuing trend to concentration of ownership and dim prospects for international competition, the twenty-six member committee reported, in convolution, that despite the industry's "wretched state," it was "inherently strong."

The committee had decided—based on the primary assumption

that the purpose of airline deregulation was to increase competitiveness and reduce fares, and fares were now actually less *on average*—that deregulation was a success.

On the other hand, there were other statistical and data sources in the U.S. that were also saying fares had actually been rising in real terms all along. One report later showed that between September 1992 and 1993, discount fares went up thirty-six per cent, the average fare was up thirteen per cent and fares for business travellers went up by almost forty per cent.

At the very moment the president's committee reported, the U.S. was littered with failed airlines and more planes than the industry knew what to do with. Except for a host of tiny, struggling new air carriers, one or two of which might be profitable for a year or so, the U.S. industry had ended up concentrating the majority of its business in the hands of three carriers—American, United and Delta. Continental had crawled out of bankruptcy protection thanks largely to Harris and Air Canada. Northwest, the nation's fourth largest carrier, had been talking to its employees about needing US $900 million in wage concessions to stay aloft. TWA crawled out of Chapter 11 on the backs of a multi-million-dollar employee bail-out. American West was still stuck in Chapter 11. USAir kept flying after trading shares for employee concessions. United Airlines, probably the only major airline not facing imminent financial grief, was talking with its employees about their unions buying controlling interest. The United board would begin unloading fifty-five per cent of its shares on its employees, with an option to buy as much as sixty-three per cent—in return for US $4.9 billion in concessions. American Airlines had just lost a total of US $1.2 billion, was about to let five thousand more employees go and was now deeper into its transitional plan. And the U.S. airline industry was "inherently strong?"

The president's committee then proceeded to recommend that the solution was more deregulation of the industry. Their primary goal was not to strengthen their airline industry to compete globally in a world where other governments actively strengthened their major national carriers. It was not to develop an industry that was strong and stable—and created more jobs than it destroyed. It was to get the consumer price of an air fare down to the tiniest sum possible, through the mechanism of more market competition. The committee even recommended, like a page from *Canadian Business* magazine, that restrictions on foreign investment in U.S. carriers be relaxed, making the foreign carriers better able to take over the U.S. airline industry. After all, according to their view of Adam Smith's thinking, this would increase competition and reduce consumer cost.

The cornerstone of their theory was better access by U.S. carriers to international markets. Then the entire airline world would be competing together on a global playing field, as level as a pool table top, with no rules to guide them, other than their inherent sense of fair play and the gratification obtained from knowing that Aunt Maude could now fly from Saskatoon to Bucharest for $17.26 less than if the industry had been regulated.

Like the spiritual heights of the Winged Gospel American air pioneers once believed in, today's Adam Smith'rs seemed to truly think that if all the players on God's earth just opened their markets to the beauty and balance of competition the only thing stopping us all from reaching Consumer Heaven would be a testy St. Peter, acting as The Regulator at The Gates.

The other blind spot Clinton's committee suffered was the emotional hype they got caught up in as they watched tiny Southwest Airlines ("tiny" in the sense that even PWA reported a billion dollars more revenue in 1992 than Southwest did) defy the industry by making a $164 million profit during the three years in which the rest of the industry lost $10 billion. Tied to Southwest's success was a whole raft of tiny airline pretenders, hoping to follow in the path of previous pretenders like People Express and American West, each apparently finding their niche in specific markets. Southwest's niche was well known. The airline was a short-haul specialist (eighty per cent of flights were ninety minutes or less), flew only one type of aircraft (Boeing 737s) to keep costs down, served no meals, and flew out of smaller, more remote airports to avoid making the mistake of competing head-to-head with The Big Guys. Southwest was referred to as the "cattle car" airline or "Wal-Mart of the Skies."

Another tiny, upstart company that helped put those "inherently strong" stars in the eyes of the president's committee was Kiwi International, run by its employees out of Newark, New Jersey. Kiwi had ten aircraft. There were also "well-known" carriers competing in the American air space with names like Branson Airlines, ATX, Destination Sun Airways and Freedom Express. One of the neatest, and perhaps the most promising to the president's committee, might have been Vintage Airways, flying between Orlando and Key West, Florida. Vintage flew DC-3s (a propeller- driven airplane first manufactured in the 1930s), dressed flight attendants in 1940s styles and offered their passengers on-board magazines and music from the same era.

There would always be a certain inevitability about the way Americans would intermingle lofty dreams about flight, business competition and religion—enough to put even the shrewdest entre-preneur into a tail spin. After four years of listening to the echoing plaudits about its success, and on its way to $154 million in net income for 1993, Dallas-based Southwest Airlines announced in December that it had bought out Morris Air. The purchase would cost $125 million in stock and Southwest would inherit Morris's twenty-one passenger jets and two thousand employees. Later, in July 1994, Southwest would step closer to the precipice when it announced it was planning to compete head-to-head with United Airlines on tougher, long-haul routes, in response to United's move to introduce its own no-frills, short-haul services. Southwest—the short-haul, no-frills jewel in the American airline crown—was getting bigger and more competitive. We all knew what that could mean.

> " 'One fact should be clear to you by now. Moneymaking is aggression. That's the whole thing. The functionalist explanation is the only one. People come to the market to kill. They say, 'I'm going to make a killing.' It's not accidental. Only they haven't got the genuine courage to kill, and they erect a symbol of it. The money. They make a killing by a fantasy . . .'
> " '. . . What makes them want to kill? '
> " 'By and by, you'll get the drift . . .' "
> —Saul Bellow, *Seize the Day*

North of the border on September 2, 1993, Air Canada and Gemini asked the Supreme Court to review the Federal Court's decision that ruled the Competition Tribunal did have the authority to break up Gemini. PWA stock was languishing in the fifty cent range and there were more doubts about CAIL making it to the December 31 deadline, given cash shortages, legal fees and the unknown cost outcome of the various legal cases.

Later in the month, Moody's Investors Service of New York assigned a single-B1 rating to about $300 million of Air Canada's long-term debt, categorizing it as "generally lacking the characteristics of a desirable investment." On a visit to Vancouver, Air Canada's Harris announced he felt that air fares should be reregulated by a federal government agency to prevent the airlines from undercutting each other further. Harris wanted "minimum fares" to be applied because he admitted candidly the airlines "don't have enough discipline to quit selling a product for below cost." A CAIL spokesperson later responded that regulated fares would "cheat the consumer." Instead, CAIL had clamoured for reregulation of capacity which, by reducing supply, would just serve to regulate the price of air fares—upwards. They were saying the same thing. Both airlines wanted to be regulated to avoid any more bloodshed. The other thing they were saying was that competition in the airline industry was inherently self-destructive.

Air Canada continued its legal torment of CAIL by filing a motion on October 7 in the Federal Court of Appeal to be allowed to argue before the federal Competition Tribunal that its $1 billion offer to PWA to buy CAIL's overseas routes (PWA claimed, after costs were deducted, the offer was worth only $100 million) was a viable alternative to the AMR deal or, certainly, to CAIL's collapse. Mid-October would bring more legal confusion with two Supreme Court rulings.

The Supreme Court would refuse to hear Air Canada's appeal of the lower court ruling that said the Competition Tribunal did have jurisdiction to decide if PWA could go free of Gemini. And it denied a PWA request to appeal the Ontario Court of Appeal ruling rejecting PWA's request to have Gemini declared insolvent. The rulings might seem unimportant, but part of the key to making the PWA–AMR deal a reality was final disposition of the outstanding $1 billion lawsuit launched by Gemini against PWA, claiming breach of fiduciary responsibility. AMR was on record as stating there would be no deal until all costs, including costs of legal actions, were quantified and assigned. The first Supreme Court ruling favoured PWA but the second meant new, unquantified costs were still in the pipeline, further disrupting chances of a December 31 closing.

There was still a lot of life left in the courts. The hearing of Air Canada's appeal to broaden the range of the November 15 Competition Tribunal hearings to include their billion dollar offer to PWA was scheduled for November 8. The legal interactions were triggering almost geometric delays. And delays meant trouble for PWA. If Air Canada lost on November 8, the airline and its partners could still appeal to the Federal Court of Appeal, further delaying the entire resolution process. If unsuccessful there, Air Canada and partners could still appeal to the Supreme Court and drag out the process even further.

By November, CAIL's condition was again becoming critical. The airline was fishing for more loan guarantees to make it to December. The Gemini issue was nowhere near resolution and the parties were far apart. Gemini had sued for $1 billion and PWA had offered $21.5 million in cash and would also throw in its $30 million portion of Gemini's estimated value.

On November 4, in a speech to the Canadian Club of Vancouver, PWA's Eyton said he "disagreed with a return to the model of reregulation of fares" proposed by Air Canada. The world airline industry was moving toward a "free market system away from the protectionist thinking of earlier decades" and Canada should not be "out of step with global trends," he added. There was more than a touch of irony to his presentation. Eyton had asked for capacity restrictions to be applied by the federal government, a pretty clear form of regulation. Eyton also acknowledged that government assistance would be required in Canada "to enforce a competitive airline policy and prevent a monopoly emerging by default."

As far as his statement about government's only role being to "enforce a competitive airline policy" was concerned, Eyton evidently missed the fundamental reality of his own argument. He was asking government to be there, so to speak, to avoid airline competitors from scratching each other's eyes out in competition. But was that not the inevitable result of free and open competition—the primal urge to make sure there was *no* competition for you at all?

Even given the benefit of the doubt, Eyton was calling for regulated cartels or duopolies, neither of which had ever had the health and care of the consumer as their primary goal. If there was room for a regulated duopoly, why not a regulated monopoly? At this time, had a consumer called the two airlines for a full-fare economy or business-class fare quote for a flight between Toronto and Vancouver, the figure he or she would receive from both airlines would be *exactly the same*, including the taxes. So much for the benefits of healthy competition.

While Eyton was musing about how the world's airlines were gearing up for increased global competition, four European airlines— Swissair, Scandinavian (SAS), Austrian Airlines and KLM—were talking about merging into western Europe's largest airline. Their intention was to beat the competition by consolidating—not competing with one another. The four European carriers were holding talks about merging and forming an airline called "Alcazar"—a Moorish term for a four-sided, unassailable fort—which would whip any airline silly enough to think the business was all about competing on level playing fields. The choice of a name for their airline was no accident. The players wanted a European Fortress from which they would compete with the rest of the world.

The fact these four influential European airlines could contemplate forming a powerhouse carrier stemmed from their philosophy about how a modern airline could best compete. Rather than the American deregulation model of individual public companies thrashing themselves in destructive domestic and international competition—with the losers coming home and unloading employees and debt losses on a country's front doorstep—the Alcazar initiative was driven by the belief systems of the four airlines' most important stockholders—the governments of each nation.

The Netherlands government owned forty per cent of KLM. The Swiss government, in various forms, held twenty per cent of Swissair. The Swedish government were into SAS for fifty per cent. And Austrian Airlines was fifty-one per cent owned by government. More cooperation-minded than their American and Canadian counterparts, these governments were not about to leave the health of their airline business to notions about strengthening airlines and countries by letting them fight it out to the grave.

The Alcazar players had also been talking with two American airlines about joining this global partnership. But they turned down Delta because it had a weak route structure and dismissed Northwest because it was too weak financially. Evidently, the world trend was not towards global competition between hundreds of airlines and away from "protectionist thinking," as Eyton might have tried to convince the Canadian Club. It was towards mega-carriers (certainly not to include Air Canada and CAIL) controlling the lion's share of the market. Governments would act as lion tamers.

Witness how British Airways PLC (BA) and Air France operated in the global marketplace Air Canada and CAIL were so anxious to enter. On May 15, 1994, an international incident was averted when British Airways agreed not to invade France.

British Airways, claiming it had a right to land its passengers where it wanted, had planned to invade Paris's Orly airport, despite France's refusal of access. Sovereign rights of nations evidently meant nothing when it came to competition in the international airline business. To combat France's rigid protection of its national carrier, the angry Brits threatened a show of force by flying ten flights into Orly—full of French and British journalists. The French had threatened to turn away the BA flights. Press reports did not indicate whether France's superior missile weaponry—such as the Exocet—would be used on this soon-to-be-levelled playing field. Predictably, both governments were called upon to intervene and prevent further corporate silliness—or the beginning of a second Hundred Years' War.

Although they would persist, it was becoming tougher for deregulationists to make their arguments hold water. Many disciples would continue to use obtuse terms like "free market system" and "open competition" and "benefits to the consumer" in public, but very often their priests would suddenly turn on them and do something embarrassing and a bit demoralizing.

In November 1993, American President Bill Clinton unilaterally forced an end to American Airlines' five-day flight attendants' strike by ruling the two parties had to get back to the negotiating table and come up with an agreement. Clinton and his economic advisers believed in enterprise and competition, but within limits. The reasons for this sudden injection of government into the deregulated airline business were not profound. The strike would cost American Airlines as much as $160 million, and a weakened American was less competitive in the international airline marketplace. It simply made no sense to let the strike damage continue. On the more prosaic side, Thanksgiving weekend was coming up and the U.S. government did not savour the thought of angry travellers complaining about an airline system that did not always serve their consumer interests as they were told it did. The lesson? Like the application of the tenets of Adam Smith, deregulation was not something etched in stone. It was a notion that had to be changed and adjusted depending on circumstances—none of them theoretical, all of them entirely practical and human.

> *"I dunno, Lou. I suppose pilots are just as good as they ever were, but they sure don't live the way we did. I can tell you that there were times when you took pride in just getting there. Flying used to be fun. It really did. It used to be fun."*
> —James Stewart in *The Flight of the Phoenix*, just before he flew into a sand storm and crashed

On November 12, 1993, PWA received a glimmer of hope when the Federal Court of Appeal rejected Air Canada's request to expand the scope of the Competition Tribunal's hearings. The decision opened the way for the tribunal to rule on whether or not to release CAIL from Gemini. On November 24, the Competition Tribunal not only ruled in PWA's favour, allowing CAIL to leave Gemini, it went further and ordered the dissolution of Gemini by November 5, 1994, providing the partners could not reach a negotiated settlement by December 8, 1993. The tribunal felt CAIL was in such a miserable financial state it was likely to collapse anyway, thus lessening competition in Canada.

The tribunal's ruling was good news/bad news. It freed CAIL to leave Gemini, but this freedom might have come too late. The airline was reportedly down to its last $120 million and considering drawing down the last of its government loan guarantees. It had admitted to the tribunal there was not enough time or money to close the deal with AMR before December 31. It now had to convince the Americans to extend the deadline. Even then, the task was more Sisyphean than Herculean.

There was still Gemini's $1 billion breach of fiduciary responsibility law suit to be settled, and until the damages were assessed and paid, AMR had made it clear there would be no deal. A substantial figure awarded by the court might scotch the whole PWA–AMR deal. As well, the entire financial restructuring plan, including the $722 million debt-for-equity swap and the CAIL employees' $200 million wage and salary concessions, teetered on the closing of the PWA–AMR agreement. A negotiated settlement on Gemini by December 8, between PWA and Air Canada, was not likely. The tribunal's ruling could also be appealed by Air Canada—rolling the rock back down the hill for PWA. Added to all this was the tribunal's sidebar ruling declaring that cash-strapped PWA–CAIL was responsible for any costs incurred by Gemini in dissolving the partnership. PWA's victory seemed to be more Pyrrhic than real.

As the PWA countdown continued, south of the border U.S. Secretary of Transportation Frederico Pena was addressing those attending IATA's forty-ninth annual meeting. The Clinton administration wanted to tear down the current bilateral airline agreement system and open the skies to more competition. The theme of Pena's pitch seemed to be: You open your skies to us and we will open American skies to you. But even in their deregulated empire, U.S. skies were as closed and as hard to enter as any country's.

Pena was delivering "simple truths" that unrestricted international airline competition was good. It led to lower fares, more travellers, more jobs and dynamic growth in the economy. While Pena was speaking of how clear the international sky might be, the five horsemen were making mincemeat out of the international and American airline business. To quote IATA director-general Pierre Jeanniot, when asked how the international airline industry did in 1993?: "Bloody awful." Despite "de-employing" over one hundred thousand airline workers over the past few years, the world's carriers could still not make a buck. International losses would stand at US $4.1 billion by year's end. And now they were discovering that fewer travellers, not more, might be flying in the future.

On December 8, the Competition Tribunal announced that although discussions between Air Canada and PWA were going poorly, the talks for dissolving Gemini would be extended to December 20. A week later the talks broke down completely. PWA was back on its emotional roller coaster ride. The Gemini lawsuit had been settled on December 10, but no terms were released. AMR was willing to extend the December 31 deadline another six months. But Air Canada's Harris announced his airline now intended to appeal the tribunal's ruling. The appeal might take to next spring to be resolved. The loser could then appeal to the Supreme Court, stretching out the deadline again and adding to PWA's bridge financing problems. Liberal transport minister Douglas Young indicated there would be no more federal loan guarantee money once the $50 million was depleted. Alberta had reduced its loan guarantee promise in October by $12.5 million, though B.C. was still in for $20 million. All this shifting of the dollar signs meant the airline's financial plan had to be restructured each time the numbers changed.

On December 16, Air Canada presented, yet again, another fresh offer to buy CAIL's overseas routes, pushing their ante up to $1.17 billion, providing CAIL stayed in Gemini until the end of the century. Although the Liberals would not provide new loan guarantees to keep CAIL in cash, they did agree on December 18 to extend the airline's repayment schedule, providing a shaky cash bridge to the AMR agreement. That left two outstanding issues to resolve: Air Canada's appeal of the Competition Tribunal's ruling and whether the remaining Gemini partners would accept PWA's offer of $20 million in cash and $30 million worth of shares as the price of its exit (on the other hand, this matter may no longer have been relevant, given Air Canada's new offer on the table). On December 21, the PWA board turned down Air Canada's $1.17 billion offer for CAIL's overseas business.

Down south on Christmas eve, United Airline's board agreed to trade US $4.9 billion in wage concessions from its employees for control of the airline. When the deal closed, United Airlines would probably become the largest employee-owned company in the country. United would also become the first financially stable carrier to sell control of itself to its employees. This initiative of employee enterprise would attract the notice of other, less stable carriers, such as Northwest Airlines and the financially troubled TWA. Even American Airlines would begin sniffing around when AMR head Robert Crandall admitted he would listen to a similar sort of offer from the airline's employees.

It was clear the ground rules of airline ownership were changing drastically. Small start-up carriers like Kiwi International were employee-owned when they began. A number of international carriers, most notably Air France, were playing "let's make a deal" with their workers. And in Canada, Canadian Airlines International was flying on a wing and a prayer thanks to its sixteen thousand employees.

There was no doubt that a final solution to keep CAIL aloft depended as well on AMR's $246 million. It also needed those government loan guarantees, not to mention the largesse of its many, now poorer, creditors. It even needed the hard work of a phalanx of lawyers. But most of all, the glue that kept the whole PWA–AMR deal together through a stormy year was the employee's $200 million wage and salary concession package. It had been the employees, through their union representatives, who kept the dream alive all along. While other parties vacillated, changed minds and numbers, slapped on new, tougher considerations for its involvement, CAIL's employees were there all along, pushing up their contribution each time the investment resolve of the other parties ebbed and flowed away.

December 31 was no longer the life-and-death deadline for PWA. It had been a year of financial tumult, politics, anguish and near-misses, but CAIL was still flying. In a year end feature the *Globe and Mail*, under the heading, "Think you had a bad year?" cited the wringer PWA's Eyton had been through. There was still uncertainty ahead for his airline. Air Canada's appeal process was still in play. CAIL was still struggling along with about $100 million in cash and was living hand-to-mouth on government loan guarantees. The airline could not enact huge employee layoffs to cut costs, certainly not with those employees holding a $200 million key to survival. CAIL was losing money daily and had been throughout 1993, though it would almost halve its losses compared to 1992. The airline had, by now, sold off much of its excess aircraft but was still looking to lose $292 million for 1993. CAIL's five-year total for losses would edge over $1 billion.

But CAIL was still flying, and Eyton's energy and persistence had a lot to do with it. The fact the airline *was* flying, against almost unseemly odds, had to be the PWA chairman's major accomplishment. It was a long, long way back to the highflying days of 1989, when Max Ward passed over the keys to his airline—along with all its problems—to Eyton.

10 / Taking Direction From Wrong-Way Corrigan

"The result is that at a revolutionary juncture in aviation history, neither carrier is in a position to invest in the future, especially in transborder markets. In consequence, they have to make their pacts where they can, with precious little bargaining leverage—except, perhaps over each other."
— James Bagnell, *Financial Times*, January 6, 1992

AS THE WORLD'S AIRLINES rushed toward new international alliances, particularly among dominating international monopoly carriers, Canada's two struggling airlines were moving further, and more permanently, apart. Although the Gemini lawsuits and disposition of assets were still in doubt as the players entered 1994, it was clear that sometime in the year the PWA–AMR deal would finally be signed—providing Canadian Airlines International did not collapse first. Canada would then have two major "competitive" airlines for a nation of twenty-seven million people. Canada had dutifully followed American free market system orthodoxy to a corporate version of nuclear weaponry's M.A.D.—Mutually Assured Destruction.

No matter what the eventual outcome between the two battered carriers happened to be, neither one would ever challenge the likes of British Airways—or even Singapore Airlines. If they were lucky, the two would continue to struggle on, fighting between themselves for a share of a relatively stagnant domestic market and an increasingly meagre slice of international business. They both would fly with operating costs higher than most competitors, with planes taking off within moments of one another and flying half-empty to the same Canadian destination. Both would continue to attempt to lower operating costs by laying off more employees. Both would widely advertize the belief they were providing travellers with something called "choice," yet an inquiry to either sales office for a full fare economy price quotation would, as we know, sound like a perfect echo.

If they were lucky, one airline would end up as a feeder airline to a foreign mega-carrier while the other would be gobbled up by its American "minority" shareholder. Either way, the U.S. certainly now loomed even larger in Canada's airline future.

We had ingested the mythology of American economic competition at our peril. Where once Canadians might have been quick to follow the light cast by the auras of Lindbergh and Rickenbacker, now we were seemingly being led by Wrong-Way Corrigan, the American aviator who, in 1938, took off from New York, bound for Los Angeles, only to end up landing in Ireland.

In January 1994, *Forbes* magazine reported that U.S. design firm Diefenbach Elkins, hired to work on Air Canada's image make-over, at one point seriously considered dropping the airline's traditional red maple leaf. It was only "after much anguish" the American design firm decided to keep Canada's national symbol. They explained they wanted to portray Canada as "a modern melting pot" and "a kind of innocent America." Perhaps to ensure no cultural mistakes were made, the firm reportedly paid $120,000 on a study to find out "what Canada really is." Had the designers been Canadian, they might have saved themselves some money—and Air Canada some embarrassment.

It was hoped by senior management that Air Canada's face lift would revitalize the carrier's image, end perceptions it was still government-owned and, mysteriously, boost sales, particularly in western Canada. Hollis Harris was quoted as saying the $22 million image make-over would translate into bottom line black ink thanks to increased sales. "We're betting on it," he was reported as saying.

Despite symptoms of a bad case of battle fatigue, the domestic combat between Air Canada and CAIL continued into what was now its third year. Just before Christmas the Liberal cabinet had passed an order extending its $50 million loan guarantee for PWA to June 30, 1997, giving CAIL's parent company more than enough time to close a deal with AMR. On the other hand, Alberta and B.C. offered their loan guarantee extensions only to June 30, 1994, perhaps hoping to push an end to this lingering denouement. But on January 26, Air Canada called a truce.

In a two-sentence media release, Air Canada announced it was dropping all litigation blocking PWA from closing the deal with AMR.

Harris had repeatedly gone on public record saying Air Canada would never allow CAIL to simply stroll away from its Gemini group partnership, because that would kill Gemini and be a severe setback to Air Canada. Now Air Canada was saying it did not matter any more.

However, the airline's one hundred and eighty degree about-face was explainable. In Ottawa, transport minister Douglas Young said he would soon announce the government's position on Air Canada's request for route access into Japan. Industry analysts suspected a *quid pro quo* was at work—if Air Canada quit the fight with CAIL, it would receive the route to Japan the airline was lusting after. Air Canada's dignified battlefield retreat would be rewarded with a juicy bone.

Denying there was a direct connection between the announcements, the next day, January 27, the federal government designated Air Canada as the second Canadian carrier into Japan, though the destination would be Osaka and not the favoured Tokyo Narita airport. Air Canada's forty-three lobbyists must have worked a lot of overtime. "Canada's two great airlines can now get on with their business," Young told the House of Commons with no small dab of political rhetoric. "They are in a position to move with confidence towards the future."

This was certainly no long-term solution to Canada's airlines' problem. Ill-considered government policy-making, questionable management decision making and an unhealthy belief—mentally and physically—that competition strengthened airlines had led the nation to the bizarre point where the Liberal government was saying more competition, this time to Japan, was just what the two Canadian airlines needed.

The Liberals were now left with the question of what to do with the Gemini group and its seven hundred employees. In another run of irony, the Liberals, in particular, Minister of Human Resources Development Lloyd Axworthy, would play the role of ideological bookends. It had been Axworthy who began the airline deregulation ball rolling and now at end game, he would be the one looking for a solution to the Gemini group closure and the possible loss of seven hundred jobs. His interest was quite practical. Many of the jobs were in Winnipeg, where Axworthy's riding was located.

Axworthy had started airline deregulation in 1984. Ten years later, he would begin to review the country's social policies, talking with a similar sense of urgency about the perceived need for a drastic overhaul of the nation's social programs, particularly unemployment insurance. A task force advising the minister initially proposed a radical redesign of unemployment insurance: cutting UI benefit periods in half and eliminating UI premiums for employers. Based on the airline deregulation case study, it would not be unfair to speculate that if the Liberals' do to the nation's social programs what they contributed to the instability of the airline industry, Canadians will be fortunate to have publicly funded poor houses when the Chrétien government is finished bending to the business community's call.

Axworthy had been on the search since December for a way to salvage Gemini by expanding the company's application from an airline computer reservation system into a broadly based data management and telecommunications network, capable of bidding on federal and provincial contracts, perhaps even using federal government loan guarantees to keep it alive. Thankfully, Axworthy deemed that last initiative not feasible. It would have been a matter of adding too much final insult to deregulation and privatization injury.

In late March, IBM Canada Ltd. announced its purchase of the telecommunication network portion of the Gemini group for $50 million. A new company would be set up as an IBM Canada subsidiary, specializing in data management and telecommunications services to IBM clients. Two hundred Gemini contract employees were to get their walking papers. Air Canada's computer reservation system would now be managed by the new Galileo Canada, a wholly owned subsidiary of the airline employing about two hundred of Gemini's former employees. The new company would be headquartered in Winnipeg. Still, the remnants of Gemini would not have existed without the intervention of Lloyd Axworthy. Realistically, he had little choice.

If one followed the Liberal and Tory efforts after a decade of airline deregulation, Canadians not only ended up with two very weak and susceptible airlines, we were also stumbling on the information superhighway. Hundreds of technologically sophisticated jobs could now fall out of the PWA–AMR deal. Oddly, as the Gemini group was being rendered into smaller parts, observers were beginning to note how sophisticated its network had been—linking most

Canadian communities with highspeed, fibre optic telecommunications. Airline deregulation had not only cost Canadians thousands of aerospace jobs, but we also seemed to be losing ground on that high-tech, information-based future. It would have been much better had the politicians let well enough alone.

While the Liberals were wrestling with the ideological residue of the nation's airline mess, the American airline industry was going through its fourth consecutive year of decline. In February 1994, American Airlines laid off more workers and reported a 1993 fourth-quarter loss of US $253 million. Barely three weeks before the PWA–AMR deal would be signed, American announced it lost an average of US $800,000 per day throughout 1993, making the air carrier portion of their business solely responsible for all AMR's US $1.2 billion losses since 1989.

Delta Air Lines, the nation's No. 3 carrier, lost US $159 million in nine months leading into March 1994, and planned to cut up to fifteen thousand employees over the next three years to stay alive. Continental's fourth-quarter loss was US $26.5 million, meaning the fifth largest U.S. carrier had lost US $38.5 million since it emerged from Chapter 11 bankruptcy protection as a "reorganized," slimmed-down carrier. The troubled airline announced at the end of April that, to keep costs down, it was cutting out meals on its money-losing flights. It was probably time for Continental to accept bankruptcy and get it over with.

American West Airlines was still avoiding imminent bankruptcy, resting in Chapter 11, at arm's length from creditors and bills. A reorganization proposal tabled in April would include an offer—led by perpetual money loser, Continental —to buy one-third ownership of the near-bankrupt company for US $245 million. And USAir of Arlington, Virginia expected to lose more than US $200 million in the first quarter of 1994 and was asking its employees for US $1.5 billion in wage and work concessions.

Later in May it would be discovered that the tiny jewel in the American airline crown—Southwest Airlines—the only large domestic air carrier to show a profit in the last four years, had realized a proportion of its balance sheet success by getting a free ride on the backs of other U.S carriers. For twenty years Southwest had been a nonpaying participant in three of the four U.S. computer ticketing systems. The operators of the three major airline ticketing systems—United-USAir's "Apollo," Delta–TWA's "Worldspan" and Continental's "System One"—would decide in May that the courtesy they had been extended to their smaller competitor was coming to an end.

Southwest officials reportedly estimated the free ride on the ticket systems saved them about US $100 million a year, a rather large part of their US $154 million net profit for 1993. When one considered that the darling of America's airline business also did not pay to be linked into a computer reservation system (travel agents booking seats on Southwest had to pick up the telephone and call the company like anyone else)—saving the airline another US $30 million a year—the mystery of how the Dallas-based, no-frills airline made a profit was a bit more evident. A large part of its operational success was less a case of overwhelming business acumen then skillfully avoiding having to pay user fees.

On February 18, Air Canada announced it was continuing "its long climb back toward financial respectability" by reporting a $326 million net loss for 1993, or -$4.23 a share. PWA also reported a $292 million loss for 1993, or -$6.13 a share. Some newspaper analysts considered PWA stock overpriced at $1.35 and recommended selling, pointing out there were many other ways for investors to make money, perhaps including opening a savings account at a chartered bank. The outlook for PWA's future was not considered that bright, despite the sell-out to AMR. Projections by analysts took into account the costly delay in closing the PWA–AMR deal and the anticipated loss in traffic CAIL would suffer when Air Canada began competing on the route to Japan.

Air Canada had also requested route access to Hong Kong, but the Liberal government had throttled back by now. There was evidently enough competitive damage and confusion littering the airline industry tarmac. The Liberals considered the request not to be urgent and reminded everyone again that it was committed to having "two, strong, viable" airlines in Canada. The secret to Canada's future airline success, the Liberals said, was to get down-and-dirty with our cousins to the south and begin negotiating an Open Skies agreement with the Americans. Open Skies would have the potential to be the diplomatic equivalent of airline deregulation.

"The concept of Canada, with a relatively small population base, having two competing international carriers is ludicrous in the extreme, particularly now."

 —Thomas S. Caldwell, President, Caldwell Securities, *The Financial Post*, September 1, 1993

The international aviation industry was no longer one industry driven by a set of simply defined theories, if it had ever been. It was, by the winter of 1994, a series of competing, and at times contradictory, business ideologies jockeying for position and dominance. And despite the howls of North American apologists, academics and acolytes calling for everyone to move to the heavens and "go global," the one consistent factor in this international turbulence was that most nations were fighting, in any way they could, to improve their position by reducing the amount of competition they faced. Only the Americans and the Canadians seemed locked in an antiquated moral certitude about the value of domestic competition, consumer sovereignty, wealth creation and free market principles. The rest of the world was getting into bare-knuckle gear. They would fight all right, sometimes perversely, but most nations were not at all prepared to succumb to the North American idealism of governments not having a major say in the competitive marketplace.

In mid-March, the BBC reported that Margaret Thatcher, the free-enterpriser and privatization moll, had threatened almost a decade ago to sabotage strategic arms limitation talks if the U.S. justice department did not back off in its intention to prosecute senior executives of then government-owned British Airways. BA was being fingered for forcing Britain's high-profile free-enterpriser, Sir Freddie Laker, out of business. To stop the justice department forays, Thatcher "bombarded the Reagan administration" with requests to cancel the investigation, including a threat to withdraw her support of Reagan and his Star Wars initiative at the 1985 Moscow strategic arms limitation talks.

Thatcher and her advisors were desperate to privatize British Airways. That would not happen until February 1987. But Thatcher felt a successful criminal action could have grave consequences for the privatization of Britain's prized international air carrier. The prosecutions never proceeded. The prime minister's blatant intervention was seen by Laker and others as a reversal of her "strongly capitalist private enterprise philosophy." Thatcher's actions revealed that all that talk about opening up skies and levelling playing fields was theoretical bunting.

Thatcher wanted one large, financially successful British airline to carry the national flag in the international marketplace, not a bunch of competing airlines, most of whom would lose money and always be one step away from embarrassing and costly bankruptcy proceedings. When played out in the real world, the security of the state and its institutions—public and private, their economic viability and ultimate success—took precedence over any notions about consumer sovereignty.

In fact, at this time there were few doctrinal systems anyone could believe in. It was mix-and-match time in the economic theory business. The global marketplace was not gearing up to enjoy the benefits of healthy competition. If anything, competition was what many members of the international airline club wanted to throttle. Talks among large national European carriers about forming Alcazar were talks about concentrating ownership and business power, and apportioning national prominence—not about increasing unrestricted competition between the parties.

Canadians seemed to have it backwards. The Liberals had just announced their support for "a strong, viable and competitive" domestic airline industry, one in which the nation's two airlines would apparently be allowed to continue to compete with one another to their mutual demise. When profit came to loss, even the American business mind was never as naive as the Canadian.

North American deregulationists and free trade advocates began to stumble across two sobering realities by 1994. First, the road to national economic growth was still to be found in domestic trade and consumption, not necessarily down the road of international trade. Second, government regulation of industry and trade barriers were actually helping to keep some nations wealthy, certainly relative to Canada and the United States.

In fact, U.S. exports still represented less than ten per cent of their Gross Domestic Product. As American economist Paul Krugman wrote, "the U.S. economy is almost ninety per cent self-contained, producing goods and services for its own use. Similar calculations for the European Community and Japan yield similar results . . . National living standards are overwhelmingly determined by domestic factors rather than by competition for world markets."

Proper government regulation and prudent restrictions on trade strengthened industries and vastly improved national wealth through economic stability—not chaos. In June 1994, international management consultant Kenichi Ohmae reminded anyone prepared to listen that nations have always regulated and protected particular noncompetitive industries to prevent unemployment and to maintain economic and social stability. Taking American free market system dogma at its theoretical word could cause worldwide catastrophe. Deregulating and opening the Japanese marketplace would result in an unemployment rate of forty per cent—compared to three per cent in 1994. The move would no doubt delight free trade theorists, but it would ruin Japan's economy.

The same degree of unemployment—forty per cent—was predicted for a deregulated, free market European Economic Community. The Swiss voted against joining the EEC. They already claimed the highest GNP in the world. Why would a nation trade that status for a tenuous and unproven theory about the benefits of unrestricted competition on behalf of the sovereign consumer?

That nether world of North American business beliefs only got more bizarre when it was reported that Adam Smith's warning—that when "people of the same trade" get together, they will immediately start conspiring to raise consumer prices—was true. On March 17, the six largest airlines in the U.S. agreed with the Department of Justice that between 1988 and 1992—during the apogee of deregulation and the healthy competition it generated—they had conspired to fix the price of air fares. The conspirators included American, Delta, Northwest, Continental, TWA and Alaska airlines. The cost of their price fixing to the American traveller was estimated to be at least US $2.5 billion.

No fines were laid and no jail sentences were handed out. Under the 1978 U.S. airline deregulation legislation, "discussions" about ticket prices were legal. As a consequence of this rather liberal allowance to business, the six air carriers just quietly bumped the discussions up to the point where they were manipulating the price air travellers were paying for their tickets. The airlines had used their airline tariff publishing computers to carry on conversations, as one assistant attorney-general put it, "just as directly and detailed as those traditionally conducted by conspirators over the telephone or in hotel rooms." Although their method was novel, the conduct of the airlines "amounted to price fixing, plain and simple."

This was the second incident of conspiracy to fix U.S. airline ticket prices since deregulation was introduced in 1978. In 1993, nine carriers had settled a class action suit with between US $450 and $600 million worth of refunds to four million travellers. As satisfying as the proof of Smith's axiom might have been to deregulation's critics, it just proved once again that the "invisible hand" could usually be found—quite visibly—rummaging through the consumer's pocket.

As if to underline this very human tendency, in late February it was reported that five top executives of Minnesota-based Northwest Airlines Inc. received bonuses of more than US $2.3 million for their work in 1993. The good news was they voted themselves the bonus after a year of hard work keeping Northwest out of bankruptcy. The bad news was the bonuses came in a year when the airline lost US $115 million—a year in which those same executives had negotiated an agreement that saw the employees of Northwest take US $886 million in pay cuts.

> *"The United States government is prepared to flex its muscles to force an open skies regime on the rest of the world. That was the hard-hitting message delivered recently to IATA members by U.S. Secretary of Transportation Frederico Pena. [He] wants to dismantle the current bilateral system in favour of multilateral and regional accords, and intends to 'tear down the barriers to competition.' "*
> —Canadian Travel Press, November 18, 1993

Stuck with one limping and one crippled domestic air carrier, faced with competition on international routes neither airline could successfully fight against, silently embarrassed by the failed promises of Canadian airline deregulation, searching desperately for an ideologically correct door out of this mess, the nation's neoconservative tub thumpers began beating their instruments to the tune of "Open Skies." Canada's airline deregulation horror could be made good again, they said, if we succumbed to the American passion for ending bilateral agreements on what airlines could fly where, and how often, across the 49th Parallel.

Report on Business columnists Terence Corcoran and Peter Cook began applauding the American move towards an Open Skies agreement with Canada, saying it would provide the thoroughly beleaguered domestic airline industry with "new room for optimism." An Open Skies agreement was always the deregulationists' version of Milo Minderbender's personal application of Catch-22. No matter how inappropriate, wrong or damaging their economic theories about consumer sovereignty, wealth generation and freedom in the marketplace were, they could always explain their lack of success by saying their theories had not been applied widely enough to be successful. Like Milo, if deregulation had resulted in immense loss and industry chaos, it was only because we had forgotten it was a universal concept. You had to open the skies *of the entire world* to make it work, they were now saying.

If one kept preaching faith in a higher level of truth to achieve market success—like Open Skies between Canada and the United States, and then, Open Skies for the Whole World—eventually, the inconsistencies of commercial competition would be levelled and consumer prices for air fares would drop. We would all then—all six billion of us, having reached that deregulated consumer heaven—be seated side-by-side with the likes of Milton Friedman ("I have yet to meet the problem for which more government regulation is the answer")—Adam Smith having vacated his seat long ago in disgust.

The Open Skies concept, like the thinking of its supporters, was quaint. Such an agreement would dismantle the current bilateral aviation arrangement in favour of multilateral and regional accords stating whose airline could fly where and when. It would be done in the interests of balance, fairness and mutual access to each other's markets—the very tenets of free trade and open competition working to make life better for the consumer. Artificial barriers such as national boundaries would be torn down in the interests of international commercial competition, leading to lower fare prices for consumers, more air travel and dynamic growth for the industry and the nation in question—just like airline deregulation had in Canada, one supposes.

But what its proponents never mentioned was that Open Skies never did mean healthy competition between Canadian and American carriers. Prodded by their industry, the Clinton administration, like the Bush and Reagan governments before it, wanted open-sky access to Canadian markets so American airlines could escape their increasingly saturated marketplace, expand their operational reach and beat the ailerons off of Canada's now-weakened and inferior Canadian air carriers.

Open Skies discussions had been going on, it seemed, forever. There had been as many as a dozen previous rounds of air service talks that went exactly nowhere. The last round collapsed primarily because U.S. airlines were not able to secure the access they wanted into Toronto, Vancouver and Montreal. Canadian representatives were not pleased with the fact Canada's carriers were being denied—at the same time—access to a number of major U.S. cities.

It was almost naive beyond belief to think the Americans were not going to negotiate from a position of pure self-interest. While the Open Skies tom-toms echoed through the commercial jungle in early 1994, Canada was poised at the brink of a potential trade war with the U.S. The issue was the unfair and highhanded way the Americans had badgered and attacked Canada's positions on trade in grain, lumber, pork and steel—under the Free Trade Agreement. In a speech in Washington in late May, Canada's trade minister Roy MacLaren openly criticized the Americans for persistently working to protect U.S. interests by unfairly blocking Canadian exports. The Americans had even badmouthed Canada's wheat export program, accusing Canada of predatory pricing, as U.S. Secretary of Agriculture Mike Espy did on a trip to Brazil. The acrimony got so intense that the U.S. ambassador to Canada, James Blanchard, came to Canada's defence over the grain dispute, criticizing Espy for attacking Canada's wheat pricing policies without presidential approval—in effect saying Espy did not know what he was talking about. Within days, and after the powerful U.S. farm lobby moved into action, Ambassador Blanchard was forced to reverse his defence of Canadian policies and say Espy was doing "a great job" and that Canada was more protectionist than the U.S.

Behind the American confrontational approach to free trade was the disturbing reality that their American accusations about Canada's trade practices had always been found, by a series of bilateral dispute-settlement panel decisions, to be patently false. But being on the side of right means nothing when dealing with the gathered might of U.S. lobbying self-interest.

On August 1, Canada was forced by U.S. threats—to impose

import restrictions on Canadian wheat—to sign an agreement to reduce this nation's wheat exports to the U.S. over the next year from 2.5 million tonnes to 1.5 million tonnes. The same day it was reported that the Japanese government had responded to a threat of U.S. trade sanctions by threatening to sever U.S. access to Japanese markets—particularly its US $10 billion a year telecommunications market. The issue in international trade was not about competition. It was about economic strength and the application of its power by governments. Some governments are evidently capable of negotiating with that power, on behalf of their domestic businesses, and some are not.

Americans do not play softball. Their trade representatives were prepared to tie up the issue, the exporters, their money and those simplistic Canadian beliefs in free trade simply because it was important that they win. And up against this kind of international hardball harassment, Canadian Open Skies advocates were still prepared to believe, and preach, that Canada would be treated ever so gently and ever so fairly in any Open Skies negotiations.

After fifteen months of no progress whatsoever, an agreement to talk about Open Skies—not negotiate, talk—was reached between Minister of Transport Douglas Young and U.S. Secretary of Transportation Frederico Pena in late March 1994. A month later, the talks collapsed—again. This time the two parties could not even agree on a basis for negotiating Open Skies—what subjects there might be to talk about—let alone talk about a new agreement. Young explained nothing would be gained at this point, the end of April 1994, by going back to the negotiating table. Pena was still eager to talk and claimed there were "enormous opportunities" in air transportation talks between the two countries. A much more subdued Young talked about the need for Canadians to ensure their airline industry had a "level playing field" and "an opportunity to survive" before proceeding further with Open Skies. Young had evidently stared into the cavernous mouth of the American Lion and it was not the animal's bad breath that made him run hastily back to Ottawa.

New PWA boss hopes to pilot 'happy times'.
"The words 'fresh start' are loaded with meaning these days for Kevin Jenkins, who last week took over the reins of PWA Corp. After dedicating the past two years to crisis management, Jenkins—who replaced company

veteran Rhys Eyton—is looking forward to a signing ceremony Wednesday that is expected to usher in a new era of 'happy times' for the Calgary-based airline company."

—Claudia Cattaneo, *Calgary Herald*, April 25, 1994

After twenty-seven years of service with the Calgary-based airline, Rhys Eyton resigned as president and chief executive officer of PWA on April 15, less than two weeks before the AMR deal would be signed. Eyton would stay on as chairman of the PWA board. He was replaced by thirty-seven year old Kevin Jenkins, a lawyer and MBA graduate from Harvard. He had been CAIL's president the past three years.

Eyton's ride at PWA was not unlike a metaphor for the airline industry. He arrived when PWA was a struggling but profitable regional airline with good future prospects. He helped raise both its sights and its profits as the airline fought its way to the top of the nation's ladder, pushing aside competitors as big as CP Air and Wardair to nestle aggressively in plane-to-plane competition with once-mighty Air Canada. And then it all began to unravel to the point where the net value of the airline Eyton was passing on to Jenkins was less than when it had all begun.

Eyton had stepped aboard a Canadian airline owned by private investors. For a time, PWA had even been owned by the Alberta government. Now its offspring, CAIL, was one-third owned by a foreign holding company and one-quarter owned by its employees. The debt-burdened airline had been saved, if that was the correct term, by the sacrifices of its employees and an embarrassed and reluctant Mulroney government. Eyton termed the airline's survival as "nothing short of a miracle."

A little over two weeks after Eyton stepped aside, only days after the PWA–AMR deal was finalized, PWA stock led the Toronto Stock Exchange in record volume trading as senior PWA creditors, it was speculated, unloaded the PWA shares they received the previous week as settlement in the debt-for-equity agreement. PWA shares ended the day trading at fifty cents. If some analysts had been urging PWA stockholders to sell at $1.35 a share, they now were probably counselling jump. At best, PWA shares were being rated on the market as speculative.

Still, everyone involved was trying to put a brave face on events. Some CAIL employees talked about "landing the big fish," though more than one thousand of them would pay for the prize with their jobs. The life-saving agreement with AMR was signed on April 27, sparking a proliferation of "new era" articles in the daily press. The deal signing meant a "fresh financial start" for CAIL. Jenkins glowed: "Unlike any other airline company I know of, we're coming out of a financial restructuring with our service levels higher," whatever that meant. It did not mean lower fares for Canadian travellers.

"AMR, PWA pact means fewer cheaper seats," the April 28 edition of the *Vancouver Sun* trumpeted quite accurately. CAIL could no longer pretend, like Air Canada, that it made business sense to fly airplanes and charge prices less than cost. The result for the Canadian consumer would be inevitable. Aircraft capacity would be cut back and fares would have to rise—by as much as twenty per cent—if there was any hope of CAIL making real money some day.

On CBC Newsworld a week earlier, Jenkins squirmed noticeably when asked if the life-saving deal would result in lower air fares for consumers. At first he avoided the question. When pressed a second time, Jenkins talked about "providing better service" for air travellers and "more choice." Canadians should be proud they once again had competition in the airline industry, he said. On the day CAIL's sword was passed to AMR, Jenkins admitted to Southam News that "stability" in the Canadian airline business would probably make it harder to find cheap seats on Canada's airlines. "There may be less deep-discount fares around because of [better] management of capacity," he was quoted. "In some ways, customers should be sending thank-yous," he went on in puzzling hubris.

Jenkins' airline would return to financial health, in part, by raising ticket prices, even though the competitive environment had stabilized, which, in theory at least, was meant to be the mechanism for making prices go down. And if Canadian consumers did not get the ticket price drop "healthy competition" was supposed to provide, they should then be happy because "service" would improve. Strange was not a strong enough word for these events.

"This was one of those rare win–win transactions that brings benefit to all parties," Jenkins went on about the finalizing of the PWA–AMR pact. "I think this is a win for consumers," because CAIL's survival meant travellers would have a choice of major scheduled airlines. But the price of an air fare in Canada, perhaps even discount fares, was going up.

If fares remained at lower levels, one or both airlines would be out of business. And then Canadians would have an opportunity to "choose" which *new*, replacement airline they wished to fly on—which was what was supposed to happen when you had true deregulation. But this was not deregulation. This was regulation by duopoly—two, semi-crippled airlines telling the consumer, by virtue of their perilous financial circumstances, and with the tacit support of frightened and confused federal governments, that they could not afford to drop their prices. They could not even afford to go out of business.

Like the Conservatives and the Liberals, airline executives were using terms that obscured, not clarified, reality. As Paul Krugman, economist and author of *Peddling Prosperity* pointed out in the spring issue of *Foreign Affairs*, too many of the world's leaders had found the "competitive" jargon useful as a political device: "The rhetoric of competitiveness turns out to provide a good way either to justify hard choices or to avoid them." What Jenkins was really saying was that he and about fifteen thousand other employees had held on to their jobs and wanted to keep them.

"We're going to be profitable next year," Jenkins predicted at the signing ceremony. Perhaps they were. The price of air fares was going up. An improving economy might allow traffic and revenues to rise. Wage and salary costs would be down $200 million over the next few years, thanks to employee concessions. And if the airline did not go out and take delivery of a scad of costly new aircraft, or start into another costly fare war with Air Canada, CAIL might just move into the black after years in the red. But, then again, it might not.

In May, Jenkins would talk about CAIL now having a "very, very strong foundation for growth." He announced his airline would move aggressively into the Asia Pacific market, but it would need to raise cash flow by another $200 million a year. He did not indicate where that surprising lump of new cash might come from. It was unlikely to come from any new issues of PWA stock.

At the same time, on the other side of the runway, Hollis Harris was admitting the international airline business was in a shambles. But Air Canada intended to get more competitive by lowering operating costs, expanding its routes and modernizing its aircraft fleet. Unlike CAIL, Air Canada was sporting a 1993 year-end cash and short-term investment kitty of $845 million, the kind of dollar power an airline could use effectively if it were inclined to put more pressure on a struggling competitor—and run it out of business. After all, this was the world of hands-off government and regulatory rules that allowed the competitors to duke it out to the last airline, was it not?

CAIL would be back in dire financial straits quickly enough if Air Canada decided to play rough again. Even with AMR on board, CAIL's survival was not at all certain. After all, AMR was the company in transition—looking for reasonable ways to bail out of the airline business. Anything could happen again in this marketplace—minus a true regulator.

CAIL would also announce on May 3 that it was taking on another money-losing route. The airline declared that after a four-year absence CAIL would be flying to Beijing again—but losing money on every flight. Airline officials admitted it would take a long time before this particular service showed a profit, but there was a "tremendous opportunity" in the long term. One could only hope the long term CAIL was planning on was not that of British economist John Maynard Keynes, when he pointed out to an overly enthusiastic critic that "in the long term, we are all dead."

When CAIL had previously flown to Beijing and Shanghai, its aircraft, on average, flew more than half empty. "This is the beginning of a new era for our company," one official announced. Following the reopening of the Beijing route, flights to Shanghai and Guangzhou would resume over the next year. It was not stated, however, whether fresh Cold Lake whitefish would be part of the cargo.

Airline deregulation in Canada had bequeathed Canadians two uncompetitive air carriers. One would now have its future, despite protests to the contrary, dictated and controlled by the instincts and presence of an American airline. To remain competitive, the other airline would have to continue to align itself with other major international carriers, perhaps at some point selling large portions of its control to them. Growth was in international, not domestic skies, and it would be impossible for either carrier, while they split markets between them, to compete successfully with the emerging mega-carriers. By July 1994, IATA would report Air Canada had now slipped to twenty-second place in the list of the world's top fifty airlines ranked by the number of passengers flown, while CAIL wallowed in thirty-first place.

Although marginal profits were a possibility, their chances of making substantial profits in the near future were problematic at best. While passenger revenue traffic was up slightly by May 1994 over the last year, both airlines still sported embarrassing load factor percentages. CAIL was flying its planes one-third empty, on average. Air Canada's load percentage had slipped to sixty-two per cent, meaning almost forty per cent of the oranges were still going bad on an average flight. Those percentages kept telling anyone who looked that we were a nation with one-too-many major airlines.

While representatives of both airlines talked enthusiastically about focusing their energies on more international travel, in May 1994, Statistics Canada published data suggesting Canadians were cutting down on travel outside the country. Chances of growth in lucrative business travel were also limited. Between 1991 and 1993, Canadian business travel dropped twenty-five per cent, while the percentage of discounted fares increased. Like their international peers, many Canadian companies and corporations were cutting back on air travel and telecommuting instead. Many who were still flying on business were choosing economy rather than business-class fares; others were even travelling on cheap, nonrefundable tickets. Even if the economy did improve and business travel did pick up, these factors would contribute to narrower profit margins and lower yields.

Both Canadian carriers would continue to fly, in the short term at least, in self-defeating, competitive route patterns, while the world's smarter nations were consolidating airline power in single, major air carriers. The day the PWA–AMR agreement was consummated, Air Canada's Harris announced that his airline had called on the federal government to "immediately" allow it to fly to Hong Kong—the fastest growing air market in the world—in direct competition with CAIL. Hong Kong represented an extra $100 million in sales and an estimated $10 million in profit for Air Canada—much of which would come out of existing CAIL business. "Now that they have a deal with American, please quit coddling and protecting the guys in the West," he was quoted by Canadian Press. "Let the federal and provincial governments quit loaning them money and let competition take place."

If the possibility of even more reckless competition between the two airlines did not hint at a bleak future for both, there was always those telltale self-destructive impulses at work. As if to polish the fortune teller's crystal ball to a higher gloss, two weeks after the PWA-AMR nuptials, Air Canada would announce it was summarily dumping its previous plan to remanufacture its fleet of thirty-five DC-9 jets rather than buy new aircraft. It cancelled its plans to launch a whole new profitable sideline of refitting DC-9s for other air carriers—the sort of job creating, socially responsible decision a government-owned air carrier might be compelled to make. Instead, Air Canada locked itself into an agreement for twenty-five new A319 Airbuses valued at about $1 billion. Air Canada's decision to acquire the A319s was based, not on any value-added benefit to this country, but simply on the urge to get their hands on more new aircraft.

Like Froggie when he spotted his first motorcar in Walt Disney's version of *Wind in the Willows*, Air Canada would go with the decision that made the least sense, in national terms, and perhaps not much business sense, either. The airline had apparently been attracted by the generous lease-back terms for the $39 million airplanes. They would begin arriving in December 1996. About that time, the impact of the decision would begin showing up indelibly on the airline's books. Battered or not, the cavaliers just could not resist the gleam of a new piece of iron.

The next day the crystal ball glowed even more ominously when Air Atlantic announced it had filed for bankruptcy protection from its creditors. Air Atlantic was a regional feeder airline, forty-five per cent owned by Canadian Airlines International. Air Atlantic operated Dash-8 aircraft, several of which were reportedly purchased with the backing of federal loan insurance. If the regional connector airline were to go bankrupt, the loss to the federal government could be as high as $53 million, if the aircraft could not be disposed of. The lenders were at no risk but the taxpayers were.

Air Atlantic president Craig Dobbin told the *Globe and Mail* he was seeking further help from the federal government, but not in the form of a cash bail-out. Instead, he wanted Ottawa to intervene and help settle a competitive battle between Air Atlantic and Air Canada's affiliate on the east coast, Air Nova. It sounded like a call for a return to airline regulation. "The aviation business in this country is a very sick baby," Dobbin said. To compete, Dobbin said Air Atlantic had been obliged to fly too many planes into too many cities. As a result, most of his planes had been flying half empty and at a considerable loss. "If this is not resolved, we're looking at a single operator in Atlantic Canada," said Dobbin, "and nobody wants that."

We certainly would not want *that* now, would we?

Air Canada profit gains altitude
"Air Canada has reported a sharp rise in profit for the second quarter of 1994 reflecting tight cost controls and a recovery in the travel industry. Coupled with similarly buoyant results from PWA *[Corp.] earlier this month, the news is leading financial analysts to predict that Canadian airlines are finally taking off after years of disastrous results."*
—The *Globe and Mail*, August 11, 1994

"The industry is on the upswing," said one analyst in response to the two airlines' 1994 second-quarter results. "The darkest days are behind them." The optimism was sparked by the announcements that PWA had achieved a $1.5 million profit in the second quarter and Air Canada had just announced a profit of $27 million—up from the $14 million reported for the same period a year ago. The *Globe* reported that PWA's financial news was the most dramatic: the second-quarter profit compared very favourably to last year's loss of $130.6 million in the same period.

A PWA spokesperson called the results "turning the corner," although he admitted the results had to be "considerably better" if the company, even with AMR's support, was to survive in the intensely competitive airline business. Air Canada's Hollis Harris was quoted as seeing "a market recovery in full progress," though his airline's results were only a $13 million improvement over 1993. He was cautiously projecting a break-even position for his airline at year-end, although some analysts could now see Air Canada finally posting a profit for 1994, after four consecutive years of losses. PWA's year-end numbers would most likely reflect a small loss, confirming the airline's statement in February that it was "poised for a return to profitability in 1995."

This renewed sense of hope ("the worst of all evils," as Nietzsche put it, "because it prolongs the torments of man") was based on a number of favourable factors: passenger numbers had risen, yields for both airlines were up and, most important, costs had remained relatively stable. Fuel, sales commissions and in-flight meal costs had remained flat or had risen only slightly. The airlines' biggest cost—labour—had remained static thanks to wage concessions, layoffs and attrition. Nevertheless, the good news did not do much to bolster investor confidence. Air Canada shares closed for the week up one-eighth to $7.00 and PWA ended the week at fifty-seven cents, after rising one cent on the announcement of its second quarter results.

To top it off, the airlines were entering their most lucrative operating period—the July-August-September third quarter of the fiscal year. In the airline business, almost everyone made money in the third quarter, even Continental. But Canada was enjoying a dramatic increase in tourism and travel in the summer of 1994—thanks to very modest economic growth and a heavily devalued Canadian dollar. More Canadians were flying on vacation travel than ever before and foreign tourists—thanks to the lower Canadian dollar—were flocking into the country in almost unheard of numbers. The two airlines could not help but benefit in the third quarter from this explosion in travel. One could almost sense the euphoria that would accompany the profit numbers when the airlines' third-quarter results were reported in late October or early November.

But close scrutiny of the numbers and factors contributing to the building optimism revealed that the two carriers could be riding the crest of a very short wave. Some hopeful analysts saw two good years for the industry. But Statistics Canada reported in August that the economic growth everyone was depending on may have already peaked. The Canadian economy "may have already achieved its high-water mark for the year." The summer of 1994 might be as good as it gets, partly because of a slowdown in economic growth, but mostly because the fundamentals of the nation's airline business were still wrong. If the airline industry had turned a corner, as some said, it should be remembered that a block was square. Turn three more times and you were back where you started.

Although the press were quick to congratulate the airlines for "controlling their costs," in fact, the major elements each had "control" of were barely controllable. The airlines still carried billions in various forms of debt. Together, they had lost over $2 billion since 1990. The scheduled purchase of expensive new aircraft waited at one of the corners. Both airlines would need to generate substantial profits to erase the burdens of the financial past as well as cope with the future. The price of fuel could rise instantly with the next angry diplomatic move in the Middle East. The price of other goods and services to the airlines had been pegged at values tied to the tail-end of a recession and were certain to begin rising again in 1995. By the time two years was up, every dollar a CAIL employee made would be worth far less than it did in 1992, thanks to inflation (particularly in high growth cities like Vancouver and Calgary where many lived) and the wage concessions made to save the airlines, possibly fuelling new wage demands. And if the enthusiasm over CAIL's 1994 second-quarter profit performance were tested against revenue generated in that period, the airline's profit margin was an astronomically thin 0.2066 per cent. Air Canada's was hardly much better at 2.79 per cent.

The sidebar comparison of the two airlines' numbers still revealed Canada had one-too-many airlines. Having both competing domestically was bad enough, but having both competing internationally was ludicrous in the extreme. Those pathetically thin profit margins were propped up with numbers that said Air Canada and CAIL were essentially splitting a market made for one.

Air Canada reported $966 million in revenue for the second quarter; CAIL reported $726.9 million. Air Canada reported 3.509 million passenger miles flown; CAIL reported 3.541 million. Air Canada reported a passenger load factor of 63.5 per cent; CAIL reported 70.5 per cent. Air Canada's efforts yielded 18.27 cents per passenger mile; CAIL's 15.3 cents per passenger mile.

However, if these were the numbers of a single major Canadian carrier—with about $7 billion in annual revenues, twenty-eight million passenger miles flown, yields of 17 cents or more per passenger mile and a profit at the end of the year instead of "break-even" or losses "considerably better than expected"—Canada would have a carrier competing in the world's top ten list of airlines, not one struggling to stay in No. 22 position and the other languishing in thirty-first place.

A day after the release of its second-quarter results, Air Canada announced it would begin sharing facilities and passengers with All Nippon Airways (ANA), Japan's largest airline. Air Canada had already signed a commercial agreement with ANA, but the alliance would now include joint promotions and operations, such as common check-in counters. Air Canada would begin service to Osaka on September 20 with four flights a week from Toronto via Vancouver. Although the

Osaka airport did not compare to Tokyo as a destination—Tokyo was CAIL territory—the commercial link with ANA, it was said, would give Air Canada better access to other Japanese cities, allowing the Montreal-based carrier to compete more effectively with its Calgary-based rival.

Competitive moves like this would continue to make it harder for either airline to realize the kind of profits each needed to ever return to full financial health and respectable growth. As rosy a picture as airline management and analysts tried to paint about prospects for 1994 and beyond, it was clear that we were witnessing the struggles of a severely fatigued domestic industry—and another weakened national institution. The folly of Canadian airline deregulation—government policy based on market forces and competition—was a failure.

One cannot strengthen a nation's economy, enhance its culture or improve its social system by making the consumer or the investor sovereign. One cannot base the foundation for a lasting nation on self-interest. The contemporary beliefs about the doctrines of Adam Smith—the advantages of individual enterprise, capitalism, free markets and the invisible hand—can perhaps make an individual rich, but they cannot make a nation—or its institutions—strong.

Adam Smith, were he to return to North America today, would be no advocate of airline deregulation. Smith saw freedom to trade motivated by self-interest, but he saw it leading to socially beneficial results—not mindless competition and the elimination of government management of the economy. He was a pragmatist. He was as concerned about working for the common good of the nation as he was about individual wealth.

When I set out to write this book, I was convinced it would simply be a story about airplanes and airlines, a bit about bush pilots-turned-entrepreneurs, a bit about the role of government and a look at the economics of a very troubled industry. It did not turn out that way. The more I read, the more traces I followed, the more I became convinced that this was a story about how we see ourselves as a nation—or do not, as the case may be. It became a story about the degree to which we value a distinctive Canadian culture, and how quickly we can be prepared to sell it out for the promise of future commercial gain. It became a story about the misconception that a satisfied capital investor is more important than real national economic growth and jobs.

It is also a story about how we make a huge, perhaps fatal, mistake when we become too enamoured by the theories, beliefs and experiences of other nations and try to make them our own. The result inevitably is not a strengthening of our nation and our economy, but a weakening.

It also became a story about valuing the things that have helped make Canadian society as distinctive as it can be and, surprisingly, the envy of much of the world. The strength of those values depends upon our collective belief that some of the things we do—the histories we attend to, the laws we make, the institutions we mould, the manner in which we wish to be governed, the way we treat each other, the way we conduct commerce—are, or have often been, superior in fact and in practice to those of other nations. When we have had so much, built so much good, it can be devastating to simply discard it all because, in a fit of economic self-doubt or national braggadocio, we try to adopt theories that run counter to our national interest and national success.

It also became a story about how Canadians now define the role of government in their lives. Increasingly, the word "government" has become a much too sullied term. For those who believe the less government we have the better, it is too often characterized by dangerously flip throw-away terms like "bureaucrats," "central planners," "command economies" and "state control." These people enjoy making government synonymous with "costly regulations," "inefficiency" and "punitive taxation," ignoring the essential and positive role good government can play in our lives.

There are times when a lessening of government regulation makes some sense, particularly when an industry has reached a proper level of maturity and the capital infrastructure has expanded excessively under monopoly protection, as in the case of telephones and telecommunications in Canada. Prudently regulated competition, not necessarily complete deregulation, then makes some sense.

There are also times when government regulations, in attempting to control cartels or monopolies, have helped make certain businesses almost unreasonably secure and profitable. A case in point is Canada's financial industry.

Under gracious regulation, in 1993, a year in which small businesses were literally crying for loans and investment funds, three of the nation's five most profitable corporations were banks. A 1994 survey revealed that Canadian businesses with fewer than fifty employees were now being turned down for loans or lines of credit by Canadian banks at double the rate they were in 1990.

But as distasteful as the excesses or inattentiveness of some regulation might seem, sweeping elimination of government regulation in all sectors is no solution at all. The solution is to regulate properly, not deregulate. There are too many weaker interests to protect in a body politic to take government out of the equation entirely.

If all that Canadians truly wanted, in this particular case, was cheaper air fares, regardless of the cost to the Canadian airline industry, then getting government out of the rule-making business might have made some sense. But you cannot make the consumer the sovereign element in a nation state without devaluing the nation itself. A consumer only demands. A citizen also gives back.

A nation—a country—cannot just be a place in which to make money, to acquire individual wealth. There must be other reasons for coming together in social compact, to contribute in various ways to each other's welfare while strengthening ourselves as a nation. The one institution responsible for guiding myriad forces in that direction must be government. It cannot be the marketplace.

"Government" is really each of us, not some spooky abstract term used to angrily define Revenue Canada or the Workers' Compensation Board. Without government setting the rules and regulations by which we all seek to benefit, we are little more than anarchists. In some cases, well-to-do anarchists, but anarchists nevertheless.

The political forces conspiring to downsize government in Canada—in particular, to deregulate and to privatize public enterprises—have been at work for almost two decades. In some instances what they recommend makes some sense, especially the less extreme efforts for controlling elements of government spending and working to reduce the national debt. But overall, the economic benefits to Canada of deregulation and privatization are highly suspect. In fact, it is conceivable that deregulation and privatization may have caused irreparable harm to the foundation of the Canadian economy. In many ways, these two misguided initiatives may have helped to widen the gap between the rich and the poor.

We were told deregulation of industry would lead to more international competitiveness, lower consumer prices and a stronger national economy. Yet, in Canada, as in the United States and Great Britain—the other two countries where both panaceas have been variously applied—the results have been nothing close to what was expected.

In the United States, the womb of modern marketplace deregulation, the biggest industrial companies enjoyed a banner year in 1993, earning $63 billion in profits—enough to wipe out the U.S. trade deficit with Japan. But total employment among Fortune 500 companies fell for the ninth straight year, while their earnings were up fifteen percent over 1992.

Those record profits were considered "American industry's steady, relentless drive to raise productivity, improve quality, and boost competitiveness." But it was at the expense of a large number of its citizens who were laid off in corporate efforts to lower costs, become "more efficient" and, in many cases, allow that higher dividends be paid to investors.

Who, then, is benefiting in such a political economy? How strong, then, are America and Canada when dividends are more important than the comfort, self-respect and security of millions of its citizens?

We make a terrible mistake when we forget that one of government's most important functions is ensuring fairness in society. One other is being vigilant, on the citizen's behalf, about checking the exploitive excesses of commercial competition. Somewhere in the misguided Canadian economic process we have decided that shareholders and the consumer are more important than the citizen.

What the tracks of the Canadian airline industry tragedy lead back to is the seductive American belief system that says wealth creation is *the* goal. The consumer is always sovereign. Governments—with their burdensome rules and regulations and taxes—should just get out of the way. Individuals, in the form of entrepreneurs or corporate representatives, will work in their self-interest. Their enhanced status will provide efficient businesses, lower prices, more jobs and a stronger economy.

But current economic realities notwithstanding, how do you

strengthen the economic and social foundations of a nation based on the primacy of a consumer and a business climate that endorses destructive competition? The answer is: You do not.

What some Americans and Canadians are only now slowly beginning to realize is that the nation which cares more about how much jingle there is in a consumer's pocket than about the formation of a strong and stable society is in deep trouble.

If the competition is over who gets to govern and who gets to make the correct political decisions, then democracy and capitalism are incompatible—as some media and business representatives are beginning to imply. But a nation, a society, is supposed to be like a warm house we share cooperatively. A society that cherishes self-interest and competition above all else is like living in a cold cave where the inhabitants "gain" by throwing rocks at one another.

If we wish to truly benefit as consumers in a national body politic we must recognize there are limits, not only defined by the damage we do with errant economic theories, but defined by our commitment to that body politic, that nation. Why else do we gather as a nation? To get a cheaper price on an air fare between Regina and Toronto?

If the consumer is to be sovereign, that sovereignty must exist within limits. It is not the best price that we are meant to enjoy, but the best price available after considering the costs and benefits to others who share our space in the body politic. And it is up to government—us—to see that the apportionment is fair.

As the notion began circulating in North America in 1993 and 1994, that a diminution of government's role in commerce, international trade and the national economy might not be such a bully idea, Canadian free market gospellers were still beating the drums for "less government"—including members of the current Liberal government. While other national governments were strengthening their competitive position vis à vis the United States—providing copious amounts of funding for research and development, facilitating access to capital, providing regulations and competitive advantages to allow their companies to compete successfully on the global battlefield, and in many cases, driving American corporations to the edge of financial ruin—Canada was doing its best, as seen through the tragic episode of deregulation of its airline industry, to compete with itself.

Index

117, 202; as information systems
supplier, 115–16; negotiations with
PWA, 3, 4, 21, 25, 26, 27, 28, 30–31,
60, 62, 63, 64, 66, 68, 113–20, 125–28,
175–76, 178–79, 180, 185; signing of
PWA–AMR agreement, 211–12. *See also*
American Airlines; SABRE reservation
system
Anacharsis, 151
Angus, Iain, 180
Asia–Pacific market, 38. *See also* Air
Canada; Canadian Airlines International
Ltd. (CAIL)
ATC. *See* Air Transport Committee (ATC)
of Canadian Transport Commission
ATCO Industries, 72
ATX Airlines, 188
Austrian Airlines, 192
Aviation Corporation of Canada, 52
Axworthy, Lloyd, 134, 139–42, 143, 144,
200–201

Bain, D.M., 54–55
Banking industry (U.S.), 86, 89
Baruch, Bernard, 93
Billman, Thomas, 89
Black box technology, 166
Blanchard, James, 209
Boeing 707, 47
Boeing 720, 47
Boeing 727, 47
Boeing 737, 57
Boeing 747, 24, 45, 47
Boeing 767, 45
Boeing 777, 47
Boeing Co., 11, 47, 168
Bombardier Inc., 171–72
Braniff Airlines, 37, 97, 99
Branson Airlines, 188
British Airways, 50, 65, 75, 193, 204
British Columbia, and PWA–AMR deal,
125, 199
"Bucket shops," 181–82
Buckley, William F., 153
Burr, Donald, 158
Bush, George, 89
*Bush Pilot with a Briefcase: The
Happy-Go-Lucky Story of Grant
McConachie*, viii, 10
Bush pilots, 9–10
Business Council on National Issues
(BCNI), 135
Byrd, Richard, 5

CAIL. *See* Canadian Airlines International

Ltd. (CAIL)
Campbell, Kim, 185
Canada: airline deregulation. *See*
Deregulation; economic philosophy,
20, 120–22, 149–51, 152–53
Canadair, 172
Canadian Airlines International Ltd.
(CAIL): and Asia–Pacific market, 26–27,
213, 214; employees. *See* Employees;
history, 54–55, 156–60, 161–62,
163–64; restructuring, 123–24, 125;
safety record, 49. *See also* Canadian
Pacific Air Lines (CPAL) ; CP Air;
Gemini Automated Group distribution
Systems Inc.; PWA Corporation
Canadian Airways, 52, 53, 54
Canadian Auto Workers (CAW), 107, 113
Canadian National Railway (CNR), 15, 51,
52, 53, 180
*Canadian Pacific Air Lines: Its History and
Aircraft*, 54–55, 67
Canadian Pacific Air Lines (CPAL), 4, 54,
55, 56, 57, 60, 144, 156. *See also*
Canadian Airlines International Ltd.
(CAIL); CP Air
Canadian Pacific Limited, 56, 59, 157, 159
Canadian Pacific Railway (CPR), 15, 51,
52, 53, 54, 55, 56
Canadian Transport Commission (CTC):
abolition of, 144; and air fares, 137; Air
Transport Committee (ATC), 131, 139,
140–41
Carter, Jimmy, 82, 88
Carty, Donald J., 62, 116, 185
Cathay Pacific Airlines, 164
Centre for Transportation studies (UBC),
113
Chrétien, Jean, 169
Civil Aeronautics Board (CAB), 88, 94–96,
131
Clark, Glen, 113
Clark, Joe, 132, 168
Clinton, Bill, 193
Competition: in Canadian airline
industry, 3, 16–17, 29, 58, 137, 139,
144–45, 146, 147, 149, 155, 156, 157,
163–64, 177–78, 191, 198–99, 219–20;
in global airline industry, 192–93, 195;
in U.S. airline industry, 94–96, 177; in
U.S. economic philosophy, 80, 102–4,
105. *See also* Monopoly
Competition Bureau, 64, 66
Competition Tribunal, 116, 180–81, 184,
190, 195, 196
Conference Board of Canada, 135, 136